The Labour Aristocracy
in Victorian Edinburgh

The Labour Aristocracy in Victorian Edinburgh

ROBERT Q. GRAY

Clarendon Press · Oxford
1976

Oxford University Press, Ely House, London W.1

GLASGOW NEW YORK TORONTO MELBOURNE WELLINGTON
CAPE TOWN IBADAN NAIROBI DAR ES SALAAM LUSAKA ADDIS ABABA
DELHI BOMBAY CALCUTTA MADRAS KARACHI DACCA
KUALA LUMPUR SINGAPORE HONG KONG TOKYO
GLASGOW NEW YORK TORONTO MELBOURNE WELLINGTON

ISBN 0 19 822442 7

© *Oxford University Press 1976*

*Printed in Great Britain
by Burgess & Son (Abingdon) Ltd.
Abingdon Oxfordshire*

Acknowledgements

I WISH to acknowledge the help and encouragement I have received from Frank Bechhofer and John Simpson (who supervised the thesis on which this book is based), from others at Edinburgh University, and from colleagues and students at Portsmouth Polytechnic. I clarified my ideas in discussions with Geoff Crossick, which touched on practically every aspect of the research. Others who have worked in the field of Scottish working-class history will know how much I also owe to Ian MacDougall. I am grateful to Richard Bland, Tony Fielding, and Peter Morse for indispensable advice and assistance with statistical and computing work, and to the staff of the cartographic section at the Department of Geography, Portsmouth Polytechnic, for preparing the maps.

This book includes material from my articles in the *International Review of Social History*, 18 (1973) and in F. Parkin (ed.), *The Social Analysis of Class Structure* (British Sociological Association/Tavistock Publications, 1974). Material from these articles is reproduced by kind permission of the editors and publishers.

Finally, I would like to thank those responsible for the trade-union and business archives mentioned in the bibliography, and the Registrar General for Scotland, for allowing me to make use of manuscripts in their care. In the case of the business archives this was facilitated by the good offices of Mr. A. M. Broom, of the National Register of Archives (Scotland), and Professor P. L. Payne. I am also grateful to the staffs of the libraries mentioned in the bibliography. I consulted a wide range of material in the local-history collection at Edinburgh Public Library, and I owe a special debt to Mrs. Armstrong and her colleagues there.

Contents

List of Tables, Figures, and Maps

Abbreviations

A.S.E.	Amalgamated Society of Engineers
C.O.S.	Charity Organization Society
Edin.	Edinburgh
I.L.P.	Independent Labour Party
P.P.	Parliamentary Papers
R.C.	Royal Commission
S.D.F.	Social Democratic Federation
T.C.	Edinburgh Trades Council

General Note

THIS book is concerned with Edinburgh proper, not with Leith (which was socially and administratively distinct throughout the period studied), Granton, or Portobello (which were both incorporated into the municipal burgh of Edinburgh only at the very end of the period). The major socio-economic overlap is in the engineering and shipbuilding trades, where it is often impossible to distinguish Edinburgh from Leith; except in this context, all references to Edinburgh should be understood to relate only to Edinburgh proper.

I   Introduction

THIS book is based on a local study of the Victorian working class. The local focus has been adopted because it seemed appropriate to the problems under investigation. The study tries to answer questions about the nature of class domination in the nineteenth century, and about the potentialities and limitations of the social forces that might have constituted a challenge to that domination. Any conclusions offered must be seen as specific to the local case; but the validity of more general interpretations can be established only when they are tested against the diversity of local experiences.

The argument is located within the Marxist tradition of socio-historical analysis. In particular, it emphasizes the distinctive position of a top layer of the working class, or 'labour aristocracy',[1] and the specific effects of this on relationships between the classes in Victorian society. This phenomenon has been discussed by a number of writers, whose emphases vary. Some accounts merely describe the diversity of economic experience within the working class, and appear to operate with implicit models, in which cultural and ideological differences passively reflect the economic structures.[2] This is a serious vulgarization, both of the 'labour aristocracy' thesis specifically and of the Marxist mode of historical analysis generally. The key question is that of the cultural mediation of different economic experiences. Marx, Engels, and Lenin were all concerned with the effects, at the ideological and political levels, of differentiation within the working class.[3]

---

[1] The leading discussion of this thesis in a British context is E. J. Hobsbawm, 'The Labour Aristocracy in Nineteenth-century Britain', in *Labouring Men* (1964), Ch. 15; see also J. Foster, *Class Struggle and the Industrial Revolution* (1974), Ch. 7.

[2] This tendency is to some extent present in Hobsbawm's treatment (op. cit.), as well as in Lenin's classic analysis: V. I. Lenin, *Imperialism, The Highest Stage of Capitalism*, in *Selected Works*, vol. i (1967), esp. pp. 759–61. For examples of the same tendency in contemporary observers see R. Samuel, 'Class and Classlessness', *Universities and Left Review*, 6 (1959).

[3] K. Marx and F. Engels, *On Britain* (2nd edn., 1962); Lenin, loc. cit.

Hobsbawm has reminded us that Lenin's views on the labour aristocracy are often misunderstood, because they are not sufficiently related to his more general view of the limitations imposed on a 'spontaneous' and 'economistic' working-class movement by the ideological hegemony of the ruling class.[1] A movement limited in this way, Lenin suggests, will be unable to move beyond defensive, and often narrowly sectional, responses to capitalist exploitation.[2] The labour aristocracy is a special case of this more general phenomenon, and it emerged under the historical conditions of later-nineteenth-century Britain. 'It arises when the economic circumstances of capitalism makes it possible to grant significant concessions to its proletariat, within which certain strata or workers manage, by means of their special scarcity, skill, strategic position, organizational strength, etc., to establish notably better conditions for themselves than the rest.'[3] In Lenin's view, this group, effectively dominating the institutions of organized labour, became the carrier of accommodative responses to industrial capitalism.

Attention has therefore to be directed, not simply to the existence of differences within the working class. Although it is true that these were exceptionally wide in the period under discussion, they are none the less a universal feature of capitalist, and for that matter of socialist, societies. We must also examine the articulation of differences in socio-economic experience with structures of ideological hegemony, and with the formation of a labour movement whose aspirations were largely defined by the upper strata of the working class. In nineteenth-century Britain the cultural distance, as well as the economic difference, separating the 'superior artisan' from lower-working-class strata has often enough been noted, but the nature of the link between them has not been explored. The cultural level is assumed, in a kind of mid-Victorian *embourgeoisement* thesis,[4] to be passively reflective of differential standards of living. And, while it is

---

[1] E. J. Hobsbawm, 'Lenin and the "Aristocracy of Labour"', *Marxism Today* (July 1970); and see Lenin, *What Is To Be Done?*, *Selected Works*, vol. i, esp. pp. 120–33, 162–5.

[2] Lenin, *What Is To Be Done?*, loc. cit.

[3] Hobsbawm, 'Lenin and the "Aristocracy of Labour"', p. 208.

[4] See Samuel, op. cit. For the concept of *embourgeoisement* see J. H. Goldthorpe and D. Lockwood, 'Affluence and the British Class Structure', *Sociological Review*, 11 (1963).

commonly suggested that such phenomena had some bearing
on the implantation of dominant values in the working class,
and on the reformist character of the British labour movement,
the exact form of the links has not been analysed. Althusser's
methodological comment, that 'Marx has at least given us the
"two ends of the chain", and has told us to find out what goes
on between them',[1] is of some relevance here. As in other
historical problems, the failure to 'find out what goes on between' the economic, ideological, and political levels makes some
discussions of the labour aristocracy seem circular, inconclusive,
and unsatisfying.

One discussion of the problem should, however, be excepted
from these strictures: that of John Foster in his *Class Struggle and
the Industrial Revolution*.[2] While some of his emphases may be
questionable—for example, he seems to exaggerate the directly
'collaborationist' nature of the labour aristocracy[3]—Foster
does indicate some important links. He suggests that 'authority
at work' was the key dimension, linking the industrial structures
emerging in the 1850s, higher wages for some groups, and the
forms of behaviour associated with 'self-improvement' and
'respectability'. Thus, it may be argued that the best-paid and
most regularly employed men were those deemed 'reliable',
and visible differences in life-style entered into judgements
about this; the social consciousness of the artisan was formed by
the fear that, like one of Mayhew's informants, he would fall
into the low-paid casual sector of the labour market, because
he 'could no longer appear respectable'.[4] In Edinburgh, for
example, it was alleged that employers preferred men who
belonged to the Volunteer Rifles, in the belief that such military
training was conducive to discipline at work.[5] The argument
of this book will follow Foster's analysis, in emphasizing the role
of 'authority at work' as the link between economic position
and those forms of personal behaviour—such as saving[6]—pre-
scribed by influential social values.

Foster's analysis also draws attention to the historical specificity of the labour aristocracy. 'Torn away from its historical

---

[1] L. Althusser, *For Marx*, trans. B. Brewster (1969), p. 111.
[2] Foster, op. cit.   [3] See below, p. 144 and footnote.
[4] E. P. Thompson and E. Yeo (eds.), *The Unknown Mayhew* (1971), p. 220.
[5] W. Stephen, *History of the Queen's City of Edinburgh Rifle Volunteer Brigade* (1881),
p. 219.   [6] See below, Ch. 6.

context, the term "labour aristocracy" means almost nothing.
By definition almost any subgrouped (or stable capitalist)
social structure will reveal groups of higher paid workers
attempting to distinguish themselves socially from the rest.'[1]
The labour aristocracy should not, for example, be confused
with straightforward craft sectionalism, and the tendency to
apply the term to any sectional grouping of highly paid workers
is altogether misleading.[2] Such sectionalism has always existed,
and perhaps always will; the formation of the Victorian labour
aristocracy is characterized by a *particular kind* of élite, based on
industrial structures peculiar to the period. And one feature of
this élite (at least in Edinburgh) was the development of a
social identity which cut across the more traditional craft
divisions of occupation, and constituted a form, albeit a limited
one, of awareness of a common position as wage-earners.[3] A
further reason for emphasizing the historical specificity of the
labour aristocracy is their domination, far more completely
than other historical examples of highly paid craft groups, of
the institutions of the labour movement as a whole. It was this
feature, rather than simply the divisive effects of socio-economic
differences in the working class, that Marx, Engels, and Lenin
saw as conditioning the reformist character of the British
labour movement.[4]

The term 'labour aristocracy' must be understood in a precise
historical sense, referring to 'a unique stage in capitalism's social
development'.[5] The thesis that the existence of the labour
aristocracy helped to stabilize the class structure of capitalist
society must be placed firmly in this context. The labour
aristocracy, it can be argued, made possible particular forms of
class rule; but other, equally powerful, forms could emerge with
the erosion or disappearance of the stratum. (Hobsbawm suggests, for example, that the reforms of the 1906 Liberal government mark the beginning of an era of concessions to the whole
working class, not just to the upper layers.)[6]

The links between economic position and ideological structures are central to my argument. The formation of a labour

---

[1] Foster, op. cit., p. 212.
[2] Ibid., p. 224.   [3] See below, pp. 91–93.
[4] Marx and Engels, loc. cit.; Lenin, *Imperialism*, loc. cit.
[5] Foster, op. cit., p. 213.
[6] Hobsbawm, 'Lenin and the "Labour Aristocracy" ', p. 210.

aristocracy made possible particular forms of ideological
hegemony, which set limits on the articulation of working-class
consciousness. This question of the ideological power of the
ruling class has been most fully explored by Gramsci.[1] He
suggested that the ruling class are able to confine working-
class struggle 'within the existing fundamental structures', by
means of a diffuse socio-cultural hegemony, exerted partly
through 'the ensemble of organisms commonly called
"private" '.[2] I shall argue that the relationship of the labour
aristocracy to other social groups can validly be seen as an
example of the process Gramsci discusses, and, in particular,
that to understand the process it is necessary to examine 'the
ensemble of organisms commonly called "private" ' (voluntary
organizations, the provision of facilities for leisure, thrift, adult
education, etc.).[3]

The process is more complex than the dissemination downwards in society of a single, dominant 'class world view'.
Gramsci certainly recognized this complexity, as his dense and
extremely subtle analyses of the structures of class hegemony
attest, but his views have sometimes been vulgarized and mis-
represented.[4] It is thus important to emphasize, as Raymond
Williams has done,[5] that hegemony should not be seen as a
static and omnipotent system, but rather as an on-going and
problematic historical process, conditioned by given structures
inherited from the past. Hegemony is correctly seen as a structured *practice*, in which diverse social practices and elements of
consciousness are ordered in a fashion compatible with the
perpetuation of the existing relations of production. A hegemonic ideology 'may therefore contain a number of "elements"
which transcribe the way classes other than the hegemonic class
live their conditions of existence'.[6] In this respect, it may be
more appropriate to refer to a 'hegemonic structuring of ideological consciousness', than to a single 'hegemonic ideology';

---

[1] A. Gramsci, *Selections from the Prison Notebooks*, ed. and trans. Q. Hoare and
G. Nowell Smith (1971).
[2] Ibid.; the phrases quoted are from pp. 181, 12.
[3] See below, Chs. 5–7.
[4] See N. Poulantzas, 'Marxist Political Theory in Great Britain', *New Left
Review*, 43 (1967), 60–1.
[5] R. Williams, 'Base and Superstructure', *New Left Review*, 82 (1973), 8–10.
[6] Poulantzas, op. cit., p. 67.

this diversity is a necessary condition of the efficacy of ideological practice in offering a plausible account of diverse social
experiences, a ' "lived" relation between men and their world'.[1]

Class hegemony is a dynamic and shifting relationship of
social subordination, which operates in two directions. Certain
aspects of the behaviour and consciousness of the subordinate
classes may reproduce a version of the values of the ruling class.
But in the process value systems are modified, through their
necessary adaptation to diverse conditions of existence; the
subordinate classes thus follow a 'negotiated version'[2] of ruling-
class values. On the other hand, structures of ideological
hegemony transform and incorporate dissident values, so as
effectively to prevent the working through of their full implications.[3] Practices and values which might challenge the established social relations are reinterpreted, giving rise to a 'contrast
between thought and action':

It signifies that the social group in question may indeed have its own
conception of the world, even if only embryonic; a conception which
manifests itself in action, but occasionally and in flashes—when, that
is, the group is acting as an organic totality. But this same group has,
for reasons of submission and intellectual subordination, adopted a
conception which is not its own but is borrowed from another group;
and it affirms this conception verbally and believes itself to be
following it, because this is the conception which it follows in
'normal times'—that is when its conduct is not independent and
autonomous, but submissive and subordinate.[4]

Hegemony, then, refers more to a *mode of organizing* beliefs and
values, than to any particular set of beliefs and values; and
the concept directs attention to the institutions and practices
that carry and reproduce ideology within a particular social
formation.

This conception, Gramsci argued, can explain the limited
character of working-class opposition to capitalism at certain
periods; a strong and class-conscious working-class movement
may still be contained 'within the existing fundamental structures', and limited to 'the purely economic sphere', in the
absence of a revolutionary practice capable of undermining the

---

[1] Althusser, op. cit., p. 233.
[2] F. Parkin, *Class Inequality and Political Order* (1971), p. 92.
[3] Cf. Williams, op. cit., pp. 11-12.   [4] Gramsci, op. cit., p. 327.

position of the ruling class in the ideological and cultural spheres.[1] This does not make class conflict any the less real, but it does mean, as Lenin showed in his analysis of 'economism' and 'trade union consciousness',[2] that a powerful pressure limits the articulation of that conflict.

The later nineteenth century saw a real growth of class-consciousness, and an occasionally bitter industrial struggle, based especially on the 'aristocratic' upper strata of the working class; but these pressures were effectively contained within a society dominated by the bourgeoisie. However, this process was problematic for all involved; and by the end of the period economic and social change and the emergence of socialist influences in the labour movement were eroding the patterns of hegemony established in the mid-Victorian decades. This study seeks to establish the reality of class hegemony, the limits it imposed on the articulation of working-class consciousness, and the dynamic and problematic nature of the relationships involved.

In the course of our analysis it will be necessary always to consider the independent effect of cultural tradition (for example, of occupational tradition in the various crafts). Modes of behaviour do not arise simply and directly from socio-economic experience, but from the interpretation of that experience with the cultural resources that people find historically available to them. The formation of the labour aristocracy, then, is the outcome of differential socio-economic experience, as this was handled through the available ideologies, and actively interpreted in terms of life-style and social imagery.

The failure of existing studies adequately to examine this process is perhaps partly a result of their general, national focus. Recent developments in British historiography have involved a recognition of the relevance of residence, neighbourhood, leisure, etc., long neglected by historians (including those who wrote about the working class), but crucial to such historical problems. They can, however, readily be approached only within a local framework. This approach is in one sense a necessary narrowing and sharpening of focus. But in another sense it broadens the field of vision; it is only in local settings

[1] Gramsci, op. cit., p. 181.   [2] Lenin, *What Is To Be Done?*, loc. cit.

that we can hope to obtain some picture of the network of formal and informal institutions that shaped the social world of working-class people. Working-class experience was local in character, and differing degrees and forms of class-consciousness must be explained in relation to the socio-economic structures of particular localities.[1]

[1] Foster, op. cit., indicates the value of a local comparative approach.

2 Edinburgh in the Later Nineteenth Century

VICTORIAN Edinburgh had many distinctive features. It was a capital city, containing national legal and religious institutions, and providing the gathering place and educational centre for national élites and a national intelligentsia. These features developed during a long history; and locally influential groups retained a strong sense of identification with this past. Large parts of the city had been built before the industrialization and urban growth of the nineteenth century. The urban community was shaped by the impact of the rapid urban growth and economic expansion of the nineteenth century on this inheritance from the past.

The kind of change most visible was the growth of population experienced by Edinburgh, as by other large cities during the period.[1] The experience of rapid population growth was, of course, common to many nineteenth-century towns. But in Edinburgh growth was less rapid than in the more heavily industrialized Scottish cities of Glasgow and Dundee. As early as the 1850s, 'it has not, for some time past, made that progress in size and population, which has so remarkably distinguished most of the large commercial towns of the empire.'[2] The half-

TABLE 2.1

*Population of Edinburgh, 1851–1901**

	1851	1861	1871	1881	1891	1901
	160,302	168,121	196,979	228,357	261,225	298,113
Percentage increase since previous census	16	5	17	16	14	14

Source: Census of Scotland, population tables; T. Thorburn, *A Statistical Analysis of the Census of the City of Edinburgh* (1851).

* All figures according to Parliamentary boundaries: for boundary changes see Appendix I. In 1901 the Municipality extended beyond the Parliamentary boundaries and had a population of 316,837.

[1] The bibliography gives fuller references to census reports, which are cited in the tables and text in summary form.
[2] *McDowall's New Guide to Edinburgh* (c. 1851).

century from 1851 saw a population increase of 80 per cent, compared to 89 per cent in Glasgow, and 101·5 per cent in Dundee.[1] Despite this difference from centres more closely associated with the industrial growth of the period, the near-doubling of population, the expansion of the urban area, the impact of such developments as railway construction, and the changing social ecology of the city enable us to refer to an experience that was typically Victorian, as well as distinctively local.

Together with this expansion went changes in the spatial distribution and social composition of the population.[2] The planned development of the New Town catered predominantly for the nobility, gentry, and wealthiest bourgeois groups, although over-building in the 1820s and a subsequent fall in rents somewhat broadened the social make-up of these areas.[3] As T. C. Smout points out, the social differentiation between Old and New Towns was not simply between the working class and middle and upper classes; many tradesmen, shopkeepers, and small entrepreneurs remained in the Old Town.[4] Population growth in the earlier nineteenth century was more rapid in the New Town; with the exception of 1811–21, the New Town had the higher rate of increase in every decade between 1801 and 1841, and between 1821 and 1841 there was an actual decline in the Old Town.[5] The mid-decades of the century saw the completion of New Town development and the beginning of Victorian suburban development; during 1841–61 there was a

---

[1] For the contrast with Glasgow, see I. MacDougall (ed.), *The Minutes of Edinburgh Trades Council, 1859–73* (1968), pp. xvi–xvii. Future references to this edition are all to the invaluable introduction and editorial matter; references to the minutes themselves are always given by date, regardless of whether they are to the period 1859–73, or to the manuscript minutes for subsequent years.

[2] The following general description of urban development draws especially on: G. Gordon, 'The Status Areas of Edinburgh' (Ph.D. thesis, Edinburgh, 1971); A. J. Strachan, 'The Rural-Urban Fringe of Edinburgh' (Ph.D. thesis, Edinburgh, 1969).

[3] Scottish landed families still kept town houses in Edinburgh during the mid-nineteenth century: J. Heiton, *The Castes of Edinburgh* (2nd edn., 1860), p. 37. For the over-building of the 1820s see T. Thorburn, *Statistical Analysis of the Census of the City of Edinburgh* (1851), p. 7.

[4] T. C. Smout, *A History of the Scottish People, 1560–1830* (paperback edn., 1972), p. 348.

[5] Thorburn, op. cit., p. 15. Thorburn adopts a strict historical definition of the Old Town, and these figures exclude the adjacent and socially similar Canongate.

34-per-cent increase in the Old Town parishes, compared to 25 per cent in the New Town parishes.[1] The growth of a wage-earning population, associated with the construction of the New Town, and with other major projects such as the railways, as well as with the general development of industry and transport in the city, comprised most of this increase. The years 1818–22 had seen the first large-scale Irish immigration (of navvies digging the Union Canal),[2] and this may explain the fact that 1811–21 is the one decade before 1841 with a higher rate of increase in the Old Town than the New Town.

Migration to the city (in so far as the census information about birth-place enables us to analyse this) seems thereafter to have followed a fairly stable pattern. In 1851, of the population aged from sixteen to sixty, 29 per cent in the Old Town, and 2 per cent in the New Town were born in Ireland.[3] In the city as a whole, the proportion of Irish-born adults (aged twenty and over) fell steadily, from 7 per cent in 1861 to 3 per cent in 1901.[4] During the same period, the proportion born in Edinburgh, Leith, and the surrounding county ranged between 39 and 45 per cent;[5] between 17 and 19 per cent were born elsewhere in the Forth–Clyde valley;[6] and between 25 and 26 per cent in the rest of Scotland.[7] The remainder were born in England, Wales, and outside the U.K.[8]

The build-up of a wage-earning population intensified long-standing urban problems of overcrowding, poor sanitation, and deteriorating living conditions. The working-class population was largely concentrated, in the 1850s, in the Old Town, the

---

[1] Population figures for Old and New Town parishes, as defined by Thorburn, loc. cit.

[2] J. E. Handley, *The Irish in Scotland, 1798–1845* (1943), p. 133.

[3] Thorburn, op. cit., p. 41.

[4] These figures are not comparable to Thorburn's, as they relate to the whole city, rather than to its core in the Old and New Towns, and adopt a different age grouping.

[5] Mainly accounted for by Edinburgh and Leith, but these must be combined with the county, as not all censuses give towns separately.

[6] The counties of Dumbarton, Renfrew, Stirling, Lanark (including Glasgow, Greenock, Paisley), Fife, Clackmannan, Linlithgow (W. Lothian), Haddington (E. Lothian); this was, and still is, the most heavily industrialized part of Scotland.

[7] This includes the less-industrialized Lowland areas, the Highlands, and the cities of Aberdeen, Dundee, Perth, and Inverness.

[8] The above analysis is based on birth-place tables in the census reports; for full references, see bibliography.

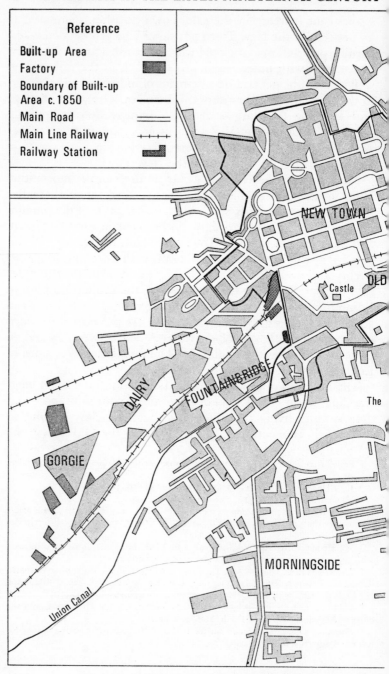

MAP 1. *Edinburgh in the Later Nineteenth Century (c. 1896)*

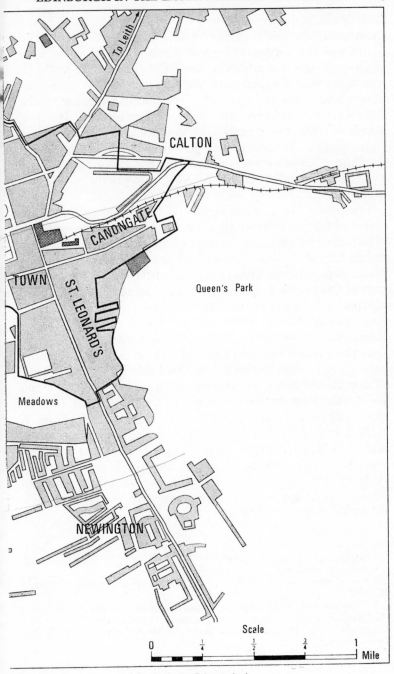

To Leith

CALTON

CANONGATE

TOWN

ST. LEONARD'S

Queen's Park

Meadows

NEWINGTON

Scale

0    $\frac{1}{4}$ $\frac{1}{2}$ $\frac{3}{4}$ 1
Mile

(Based on street maps from *P.O. Directories*)

Canongate, and the poorer streets in the district known as the 'Southside' (the area bounded by the southern fringe of the Old Town and the northern fringe of the later suburban developments in Newington and Morningside).[1] These were predominantly areas of decayed slum housing, interspersed with some newer, and frequently jerry-built, speculative tenement blocks. In 1861 the Canongate and St. Giles Registration Districts, which covered the central Old Town–Canongate area, had respectively 47 per cent and 43 per cent of families in one-room dwellings.[2] Death-rates per 1,000 in 1863 ranged from 29 to 37 in these central areas, compared to 15–17 in the New Town areas.[3]

Conditions improved somewhat after the 1860s. Successive waves of further urbanization created extensive new working-class industrial districts; densities in the older slum areas were reduced by slum clearance, as well as by 'spontaneous' movements of population. During the period 1861–1901 the population of Canongate Registration District increased 49 per cent, compared to 78 per cent for the whole city, while in St. Giles Registration District there was an actual decline.[4] (These Registration Districts are larger and less homogeneous areas than the wards of the same names shown on the map of housing conditions, or than the areas listed in Table 2.2.)[5] In the areas of new development to the west and south (St. George's and Newington Registration Districts), on the other hand, population increase was more rapid than for the city as a whole. A table prepared by Dr. Littlejohn (a noted sanitary reformer, and M.O.H. for the city) for the Royal Commission on Housing, gives a more precise picture of the process (see Table 2.2). Although the exact boundaries of the areas referred to are not stated, the broad pattern of movement to the areas of new urban development is clear enough.

[1] Gordon, op. cit., pp. 36, 45, 69.
[2] Calculated from table in 1861 census report.
[3] *R.C. on Housing (Scotland)*, P.P. 1884–5 XXXI, Appendix B to evidence of Dr. Littlejohn (q. 18996).
[4] Canongate Registration District had vacant land on its north-eastern edge at the beginning of the period; whereas St. Giles District was completely enclosed.
[5] Details of the various administrative units in the city were found in the *Post Office Directories*.

TABLE 2.2

Population Change in Selected Areas, 1861–1881

	Population 1861	Change 1881	Percentage Change
Old Town Central areas			
Canongate	12,200	−1,642	−13·5
Tron	11,636	−5,030	−43
St. Giles	15,967	−2,555	−16
Grassmarket	5,227	− 729	−14
Areas adjoining open land in 1861			
Fountainbridge	9,880	+4,537	+46
Pleasance/St. Leonards	11,104	+7,608	+68·5
Calton/Greenside	10,984	+6,588	+60
West End*	7,748	+19,386	+250

Source: R.C. on Housing (Scotland), Appendix B to evidence of Dr. Littlejohn (q. 18996). 'Central' and 'open' areas in 1861 identified from *P.O. Directory* maps.
  * Probably means the area immediately south-west of Princes Street station, and toward Dalry.

This movement relieved pressure on the central areas. Between 1861 and 1881 the percentage of families in one room fell from 47 to 37 in Canongate Registration District, and from 43 to 36 in St. Giles; and corresponding increases in the proportions in two and three rooms suggest that this reflects a change in working-class conditions, rather than in the social composition of the areas.[1] Dr. Littlejohn's table shows a fall in persons per acre, and marked improvement in the death-rate in the central areas.[2] But this improvement was not uniformly distributed; indeed, its unevenness is a central factor in working-class development, with, for example, a marked differentiation in housing within the working class.[3] The over-all reduction in death-rates by no means wiped out the differences between parts of the city; the highest death-rate in 1883 (29 per 1,000 in Tron) was twice the lowest (14 per 1,000 in Broughton).[4] Housing data for municipal wards (smaller and analytically more useful units than the large and heterogeneous Registration Districts) from the 1901 census enable us to draw a 'social map' of the city at that date. The areas of more crowded housing form a central belt, between the New Town and the more spacious suburbs to the south; the newer industrial areas along

---

[1] Calculated from tables in census reports.   [2] *R.C. on Housing*, loc. cit.
[3] See below, pp. 95–8.   [4] *R.C. on Housing*, loc. cit.

the railways, 'groups of ill-planned factory buildings and stores and beyond a conglomeration of houses for the working classes',[1] are connected to each other by the older central working-class areas of the Old Town and Canongate. These areas of crowded housing contained most of the city's large-scale industry, as well as the railway lines and sidings and the Union Canal. The social contrasts between areas of the city were striking—indeed, they may have become more so, as distinctively Victorian urban-industrial areas developed, with streets of grimy tenements sandwiched between railway lines, and often overshadowed by the foundries and breweries where their inhabitants sought employment.

These developments superimposed new patterns of social segregation upon the distinction between Old and New Towns. Although that distinction was a well-established one, there were elements of heterogeneity. The back lanes of the New Town and areas like Canonmills provided 'the operative and occasional menial aid, which in most cases will be found in close proximity to the residences of the wealthy classes'.[2] Thus, in the jewellery trades, 'the workshops of the small masters are situated in out-of-the-way lanes in the New Town'; and some important printing firms were located in the same lanes, or in the Old Town 'down the closes or lanes or in some blind alley approached from the High Street or the Cowgate'.[3] During the final quarter of the nineteenth century, however, the bigger printing firms were moving to purpose-built factories in 'the more commodious outskirts'.[4] The concentrations of heavier industry around the railways and the development of large tracts of working-class housing created a distinctively industrial element in the urban scene. Working-class dwellings, one commentator noted, were 'now so numerous that had all been built in near neighbourhood they would have formed a considerable town'.[5]

---

[1] Institute of Public Administration, *Studies in the Development of Edinburgh* (1939), p. 19.

[2] Thorburn, op. cit., p. 10.

[3] D. Bremner, *The Industries of Scotland* (1869), p. 123; *The Ballantyne Press and its Founders, 1796–1908* (1909), pp. 143–4.

[4] *Ballantyne Press*, loc. cit.

[5] F. H. Groome (ed.), *Ordnance Gazetteer of Scotland* (1885), p. 529.

There was also a marked growth of middle-class suburbs, themselves finely stratified by style and cost of housing, and certainly embracing a wider social range than the highly select New Town. Those groups that had not shared in the movement to the New Town earlier in the century could establish their distance from the manual workers by moving to the new petty-bourgeois suburbs of the later nineteenth century.

The social conditions of the middle class, at least prior to the sixties, were simpler, less comfortable, and certainly less pretentious than those which prevail in a similar section of society now. Well-to-do tradesmen and other substantial members of the middle classes were content to dwell in tenement houses of limited accommodation, generally consisting of only one public room for the family, a small

Wards with 1·5 or more persons per room

MAP 2. *Housing Conditions, 1901*

number of bedrooms, and a kitchen with a dark closet, in which the single servant lassie slept.[1]

According to a rather impressionistic account of 1908, the residents of Newington were the 'aristocracy of retail trade', those of Morningside and the south-western suburbs 'solicitors, accountants, stockbrokers and insurance men', etc.[2]

The period therefore saw a near doubling of population, the growth of districts of industrial land-use and working-class housing, and predominantly middle-class outer suburbs. The over-all effect was to intensify residential segregation. This development was superimposed on the activities traditionally associated with the city; and groups engaged in those activities continued to play a prominent role in local life. The growing industrial, financial, and commercial activity of the period was, on the other hand, reflected in the emergence of newer social groups.

Non-industrial employments have always been regarded as a distinctive feature of Edinburgh. 'The city has a calm, steady character, in keeping with the predominance of legal, educational, literary and artistic pursuits, from which it derives its chief maintenance, and contrasts broadly with the fluctuations, excitements, and mercantile convulsions, which produce so much vicissitude in manufacturing towns.'[3] It is this image, and the rich local associations with a history stretching from the Middle Ages to the Scottish Enlightenment, that figures in the extensive literature about the city.

This impression of the city is to some extent supported by the evidence of the census tables, although the figures derived from these tables cannot be regarded as precise. Their drawbacks are discussed in Appendix I. The census reports are none the less the best evidence available, and at least indicate the broad shape of the occupational structure. The figures in Table 2.3 reveal a considerable proportion in administrative, professional, and service occupations; while the size of the domestic-service group is a powerful indicator of the local concentration of the wealthier classes generally. The census reports also contain some comparative evidence that this was a distinctive feature of Edinburgh.

[1] 'J.B.S.', *Random Recollections and Impressions* (1903), p. 23.
[2] A. Keith, *Edinburgh of Today* (1908), pp. 144–6.
[3] Groome (ed.), op. cit., p. 534.

In 1901, for example, 9 per cent of males in the city were in what is called the 'professional class', the next-highest figure among the four largest Scottish cities being 5 per cent for Aberdeen, with lower proportions in Glasgow and Dundee; similarly, 1·5 per cent were in the 'domestic class', again followed by Aberdeen (0·8 per cent). Figures for the 'industrial

TABLE 2.3

Administration, Professions, Commerce, and Services
as Percentage of Total Occupied Population, 1881 and 1901

	1881	*1901*
Administration, professions, etc.	11·17	8·81
Commerce	5·26	7·25
Domestic service	20·51	16·05
Administration	1·68	1·69
Church	0·29	0·30
Law	0·54	0·72
Medicine	0·32	0·42
Teaching	1·80	1·91
Other services, etc.	6·54	3·77
Insurance	0·35	0·40
Commercial traveller	0·73	0·93
Commercial clerk, etc.	2·75	4·55
Bankers, bank officials, clerks	0·47	0·46
Other commerce	0·96	0·91

Source: Census occupation tables. See Appendix I for details of definitions and procedure used in this table.

class' fall into precisely the reverse order (ranging from 52 per cent for Edinburgh to 66 per cent for Dundee).[1]

Edinburgh contained an unusually large professional and administrative middle class. The city also to some extent retained its traditional character as a seasonal gathering place for the wealthy. But this should not be allowed to obscure the effect of economic and social change on the occupational composition of the middle class. The figures for commerce in Table 2.3 indicate an increase in this category, although one has to be extremely cautious in drawing inferences, in view of possible

---

[1] *Census of Scotland*, 1901, vol. iii, p. xl. The 'classes' referred to are not comparable to the categories in Table 2.3; and the figures are based on total, not occupied, population.

shifts in classification procedures (especially for such designations as 'clerk'). It is certainly true that Edinburgh became a
centre of banking, insurance, and allied activities, 'engrossing
all the top legal and much of the top financial business of a
country which was . . . already achieving industrial and commercial eminence'.[1] Moreover, the growth of the professions,
so often seen as distinguishing Edinburgh from most cities of
comparable size, was itself in part a consequence of the development of industry and commerce, and of the industrial and
commercial bourgeoisie. Much of the business handled by
Edinburgh lawyers must have been linked to the growth of
Scottish industry and commerce; accountancy in Scotland, for
example, was regarded originally as a branch of the legal
profession.[2]

Industrial and commercial activity seem to have been of increasing importance, both in the direct impact on occupational
structure, and indirectly through the changing pattern of demand for those professional services in which the city specialized.
But it is, as we have seen, difficult to measure from census
figures such trends as the growth of white-collar commercial
occupations. For other middle-class occupations developing in
the nineteenth century it is still more difficult, even to make estimates. The census figures cannot take us far beyond impressionistic statements as to the changing composition of the local
middle class. That its composition was indeed changing, and
that Edinburgh was unusual in the size and heterogeneity of its
middle class is perhaps the firmest conclusion that we can draw.
A section of the professional middle class retained an identity
linked to the traditional role of the city in national life, as a
centre of law and administration, and a focal point in the social
life of the landed class; other professional and business groups
were associated with the economic changes of the Victorian
period. The city's notorious snobbery seems to have derived
from social and political rivalries encouraged by this heterogeneity of the wealthier classes. Heiton, writing in the mid-
nineteenth century, characterized Edinburgh as a society of
'castes', ranging from the 'titular Lord to the Applewoman';
the top professionals were grouped beneath the aristocracy, the

---

[1] G. Best, *Mid-Victorian Britain* (1971), p. 49.
[2] A. M. Carr-Saunders and P. A. Wilson, *The Professions* (1933), p. 209.

merchants 'stand between the Professionals and the Shop-keepers', while the latter are themselves 'striving to be great in their shopocratic . . . way'. In the 'war of energy and pride between caste and caste', 'the entrenchments become the firmer and firmer as you ascend'.[1] In the 1900s, Keith evokes a similar image of local society: the 'Old aristocracy of Scot-land', and 'the modern professional aristocracy' were obliged to 'tolerate . . . persons who have soiled their hands with trade, but are forgiven the offence on account of the trade having proved lucrative'.[2] The status aspiration and rivalry involved in the rise of new middle-class strata had an impact on political life in the city. Williams sees the overthrow of the Whig 'old guard' by a Liberal coalition as a challenge by business groups to the traditional dominance of an élite of lawyers.[3] While religious cleavage also made for tensions within the middle class.[4]

The formation of a working class occurred in a community without a unified industrial bourgeois élite; the most prominent middle-class groups were not directly involved in relations of production with the manual working class, but were engaged in the professions, wholesale and retail distribution, commerce, and finance. The industrial structure was itself heterogeneous, with a considerable amount of smaller-scale labour-intensive industry and a consequent diffusion of ownership. The relation-ships of industrial employment did not figure prominently in local affairs. Industrial groups, whether employers or workers, are not included in the images of a 'caste' society discussed above.

The concentration of middle-class groups in the city had a bearing on the distribution of industrial employment. Small-scale crafts, catering for a 'luxury' market, constituted an im-portant part of this employment.

Edinburgh . . . has not, and never had, any considerable staple of produce for the supply of the general market. Her manufactures, perhaps, are more diverse, exhibit a larger aggregate of genius than those of any other great town; but some are of the common kinds for

---

[1] Heiton, op. cit., pp. 4–7, 204.
[2] Keith, op. cit., pp. 204–5.
[3] J. C. Williams, 'Edinburgh Politics, 1832–52' (Ph.D. thesis, Edinburgh, 1972), pp. 3–6, 374–5.   [4] Ibid., pp. 12–30.

the supply of local wants, and therefore need not be mentioned, while the rest are all on so limited a scale as to require only the briefest notice.[1]

Local industry had a reputation, in keeping with the more general image of Edinburgh as a city 'peculiarly free from the

TABLE 2.4

Industrial Occupations as Percentage of Total Occupied Population, Edinburgh, 1841–1901

A. *Industrial Groups*	*1841*	*1861*	*1881*	*1891*	*1901*
1. Printing	3·04	4·28	4·57	4·45	4·42
2. Building	10·49	7·30	9·34	6·96	8·49
3. Engineering and Metals	3·85	4·19	3·93	4·02	4·49
4. Clothing	14·09	12·59	9·27	9·23	7·01
5. Transport	2·17	4·21	5·41	5·88	7·12
1. Printer	1·94	2·17	2·52	2·53	2·83
Book-binder	0·95*	1·48	1·55	1·31	1·15
Lithography	0·11	0·45	0·33	0·44	0·44
Other printing	0·04	0·18	0·17	0·17	–
2. Mason	4·49†	2·36†	1·97	1·26	1·66
Joiner	1·84	2·19	2·70	1·68	2·23
Painter	3·64	1·14	1·50	1·26	1·45
Slater, tiler	0·23	0·28	0·29	0·25	0·28
Plasterer	0·20	0·39	0·52	0·30	0·40
Plumber, gas-fitter	– §	0·62	0·95	0·85	0·97
Building labourer	–	–	1·03	0·97	1·06
Other building	0·09	0·32	0·38	0·39	0·44*
3. Engineer	0·38	0·72	0·87	1·05	1·34
Blacksmith	1·76	1·39	0·99	0·81	0·81
Brass manufacture	0·67	0·89	0·78	0·71	0·61
Iron manufacture	0·20	0·36	0·49	0·55	0·42
Tin-worker	0·36	0·33	0·38	0·38	0·37
Electrical apparatus	–	–	–	0·06	0·35
Other engineering	0·48	0·50	0·42	0·46	0·59
4. Shoemaker	4·53	3·06	1·65	1·43	0·91
Tailor	3·28	2·33	2·32	2·24	2·04
Other clothing‡	6·28*	7·20*	5·30*	5·56*	4·06
5. Rail	0·01	0·86	1·39	1·78	1·98
Cabman, coachman	–	0·71	0·47	0·43*	1·07
Carrier, carter	0·77	0·88	1·30	1·44	2·02
Tramway	–	–	0·10	0·28	0·38
Messenger, porter	1·39	1·76	2·15	1·95	1·67

see Notes next page

[1] Groome (ed.), op. cit., p. 535.

TABLE 2.4 (Continued)

B. Other Occupations	1841	1861	1881	1891	1901
Furniture trades	2·59	2·28	1·95	1·34*	1·25*
Cooper	0·23	0·24	0·36	0·48	0·45
Other wood	0·46	0·39	0·23	0·22	0·32
Leather	0·71	0·70	0·58	0·57	0·42
Jewellery, precious metals, watches, etc.	0·81	0·83	0·72	0·59	0·51
Baker	1·47	1·34	1·34	1·54	1·69
Brewer	0·25	0·32	0·57	0·77	0·54
Other food and drink	0·70*	0·94	0·88*	1·16*	0·53
Paper-making	0·04	0·20	0·46	0·60	0·76
Type-founder	0·60	0·50	0·42	0·38	0·24
Coach-maker	0·60	0·47	0·35	0·32	0·29
Brush-maker	0·15	0·16	0·13	0·09	0·06
Glass	0·19	0·28	0·26	0·23	0·39
Rubber	–	0·33	0·54	1·17	0·82
Merchant seaman	0·08	0·13	0·15	0·15	0·35
Stone quarrier	0·07	0·12	0·10	0·11	0·17
Paviour, road labourer	–	–	0·10	0·11	0·17
Gas	0·02	0·22	0·27	0·29	0·37
General labourer	3·64	2·31	1·90	2·62	1·63
Undefined manufacturing	0·03	0·20	1·00	0·91	0·78

Source: Census occupation tables.

Notes: See Appendix I for classification scheme and procedures.
* Figures based partly on estimates: See Appendix I.
† Probably includes masons' labourers: not strictly comparable to later figures.
‡ Mainly female (i.e. seamstresses, dressmakers, etc.).
§ Included with Painter.
– Not separately enumerated.

taint of the ledger and the counting-house',[1] for high quality hand-made goods. In jewellery, for example, 'all the work done is of a superior kind, no attempt being made to vie with Birmingham in the production of cheap and showy articles, the ✓ beauty of which is as transient as that of a flower'.[2]

The evidence of the census lends some support to this picture of the industrial structure; but a closer examination suggests important qualifications. We are again faced with the difficulties of interpreting Victorian censuses. In analysing the figures, Booth's scheme as recently presented and developed by Armstrong,[3] has been used to estimate the size of five major industrial groups. Part A of Table 2.4 gives totals and the more important individual occupations, for printing, building,

[1] Ibid. [2] Bremner, op. cit., p. 131.
[3] W. A. Armstrong 'The Use of Information about Occupation', in E. A. Wrigley (ed.), *Nineteenth Century Society* (1972).

engineering and metals, clothing, and rail and road transport. These are based on Armstrong's classification, modified by the exclusion of census designations definitely referring to employers (for example, 'builder', as opposed to the specific building trades), and by a number of minor changes. Reference should be made to Appendix I for a fuller account of these procedures. Part B of the table gives all occupations with 100 or more (= 0·09 per cent of occupied population) in 1881, some of which are combined for convenience of presentation.

The figures point to the importance of consumer crafts. Apart from building, clothing constitutes the largest industrial group throughout the period, while the furniture, leather, jewellery, and coach-making trades together account for a considerable proportion of industrial employment.[1] The local importance of a middle-class consumer market is perhaps also indicated by the fact that domestic service was far larger than any industrial group (see Table 2.3). Large-scale mechanized industry was correspondingly of less importance than in many cities of Edinburgh's size. 'Edinburgh's heavy industry is composed largely of single firms of outstanding reputation in each sector. In that it differs from the concentration of similar firms which we find in large conurbations such as Clydeside or Birmingham.'[2]

We must, however, qualify the picture of an occupational structure dominated by small-scale consumer trades. Although this was an important sector, the proportion engaged in it declined over the four censuses, while that in the heavier industries —engineering, brewing,[3] rubber—either grew or remained stable. Moreover, the importance of this sector to the local industrial economy was probably greater than its effects on the occupational structure, since it included a number of leading firms with widespread markets. The same applies to printing, which was probably more heavily concentrated in Edinburgh than in any other town, developing from its traditional role as an ancillary activity to the legal, administrative, and literary life of the capital, to become an industry of far wider importance.

[1] Cf. MacDougall, loc. cit.
[2] 'The Edinburgh Story', *Scotsman*, 25 Apr. 1960.
[3] The breweries certainly also employed the growing numbers of coopers, who are separately listed in Table 2.4.

Local firms included several leading publishers, and such specialized branches as Bartholomew, the map-makers. In the 1900s, publishers who had moved their offices south continued to use printing facilities in Edinburgh.[1]

The growing importance of the more heavily capitalized industries with extra-local markets is brought out more clearly by changes in the absolute, rather than proportionate, numbers employed. Table 2.5 indicates that the numbers of printers, engineers, engine-drivers, rubber-workers, and brewers grew faster than the total occupied population, while domestic service, tailors, and cabinet-makers lagged behind, and shoe-making underwent an absolute decline. This suggests that, despite the local concentration of the consumer crafts, the larger-scale industries were the more dynamic sector of the local economy. This point is reinforced when we consider the effects

TABLE 2.5
Percentage Change in Numbers in Selected Occupations,
1841–1901

Total Occupied Population	+164
Printer	+287
Engineer	+886
Engine-driver*	+544 } 1861–1901
Rubber	+890 }
Brewer	+459
Domestic servant (female)	+ 40
Tailor	+ 64
Shoemaker	− 34
Cabinet-maker†	+ 28

* Included in 'Rail' in Table 2.3.
† Included in 'Furniture trades' in Table 2.3.

of female employment (much of it probably part-time), which was heavily concentrated in domestic service and the clothing trades. In 1881 building and engineering account for a considerably larger proportion of occupied males than of the total occupied population, while clothing accounts for only 6 per cent of occupied males, compared to 9 per cent of the total occupied population.[2]

In the pattern of growth for the building industry we find a fluctuation in the numbers employed, according to the movements of the building cycle. As Table 2.4 indicates, there is a

[1] Keith, op. cit., p. 10.
[2] Industrial groups and domestic service, 1881:

fall in 1891, following the depression of the 1880s, then a rise in 1901, following the boom of the 1890s. (The 1911 census again shows the effects of the chronic slump of the preceding years, with a halving of the numbers of masons and masons' labourers since 1901.)[1]

We therefore find three types of pattern of occupational growth. The first type, old-established handicrafts catering for the local 'luxury' market, remained of considerable importance, distinguishing the pattern of industrial employment from that of more industrialized cities, such as Glasgow.[2] But an examination of the figures shows a marked tendency to a relative, and in some cases absolute, decline in industries of this type.

TABLE 2.6

Percentage Distribution of Total and Male Employment, 1881

	Percentage of total occupied population	Percentage of occupied males only
Domestic service	20·5	4
Printing	5	5
Building	9	15
Engineering	4	6
Clothing	9	6
Transport	5	8

Employment in the second type, larger-scale industry and transport, grew more rapidly, suggesting their relatively greater importance to the local industrial economy. Finally, the building industry shows a pattern of cyclical fluctuation in the numbers employed.

The industrial working class in nineteenth-century Edinburgh was thus marked by a considerable occupational diversity. A range of old-established crafts catered for the large middle-class consumer market, while newer, more capital-intensive enterprises were geared to national and world markets. One feature common to many local industries was their high proportion of skilled labour. Shoemaking, tailoring, furniture, and other consumer trades were labour-intensive and—at least in the high-quality bespoke sector—relied heavily on traditional craft skills transmitted by apprenticeship. Building was likewise marked by the persistence of craft methods. In printing and

[1] J. J. Cossar and A. Froude, *The Census Returns of Edinburgh* (c. 1911), pamphlet in Edinburgh Public Libary.
[2] MacDougall, loc. cit.

engineering the effect of technical change was to create new skills (for example, those of printing machinemen and engineering fitters) as well as to make more efficient and intensive use of older ones (for example, compositors and bookbinders).

There was a considerable diversity in the industrial situation of skilled labour, while the changing importance of different industries, revealed by the analysis of the census figures, affected the occupational composition of the working class. My analysis of class structure will adopt a comparative focus, concentrating on selected skilled trades (though other occupations will be considered where data are readily available). The occupations selected include important trades from all the industrial groups in Part A of Table 2.3, with the exception of transport. Printing, a key local industry, is represented by compositors, machinemen,[1] and bookbinders; building by masons, joiners, and painters; engineering by engineers[2] and ironmoulders;[3] clothing by shoemakers. The reference is in all cases to *adult male skilled workers*, and not to semi- and unskilled workers who may sometimes be covered by the same general title (for example, the census designations 'printer' and 'bookbinder' both comprise about 50 per cent semi-skilled women).

A number of criteria have determined this selection. In the first place, it is desirable to include the important sectors of local industry, and to obtain a cross-section of the range among skilled trades, in terms of social experience and of historical tradition. Secondly, it is necessary to bear in mind the availability of documentary sources relating to the various occupations. These requirements have not in practice been incompatible. The data reveal a considerable range of variation in class situation, both between and within the selected trades; and, although the documentary material is far richer for printing than for other occupational groups, it nevertheless provides some evidence for all the trades. The diversity of local industry, and the impact of changes in the economic and occupational structure thus facilitate a comparative approach.

[1] These two trades are quite distinct, though they are often lumped together under the heading 'printer' (e.g. by the census).

[2] This refers mainly to the two major engineering trades, fitters and turners, but the designation 'engineer' may sometimes also include millwrights, etc.

[3] The census does not distinguish the skilled moulders from other foundry workers.

3   Industrial Structures

GIVEN the diversity of Edinburgh's industrial economy one cannot point to any single industry, whose structures dominated the social experience of working-class people in the city. The first point to be made about the local industrial structure is its diversity, in terms of such variables as scale of enterprise,

TABLE 3.1
Labour Force and Steam Power in Local Industries,
1871 and 1901

| | 1871 (Factory Returns) | | 1901 (Census) |
	Steam h.p. per worker	Mean workers per employer	Mean workers per employer
Printing*	0·10	47	74
Masons	0·08	18	14[+]
Joiners	0·03	9	9[+]
Painters	–	7	8[+]
Engineering†	0·14	83	43[‡]
Shoemakers	–	6	8
Tailors	–	9	19
Precious metals, Jewellery	–	8	6
Clock and Watch	–	4	4
Tanners, Curriers	0·29	19	14
Bakers	0·04	4	16
Cabinet-makers	0·03	14	10
Glass	0·21	119	120
Rubber	0·45	337	262

Source: Calculated from: *Return of Factories,* P.P. 1871, LXII; census occupation tables, 1901.

* 'Printers' and 'bookbinders' combined (also litho printer, etc. 1901): this seemed the best course in view of the doubtful status in the figures of the many firms combining both operations.

+ Employers described as 'builders' are added to those in specific trades.

† 'Machine-makers' and 'foundries' combined, 1871: all trades in census order X.3, 1901; the same point applies as in printing.

‡ This is undoubtedly an underestimate, unavoidable because of the problem of blacksmiths. Journeymen smiths worked either in large engineering shops, or in small blacksmiths' (smiths account for 55 out of 164 employers in the engineering group). Excluding smiths (both employers and workers) gives a figure of 62 workers per firm, but this is still an underestimate, since we have thereby excluded a large number of smiths employed in engineering shops, as well as those in small smithies.

technology, and productive organization. An otherwise diverse
industrial experience was, however, to some extent unified by
analogous features in the organization of work, and especially
the distinctive position of sections of the skilled labour-force.
This dimension of 'authority at work' was of critical importance
in the formation of a labour aristocracy.[1]

Analysis of the industrial structure has to be based on rather
fragmentary and unreliable official statistics. Figures for steam
power given in the 1871 factory return may be used to give a
rough indication of the amount of fixed capital employed; and
both this return and the 1901 census enable us to estimate the
mean size of firm (employees per employer).[2] In both respects,
the main interest is in establishing the *general direction* of differences between industries, rather than in precise quantitative
estimates of the magnitude of such differences; given this
limited goal, the many problems of definition, comparability,
and reliability that arise in using the data are less serious. The
figures (Table 3.1) do show some measure of agreement between the factory return and the census, in the ranking of
industries by firm size; and the general pattern is in line with
what one would expect from general descriptions of the industries concerned. The building trades, and such consumer crafts
as clothing, jewellery, and furniture, have little or no steam
power, and an average of under twenty workers per employer;
while engineering, printing, glass, and rubber-manufacturing
are carried on in larger firms, with a greater application of
steam power. This indicates a broad contrast between the local
consumer and building crafts, and larger-scale more modern
industries.

Given the rather dubious status of the figures, we have to be
more cautious about inferring structural change between the
two dates. Apart from the problem of different classification
procedures, some differences may be accounted for by the fact
that the relevant legislation in 1871 covered all workers in
printing, engineering, glass, and rubber, virtually all cabinet-
makers, 80 per cent of tanners and curriers, and varying

---

[1] Foster, *Class Struggle and the Industrial Revolution*, pp. 223 ff.
[2] See Table 3.1 and sources there cited.

proportions in the other industries.[1] The apparent increase in firm
size in printing, however, is in line with other evidence. The
final quarter of the nineteenth century saw the migration of
most of the leading firms to purpose-built suburban factories.
'Many of the larger printing-offices have, within the last thirty
years, removed their premises to the more commodious outskirts of the city.'[2]

It is likely that a disproportionate amount of employment was
in the larger firms. Indeed, several firms, especially in printing
and metal-working, seem to have been considerably above the
mean size for their industries. Nelson's, the largest local printing
works, were said to have 440 workers about 1867; the same
source gives a figure of 350 for Milne's brass foundry.[3] As early
as 1853 one ironworks had 700–800 workers.[4] Table 3.2 gives
some figures for particular firms at the turn of the century; all
of them are—not unexpectedly, in view of the pre-eminence
implied by the survival of records—larger than the mean firm
size for their industries indicated in the census. There is, moreover, some direct evidence for the increase in plant size. The
Scotsman newspaper employed thirty-two printers (compositors
and machinemen) in 1855, 103 ten years later; Constable's
employed eighty-four in 1856, rising to 256 in 1900.[5] For the
building trades, we have no evidence of this sort, but size of
firm (as given in Table 3.1) is less meaningful here than in
other industries; the work force in building would often be
assembled for particular projects, and gangs on large sites
might well be much larger than is indicated by the figures. In
1876 thirty-six employers were reported to have conceded a rise
to 600 joiners; this indicates a mean firm size about twice that
shown by the 1871 returns.[6]

It is possible from business records to discover the size of

[1] Numbers in factory returns, as a proportion of estimated totals in relevant
occupations (average of 1861 and 1881 censuses).

[2] *The Ballantyne Press*, p. 157.

[3] Bremner, *Industries of Scotland*, pp. 504, 136.

[4] 'The Condition of the Working Classes in Edinburgh and Leith', *Edinburgh
News*, 10 Sept. 1853. All future references to the *Edinburgh News* are to this series of
articles.

[5] *Scotsman* and Constable wage books; Constable, 'List of Parties Employed,
1833–56' (manuscript notebook). These, and the other wage books used for Table
3.2, are in the archives of the firms concerned.

[6] Edin. Central Branch, Associated Joiners, Minutes, 29 May 1876.

particular departments, as well as of the total work force. Table
3.2 gives department size in the two printing firms for compositors and machinemen (Bartholomew, being lithographic rather

TABLE 3.2
Numbers employed by Firms, April 1900

Firm	Industry	Department	Number Employed
Constable	Printing	Compositors	97
		Compositors (female)	12
		Machine room	64
		Others	83
		All	256
Bartholomew	Litho printing (maps)	Machine men	9
		Machine girls	11
		Others	79
		All	99
Allan	Shoemakers	All	45
Hamilton & Inches	Silversmiths etc.	All	15

Source: Wage books of firms. Numbers were counted as at the first pay day in
April; clerical, retail, and managerial employees being excluded.

than letterpress printers, had no compositors). Some other
pieces of information may be cited. Towards the turn of the
century Neill's had accommodation for 200 compositors in a
special office they opened for government work;[1] in 1865 the
Scotsman employed seventy-three compositors and thirty in the
machine room.[2] In the foundries, large numbers of skilled ironmoulders seem likewise to have worked in the same shops: in
1900 three foundries had sixty or more union members, and
another five had twenty or more (these are minimum figures
for the totals employed).[3] According to their union secretary,
the ratio of skilled moulders to foundry labourers was 11 : 6 ✓
in 1893.[4]

[1] *History of the firm of Neill and Co.* (1900), p. 14.
[2] *Scotsman* wage books.
[3] Membership figures for shops in Edinburgh and Leith, Associated Ironmoulders, *Reports*, 1900.
[4] *R.C. on Labour, group A*, P.P. 1893–4 XXXII, q. 23454. There were also
4,000–5,000 irondressers and 4,000 'boys' to the 11,000 skilled moulders in Scot- ✓
land.

The evidence suggests that firms in printing and engineering were larger and more capital-intensive than in building and shoemaking, and that the size of firms in printing tended to increase during the half-century from 1850. However, social relations in the work place are by no means the automatic consequence of some inexorable 'size effect'.[1] They depend also on the nature of technology, the division of labour, the deployment of managerial authority, etc.; while these things are themselves conditioned by the wider structures of the economy, by the employers' strategies to extend or intensify exploitation, and by the workers' formal or informal counter-strategies. Under nineteenth-century conditions, the expansion of firms did not necessarily lead to the development of formal management hierarchies. Various kinds of incentive scheme or subcontract might, for example, be an easier way of controlling large numbers of workers.[2] Although subcontract was of little importance in Edinburgh, the authority and responsibility exercised by some skilled men, and the higher wages and greater security that went with this, meant that there was an analogous devolution of the tasks of managerial control. Information about such things as plant size has therefore to be interpreted in the light of a detailed examination of productive processes and of the social relations of production in particular sectors of industry.

Even in the largest local factories, it was possible for the employer, or his agent, to exert a personalized authority. William Nelson's biographer tells us how:

Two navvies were engaged one day at Hope Park turning a crank when Mr. William Nelson was passing. He paused for a moment and looked at the men, who seemed to go about their work rather leisurely. He then came forward to them, and asked, in a gruff manner, if they could not work a little harder and turn the crank quicker. They answered at once 'they could not; it was a stiff job, and very fatiguing.' 'Nonsense', he replied; 'let me try.' Seizing one of the handles, he did try; but, after giving the handle two or three turns, desisted, for it made the perspiration pour from him. Then he

[1] G. K. Ingham, *Size of Industrial Organisation and Worker Behaviour* (1970).
[2] See R. Bendix, *Work and Authority in Industry* (1st paperback edn., 1963), Ch. 4; E. J. Hobsbawm, 'Custom, Wages, and Work-load', *Labouring Men*, Ch. 17; S. Pollard, *The Genesis of Modern Management* (Pelican edn., 1968).

remarked, 'Ay, just go on as you've been doing'; and, putting his hand into his pocket, added, 'there's half-a-crown between you'.[1]

The obituary column of the printers' union journal noticed the deaths of master printers—with their individual quirks, strengths, and weaknesses—as well as of leading union members.[2] This was not simply a question of 'paternalism', but rather of the way in which the personality of a known individual could affect behaviour in the workshop (including conflict behaviour). The founder of Hunter & Foulis, bookbinders, an ex-journeyman, 'could not be taught anything about the time required to do any binding process, his views being based on hard-earned personal experience', and this led to frequent disputes about the intensity of labour.[3] Something of the heroic aura of the 'captain of industry' could be attached to the very ruthlessness of Victorian capitalists.

Despite the marked contrast between small-scale, labour-intensive and large-scale, capital-intensive industry, the experience of industrial labour had common features. Even in heavily capitalized sectors, the tendency for authority to de- ✓ volve onto sections of skilled labour, and the personalized role of the employer, limited the need for elaborate management hierarchies.

PRODUCTION PROCESSES

Printing

The two basic letterpress printing processes—the arrangement of movable types to form the text of the matter to be reproduced, and their application to paper by means of the press—had long been regarded as separate occupations, at least in the major centres, such as Edinburgh. There is a clear distinction between compositors and pressmen in the *History of the Art of Printing* (Edinburgh, 1713).[4] The technique of typesetting by hand changed little until the advent of the linotype

---

[1] D. Wilson, *William Nelson: a memoir* (privately printed, 1889).

[2] *Scottish Typographical Circular*, e.g., editorial tribute to Andrew Balfour, March 1863.

[3] *A Hundred Years of Publishers' Bookbinding, 1857–1957* (privately printed, 1957), pp. 16–17.

[4] E. Howe (ed.), *The Trade: passages from the literature of the printing craft* (1943), pp. 26–8.

and monotype, the first really efficient type-setting machines, in the late nineteenth century; and these machines were at first confined largely to newspaper work, where speed was at a premium. A large part of the hand-compositor's skill resided in the correct spacing of the matter, the 'making up' of lines into pages, and general familiarity with the range of sizes and styles of type and ability to find his way around the case room. There was thus a considerable measure of variety and initiative in his work.[1] The growing size of firms, and changes in the other processes in the industry (especially the enormous increase in productivity from the application of steam power to the printing press) must none the less have affected the hand-compositor. There is some evidence of a growth of specialization in particular classes of work, and particular parts of the type-setting process. Newspaper work, for example, demanded rather different aptitudes from book or jobbing work; the newspaper compositor 'should be expeditious and careful', and 'good spacing has very largely to be sacrificed'.[2] There may, then, have been a relative decline in the versatility and initiative of the compositor, which led some commentators to refer to the 'deteriorating result of the close adherence of so many of our larger printing businesses to the system of division of labour'.[3]

The growing use of the 'stab, or time-rate, system of payment was an important aspect of this division of labour.[4] The 'stab system made it possible to retain a nucleus of more regular and 'reliable' employees, while wage costs were cut by allocating the best-paid items on the piece-work scale to this minority of time-workers. Compositors also complained of the use of apprentice and female labour;[5] and this led to the specialization of some journeymen in the more skilled parts of the work, and in the heavy work of carrying 'formes', 'making up', etc.[6] The

---

[1] Cf. R. Blauner, *Alienation and Freedom* (1964), pp. 40–1; I. C. Cannon, 'The Social Situation of the Skilled Worker: a study of the compositor in London' (Ph.D. thesis, London, 1961), p. 229.

[2] S. T. Jacobi, *Printing* (5th edn., 1913), p. 129.

[3] Letter in *Scottish Typo. Circular*, March 1896.

[4] See below, pp. 58–9, for the growing gulf between piece- and time-workers in Edinburgh.

[5] Edin. Typographical Society, *To the Master Printers of the City of Edinburgh* (1891).

[6] J. R. Macdonald (ed.), *Women in the Printing Trades* (1904), p. 48.

persistence of handicraft technique in type-setting did not therefore mean that there were no significant changes in the structure of the labour force and the organization of production. The heavier capital investment and increased scale of enterprise associated with mechanization in the press room were accompanied by attempts at rationalization and new divisions of labour in the type-setting process. And in the 1890s these pressures were intensified by the advent of the 'iron compositor',[1] type-setting machines, which seemed to threaten established wage rates and working practices, if not the complete displacement of the skilled compositor.[2]

Skilled machinemen worked in a rapidly changing technological environment. The powered press created new kinds of skill, as well as making possible the expansion and cheapening of the output of all sorts of printed matter; the machineman was generally agreed to be a superior class of worker to the old hand-pressman (who used to be known as 'pig' from the grunting occasioned by the heavy work of pulling the bar).[3] There was, throughout the period, a constant proliferation of new, faster, more specialized machines.[4] The skilled machineman had to master this changing technology. 'If youths who do not know (and men, too, for they exist) would only endeavour to help themselves by studying the current literature of their trade—and there is good and plenty of it in our own business—they might be able to help themselves forward very materially', urged the introduction to one technical handbook.[5] The machineman had an over-all responsibility for his machine, as well as for supervising its complement of semi-skilled feeders etc. One common type of machine had eleven preparatory steps and eighteen possible adjustments during running.[6] The initial

---

[1] *Scottish Typographical Circular*, Jan. 1896.

[2] Fears of the complete elimination of skilled labour were certainly exaggerated; but the uncontrolled use of the machines could erode wages and conditions; see below, p. 171, for the main dispute arising from this threat.

[3] *Edin. News*, 25 May 1853; S. Kinnear, 'The Future of our Young Compositors', in scrapbook of his writings in Edin. Public Libarary (dated July 1891, source unattributed); J. Child, *Industrial Relations in the British Printing Industry* (1967), p. 37.

[4] Child, op. cit., pp. 108–9, 158–9.

[5] 'Old Machine Manager', *The Printing Machine Manager's Complete Handbook and Machine Minder's Companion* (1889), p. vii.

[6] Ibid., pp. 8–10.

adjustment needed to ensure a clean and even impression demanded considerable skill and judgement.[1] Here again, versatility and initiative characterized the work situation of the skilled worker. The machinemen seem, however, to have been more subject to the exigencies of managerial control than the compositors. At Constable's machinemen were liable to fines for spoilt work.[2] The less stable technology, as well as the capital costs involved, therefore increased the role of management: 'The manager of a machine-room should be a man of firm character, and one who has a large amount of mechanical ingenuity and experience. The management of the machine department needs careful watchfulness.'[3]

In bookbinding a series of technical innovations, the subdivision of processes, and the adoption of cloth bindings for the new mass market restricted the skilled men to certain specialized tasks within a system of batch production.[4] This rationalization was evidently carried furthest at Nelson's, producing cheap editions for a newly developed mass market.[5] This led, according to one authority, to an increased level of skill in those tasks still performed by the apprenticed man, whose 'touch' was no longer spoilt by working at the heavier parts of the process.[6] Subdivision and mechanization clearly continued throughout the period; at Nelson's, whereas in 1867, 'a large amount of hand-labour is indispensable', by 1908 the only hand operation was the 'laying on' of gold lettering.[7] By the 1900s binding was 'sub-divided to such a degree that a man could be . . . taught some particular part of the process in a few months.'[8] Bookbinding thus exemplifies the adaptation of an old craft to skilled operations within a factory system of rationalized mass production. In the mid-nineteenth century the *Edinburgh News* commented on the work discipline of the bookbinders; the men

---

[1] Blauner, op. cit., pp. 41–2.

[2] Constable, press-department wage books.

[3] A. Oldfield, *A Practical Manual of Typography* (n.d., c. 1891), p. 115.

[4] C. White, 'A Century of Bookbinding in Edinburgh', *Edin. Journal of Science, Technology and Photographic Art* 16 (1941), 15.

[5] Bremner, op. cit., pp. 502–4; Wilson, op. cit., pp. 68–9; D. Balsillie, 'Nelson's 7d Library: how it is produced', *Bookbinding Trades Journal* (1908).

[6] White, loc. cit.

[7] Bremner, op. cit., p. 503; Balsillie, op. cit., p. 285.

[8] O. Gordon, *A Handbook of Employments* (1908), p. 149.

were punctual, there was little absenteeism or drinking during working hours, and generally 'the very best order is maintained in the workshops'.[1]

Building

In the building industry there was little change in technology, and the need to assemble a work force according to the demands of particular projects made 'craft administration' the most viable form of organization.[2] There were differences between the building trades, especially in the extent of specialization and subdivisions of skill within the trade. The most versatile, according to the *Edinburgh News*, were the joiners; the joiner was 'comptroller-general of the whole work' in housebuilding, and was therefore required to work from drawings.[3] The masons were also versatile: 'Nearly all Edinburgh masons can cut mouldings, however difficult'; but they were divided into two distinct branches, hewers and builders.[4] The painters, on the other hand, had marked 'professional gradations', arising partly from the influx of unapprenticed labour; consequently, 'there are very few painters indeed, in Edinburgh, who excel in every branch of their business.'[5] Skilled building workers, especially the masons, worked with labourers; the craftsman : labourer ratio was apparently similar to that in the iron foundries, with 0·52 labourers to every mason at the 1901 census. There were strong customs regarding working practices and job demarcation. 'Masons, having trade privileges, were bound to maintain them, without submitting to have them discussed by any other body of men, not even by labourers who might be subject to the injustice of those privileges.'[6]

Engineering

The second half of the nineteenth century saw the diffusion of the new techniques developed for the construction of the locomotives and textile machines of the Industrial Revolution,

---

[1] *Edin. News*, 30 July 1853.
[2] A. L. Stinchcombe, 'Bureaucratic and Craft Administration of Production' *Administrative Science Quarterly* 4 (1959).
[3] *Edin. News*, 9 Oct. 1852.   [4] Ibid., 2 Oct. 1852.   [5] Ibid., 20 Nov. 1852.
[6] A. Somerville, *The Autobiography of a Working Man* (1951; original edn., 1848), p. 88.

and the growth of specialized branches of engineering.[1]
Edinburgh's engineering industry was relatively 'conservative'
at mid-century; the first diffusion of capital-intensive methods,
using new types of machine tool, was localized to the textile
areas of the north of England, and rather narrowly based on the
manufacture of textile machinery and locomotives.[2] Burgess
suggests that the proportion of millwrights (the old established
all-round craft workers in engineering) is indicative of local
differences in the nature of the industry.[3] At the 1841 census,
millwrights accounted for only 7 per cent of all engineering
workers (millwrights, fitters, and turners, and engine- and
machine-makers combined) in Oldham, but for 18 per cent in
Edinburgh and Leith.[4] The engineering industry in earlier-
nineteenth-century Edinburgh would therefore seem to be
comparable to that of London, with a proliferation of small-
scale, highly skilled, and versatile craft workshops.[5] (As in the
English capital, the presence of scientific and medical institutions in the city may have encouraged such small shops,
manufacturing apparatus to standards of precision as yet in-
applicable to the manufacture of capital goods.) This milieu
was conducive to invention and the formation of entrepreneurs
and technicians, but not to the systematic application of new
technical knowledge; James Nasmyth, for example, took the
range of machine tools he had developed in a small experimental workshop in Edinburgh with him to Lancashire, where
he became a pioneer in the application of these new methods.[6]

The late 1840s and early 1850s saw a crisis and turning-point
in the development of the engineering industry, and of industrial capitalism generally, in Britain.[7] The crisis of over-
investment was overcome by broadening the base of the industry
and selling its products in export markets protected by Britain's
lead in advanced techniques and productive capacity. The

  [1] J. B. Jeffreys, *The Story of the Engineers* (1945), pp. 51–7.
  [2] K. Burgess, 'The Influence of Technological Change on the Social Attitudes
  and Trade Union Policies of Workers in the British Engineering Industry, 1780–
  1860' (Ph.D. thesis, Leeds, 1970), Ch. 2.   [3] Ibid., Ch. 3.
  [4] Census occupation tables, 1841. Edinburgh and Leith were combined, in
  view of the difficulty of distinguishing their engineering industries from each other.
  [5] For London see Burgess, op. cit., pp. 14–30, 146–7.
  [6] S. Smiles, *Industrial Biography* (1863), pp. 281–2.
  [7] Burgess, op. cit., pp. 72–5; Foster, op. cit., pp. 224–9.

basic machine-tool innovations of the earlier nineteenth century were refined, modified, and applied to a widening range of specialized branches of machine-making. Local engineering specialisms were emerging in the 1850s and 1860s; Bertram's of Edinburgh were already noted manufacturers of paper-making machinery in 1853, and certain specialized kinds of marine engineering, as well as some repair work, were carried on at Leith, despite a general decline of shipbuilding there.[1] Such new fields as the manufacture of electrical equipment had been added to these by the end of the century.[2] This development can be traced from the occupational breakdown of engineering employment; the proportion of millwrights in Edinburgh and Leith fell steadily from the 1850s, and new members of the A.S.E. followed the national pattern of a preponderance of fitters and turners.[3]

The effect of these trends was to decompose the all-round skills of the old millwrights, but also to create new skills (fitters and turners) with less versatility, but the greater accuracy and speed appropriate to the new methods. At the same time, the privileged position of British engineering in the world market, and the nature of the techniques employed, limited—but by no means eliminated—the pressures of further rationalization and displacement of skilled men. Here again, the role of a section of artisans in managing the production process, solving technical problems, etc., was as important to their privileged economic position as simple manual skill. Engineering products in the capital-goods sector were generally made to order, rather than for stock, even if the range of designs was standardized. The work of the skilled engineer was therefore likely to vary from job to job. The relatively high tolerance of machined components at this time made fitting very dependent on the skill of the fitter.[4] None the less, the steady improvement in machine tools must have had some impact. The use of excess

---

[1] *Edin. News*, 3 Aug. 1853; Bremner, op. cit., pp. 74-5; Institute of Public Administration, *Studies in the Development of Edinburgh*, pp. 23-34.

[2] Institute of Public Administration, loc. cit.

[3] Census occupation tables, 1861-1901; trades of new members of Edinburgh and Leith branches from A.S.E. *Reports*, 1865-9, 1875-9, 1885-9, cf. Jeffreys, op. cit., p. 59, for the national pattern at the same periods.

[4] Jeffreys, op. cit., pp. 122-4; D. S. Landes, *The Unbound Prometheus* (1969), pp. 305-7.

numbers of apprentices as semi-skilled machinists was alleged to
be especially bad in the Edinburgh District during the 1890s;[1] in
1908 a guide to employment for young people in Scotland noted
the emergence of the machinist, 'something between labourers
and tradesmen'; lathes, however, remained the preserve of
apprenticed turners.[2]

There was, on the other hand, a sector of the metal-working
industry that early adopted the 'division of labour principle'.
In brass-founding the existence of a mass market for gas and
plumbing fittings encouraged standardization and subdivision;
high piece-rates were paid for repetition turning of standardized
components.[3] At Milton House brass foundry in the 1860s the
moulding work—the making of a mould in sand from a wooden
pattern, into which the molten metal was poured, generally
regarded as a skilled trade—was said to be 'easy' and done
largely by boys; women were employed in the repetition drilling
of gas burners, and meters were assembled on the batch mass-
production system.[4] In the iron foundries, although moulding
was 'a delicate operation, and requires both tact and taste',
much of the work was 'mechanical' as well as 'very heavy'; part
of the iron trade in Edinburgh apparently consisted of the mass
production of standardized gates, fencing, girders, etc.[5] The
making of castings for machinery, on the other hand, required
a greater degree of skill and precision. The work experience of
engineering and foundry workers thus depended to a large
extend on the sector of metal-working in which they were
employed, and especially on the degree of product standardization and on whether production was for stock or to order.

Shoemakers

Shoemakers traditionally worked at home and by hand. This
remained the case throughout the trade, until the provision of
workshops by those employers who recognized the union,
apparently in the 1860s (and home work no doubt persisted in
the unorganized sections therafter). Despite the prevalence of

[1] A.S.E. *Quarterly Report*, May 1894.   [2] Gordon, op. cit., pp. 214–15.
[3] *Edin. News*, 10 Sept., 1853.   [4] Bremner, op. cit., pp. 136–8.
[5] *Edin. News*, 20 Aug., 10 Sept. 1853.

home work the process was subdivided by the 1850s: the cutting out of the leather, 'closing' (or the sewing together of the uppers), and 'making' (or the attaching of the sole to the uppers) were all separate processes (though not perhaps altogether separate occupations).[1] 'Making' was said to be the most skilled and arduous task.[2] Working at home, 'the men are thus their own masters, in so far as the disposal of their time is concerned', with a marked aversion to workshop employment, a 'hereditary and deeply-rooted dislike to be called a servant'.[3] Mayhew similarly attributed the London shoemakers' reputation for cantankerousness to the individualism engendered by their work situation: 'They appear to be a stern, uncompromising and reflecting race. This, perhaps, is to be accounted for by the solitude of their employment developing their own internal resources . . . The shoemakers are distinguished for the severity of their manners and habits of thought, and the suspicion that seems to pervade their character.'[4] The advent of workshops seems to have been linked to the introduction of the sewing-machine in the 1860s: in 1863, the *North Briton* noted the improvement in sobriety and work discipline associated with this trend.[5] After the introduction of sewing-machines and workshops the mass and bespoke sectors differ increasingly in their techniques of production. During the last quarter of the nineteenth century the making of shoes for the mass market was further mechanized and broken down into semi-skilled operations.[6] This process was associated with the localization of the new factory shoe industry in Leicester, Northampton, and other centres; that it none the less had effects in Edinburgh is indicated by the existence from 1881 of a branch of the Boot and Shoe Rivetters (the predecessor of the National Union of Boot and Shoe Operatives), which catered for workers in the mechanized sector.[7] The large luxury market in the city, on the other hand, supported a number of 'first-class firms who make a speciality of hand-made goods'.[8] Thus, the mechanization of production for the mass market increased the occupational

---

[1] *Edin. News*, 15 Mar. 1853.   [2] Ibid., 18 Mar. 1853.   [3] Ibid., 2 Apr. 1853.
[4] E. P. Thompson and E. Yeo (eds.), *The Unknown Mayhew*, p. 232.
[5] *North Briton*, 18 Aug., 1863.
[6] A. Fox, *A History of the National Union of Boot and Shoe Operatives* (1958), Ch. 2.
[7] T.C. Minutes, 11 Oct. 1881.   [8] Gordon, op. cit., p. 155.

distinctiveness of the craft shoemaker—whereas the old sweated trade had used the same basic techniques, albeit less competently. Shoemaking is an instance of the persistence of craft methods for the luxury market in an industry increasingly using mechanized mass-production techniques. Both sectors appear to have existed in Edinburgh, but the local importance of a wealthy market no doubt made the craft sector of greater significance than in most large cities.

In all the industries discussed, skilled labour had considerable autonomy in the workshop. Productive techniques were by no means static—even in trades unaffected by mechanization there were signs of a more rigid division of labour, and hierarchy of specialization—but these changes did not destroy the distinctive position of the artisan, or the *de facto* authority he exerted in the work place. (There is, on the other hand, a good deal of evidence,[1] that this position was subject to intensified pressures in the 1890s, with such developments as the acceleration of technological change.)

This workshop autonomy was both cause and effect of the strongly marked occupational 'craft cultures' of the artisan strata. Craft customs and traditions, and the powerful defensive practices they often embodied, are a well-documented feature of Victorian artisan life. But differentiation of work roles operated within the skilled trades themselves, and may have undermined the homogeneity of 'craft communities', partially detaching some members of the trade from those communities.[2] The growing division of labour in skilled occupations, and the associated distribution of authority at work, means that the situation of the skilled worker cannot be described simply in terms of craft autonomy. Changing techniques and scale of production, within an expanding capitalist economy, created new forms of hierarchy and division among manual wage-earners, which operated *within the skilled labour force*, as well as in its relations with less skilled groups of workers.

---

[1] See below, pp. 167–9.
[2] Cf. Foster, op. cit., pp. 223–4, 228; and below, pp. 93–4.

4   Wages and Standards of Living

To delineate the economic situation of the artisan it is necessary to make three sets of distinctions: between skilled and unskilled labour; between different skilled trades; and within certain trades. The first and second sets of distinctions are, in themselves, relatively poor predictors of the economic circumstances of any particular person. As Mayhew argued: 'It becomes most important in speaking of wages, and in citing individual earnings, to state the portion of the trade for which the man is working, or else egregious blunders and confusion, and injustice, may be the result.'[1] The economic differences within the working class are rather more complex than the familiar distinction between the artisan and the labourer. It is certainly true that skilled labour in general was advantageously placed, relative to the unskilled. But the evidence suggests also a considerable range between and within the skilled trades themselves.

Certain methodological problems arise in the investigation of these issues. There is a considerable literature about standards of living during the nineteenth century. Much of the evidence presented in it is at what could be called the 'aggregate' level of analysis—it gives data not broken down further than by occupation. This has been a result partly of a necessary dependence on trade-union or other reports of standard wage-rates, but partly also of a preoccupation with the construction of national indices, and with such issues as factor shares of the national income.[2] Whatever its merits, this approach is by itself inadequate: what matters, for a local study, is the experience of identifiable individuals over their lifetimes.[3]

---

[1] Thompson and Yeo (eds.), *The Unknown Mayhew*, p. 472.
[2] See A. L. Bowley, *Wages and Income Since 1860* (1937); P. Deane and W. A. Cole, *British Economic Growth, 1688–1959* (2nd edn., 1967), Ch. 7 and sources there cited.
[3] See R. S. Neale, 'The Standard of Living, 1780–1844: a regional and class study', *Economic History Review* 2nd ser. 1 (1 66).

That experience is extremely hard to penetrate, but we can make informed guesses, provided that we move from the aggregate level to a closer examination of the processes shaping the experience of men in particular occupations. The evidence is inevitably fragmentary, and the most that can be achieved is some picture of the rough location of different occupations in the economic hierarchy, and of the range of variation within the skilled working class as a whole, and within specific trades. We can, on the other hand, make use of statistical data relating to individual workers as a partial test of this account of occupational differences.

One aspect is neglected in the following analysis; the movement of prices. Students of living standards have rightly been concerned to obtain reliable price indices.[1] In the present study, on the other hand, no effort has been made to estimate real, as opposed to money, wages. The main reason for this is that the work of collecting local data for rents and retail prices did not seem justified, given the chronological scatter and dubious reliability of the figures for wages. The price history of the period should, however, be borne in mind—in particular, the cheapening of foodstuffs generally held to have contributed to improved real wages in the 1880s and 1890s.[2] There is no special reason to suppose that working people in Edinburgh failed to benefit from this trend.

I. AGGREGATE INDICATORS

Table 4.1 shows the distribution of occupations over the range of standard wage-rates for adult male labour in Edinburgh.[3] (Here, as for most of this discussion, the interest is in the *adult male*, whose wage was in theory supposed to constitute the means of subsistence for a family, at any rate in skilled trades; various figures for juvenile and female labour have therefore been ignored.) The figures are apparently based mainly on trade-union returns; in some cases the weekly rate has evidently been computed by multiplying an hourly rate by the full working

---

[1] See, e.g., B. R. Mitchell and P. Deane, *Abstract of British Historical Statistics* (1962), pp. 343–5 and Ch. 16.   [2] Ibid.

[3] All statements regarding standard wage-rates or hours not otherwise substantiated are based on the sources for this table.

week. There is no allowance for fluctuations in employment. ✓ And, in the case of the printer's rate, a further complication is the prevalence of piece-work among compositors. Finally, one must bear in mind the rather selective occupational coverage of the table (which is confined to occupations for which figures are given at both dates).

TABLE 4.1

*Distribution of Standard Weekly Wage-rates, 1866–1867 and 1890:
Positions of Occupations by Quartile Intervals*

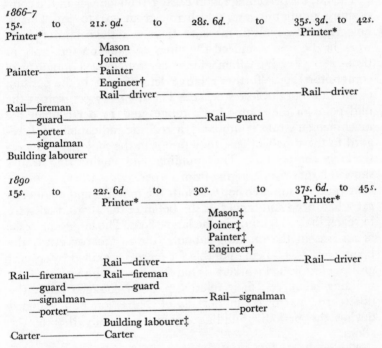

1866–7
15s.   to   21s. 9d.   to   28s. 6d.   to   35s. 3d.   to   42s.
Printer*————————————————————————————Printer*
            Mason
            Joiner
Painter————— Painter
            Engineer†
            Rail—driver——————————————Rail—driver
Rail—fireman
    —guard——————————————Rail—guard
    —porter
    —signalman
Building labourer

1890
15s.   to   22s. 6d.   to   30s.   to   37s. 6d.   to   45s.
            Printer*————————————————————Printer*
                    Mason‡
                    Joiner‡
                    Painter‡
                    Engineer†
            Rail—driver——————————————Rail—driver
Rail—fireman——— Rail—fireman
    —guard—————————guard
    —signalman——————————————— Rail—signalman
    —porter——————————————————porter
            Building labourer‡
Carter—————————Carter

Source: A. L. Bowley and G. H. Wood, 'The Statistics of Wages in the United Kingdom during the last Hundred Years', *Journal of the Royal Statistical Society*, 62–8 (1899–1905) (series of articles); Bremner, *Industries of Scotland*, (1869); *Returns of Wages, 1830–86*, P.P. 1887 LXXXIX; *Report on the Strikes and Lock-outs of 1890*, P.P. 1890–1 LXXXVIII, Appendix vi; *General Report on Wages*, P.P. 1893–4 LXXXIII, Pt. ii.

Notes: ——————— indicates range of rates for the occupation.
 * Compositors and machinemen are not distinguished.
 † Fitter and turner (both rates fell in the same bracket).
 ‡ Summer hours.

For these reasons the information can be regarded as at best a rough guide. It is nevertheless worth noting a distinct diminution in the bunching of occupations in the lower intervals, skilled trades disappearing entirely from the bottom quartile (with the exception of rail guards, firemen, and signalmen who are classified as skilled workers throughout this study). The picture shows a general improvement in standard rates, but also continuing, and possibly increasing, differences between occupations, especially between skilled and unskilled.

The largest percentage gain during 1866–90 was in the compositor's minimum rate, which rose from 20s. to 30s. This is, however, not a realistic measure, in view of the extent of piecework in the trade—indeed the effect of gains on the 'stab, or time-rate (covering all machinemen, but only a minority of compositors), was 'further relative deterioration in the position of the Edinburgh piece worker'.[1] The rise of 17 per cent at the mid point of the compositor's range, and 15 per cent in the machinemen's rate is probably a realistic indication, with regard to the time-workers, though not to the majority of piece-working compositors. The building and engineering trades showed larger rises, ranging from 17 per cent (turner) to 26 per cent (mason, summer hours). Both the mason's and engineer's rates had been still higher in the boom of the 1870s, and were to reach their maximum in the later 1890s. The largest increase of all was in the building labourer's rate (30 per cent), the boom of 1889–90 being notable for increases gained by several groups of unskilled workers. Whatever the absolute gains of the building labourers, their relative position changed little: the differential narrowed in periods of depression and widened during the periodic building booms, especially that of the 1890s.

The available information about standard hours presents a similar picture of general improvement, especially in building and engineering, but persistent differences between industries. The masons took the lead in shortening hours, winning the nine-hour day (or fifty-one-hour week: nine hours, and six on Saturday) in 1861; this was then quickly extended to the other

---

[1] S. C. Gillespie, *A Hundred Years of Progress: the record of the Scottish Typographical Association, 1853–1952* (1953), p. 66.

building trades.[1] The engineering and metal workers won the fifty-one-hour week in 1872, but this was lengthened to fifty-four hours during the depression.[2] The printing trades won the fifty-four hours in 1871 (but failed to gain another reduction in a bitter strike the following year), with further reductions in the 1890s (especially among the more prosperous sections, such as lithographers and bookbinders). We know less about hours in tailoring or shoemaking. Those shoemakers in workshops worked a ten-hour day in 1872.[3] In general, piece-workers' hours fell less than time-workers'. According to the Webbs, the press and machinemen broke away from the Edinburgh Typographical Society because they 'did not pull well together with the comprs. [sic] (piece workers) who wanted hours as they were whilst machinemen (time workers) wanted them reduced'.[4]

As we know more about standard wage-rates than about actual earnings, so we know more about the standard working week than about actual hours worked. The tendency for over-time payments, designed as a disincentive to the employer, to be perverted into an incentive to the worker, is certainly visible in nineteenth-century industry. At the Royal Commission on Labour (1892) the engineers complained that 71·7 per cent of A.S.E. members in Edinburgh were in shops that worked systematic overtime at boom periods; whereas the masons and joiners reported little overtime working.[5]

TABLE 4.2
Standard Hours, 1860–1900

	1860	1866–7	1872	1900
Building	57*	51	51	51
Printing	–	–	54	52½
Bookbinding	60	57	54	52½
Engineering	60	57	51†	54
Shoemaking	–	60	–	–

Source: As for Table 4.1.
* 60 in some trades.
† Lengthened to 54 in late 1870s.

[1] MacDougall (ed.), *Minutes of Edinburgh Trades Council*, pp. xxxvii–xxxviii.
[2] Ibid.; T.C. Minutes, 20 Aug. 1877, 12 Sept. 1878.
[3] Edin. Operative Cordwainers' Society, *To the Master Boot and Shoemakers* (1872).
[4] S. and B. Webb, Manuscript Notes (Webb Trade Union Collection A.7. ii).
[5] *R.C. on Labour, group A*, P.P. 1892 XXXVI, pt. iii, appendix xlvi, special report by the A.S.E.; *R.C. on Labour, group C*, P.P. 1892 XXXVI, pt. ii, qq. 17977, 17646.

TABLE 4.3

Methods of Payment in Edinburgh Skilled Trades

	Piece	Time
Printing	Most compositors	Some compositors
		Machinemen
	Some bookbinders	Most bookbinders
Building		All
Engineering	Brass workers	Engineers
	Various metal trades	Smiths
	(meter-making, possibly	Ironmoulders
	rail workshops)	
Clothing	Tailors	
	Shoemakers	
Wood and Furniture	Cabinet-makers	
	Coopers	
Other	Curriers	
	(possibly other leather	
	trades)	
	Some coachmakers	Some coachmakers
	Glass workers	
		Jewellery and
		precious metals
	Some type-founders	Some type-founders
	Comb-makers	
	(rubber factory)	

Source: Mainly as for Table 4.1: othersise miscellaneous references in trade-union sources etc.

The system of payment also had a bearing on wages and working hours. Piece-work existed in two sorts of situation. First, in labour-intensive handicrafts with market conditions subject to seasonal or other short-run fluctuations. Second, in larger-scale, more heavily capitalized industries, where the product was standardized to such an extent as to allow of piece-work. In the latter case the system is associated with standardization, in the former with its absence. This point is illustrated in Table 4.3: the piece-work trades include the clothing trades (which belong to the category of labour-intensive handicrafts) and workers in such capital-intensive industries as glass and metal-working.

Many workers believed that piece-work was to their detriment. The printers' delegate at the Trades Council (no doubt thinking of the piece-working compositors) declared that the piece system 'tended to Keep Down men in every form',

although the tailors and cabinet-makers defended the system.[1]
The engineering trades condemned piece-work (as was the
policy of their unions).[2] Piece systems were judged according
to whether they were believed to secure for particular trades
their expected norm of a 'a fair day's work for a fair day's wage'.
As the saddlers' delegate put it, the system was acceptable
'wherever the men were able to enforce their claim to have A
Voice in the setting of the Piece Prices'.[3] On the other hand, the
introduction of piece-work might powerfully reinforce the
growth of the casual-labour market (as was allegedly the case
with the London tailors).[4] Although the piece trades do not
have the same history of wage reductions and recurrent large
disputes as the engineering or building trades, there was un-
doubted scope for employers to exert pressure in other ways,
altering the interpretation of the agreed lists (which were often
extremely complicated), manipulating the classification and
allocation of work, and so on. While the combination of piece-
work with casual labour and sweating weakened the capacity
to resist, 'causing jealousy and ill feeling in every instance and
often causing men to bring themselves to the level of Slavery'.[5]
Thus, although the incidence of unemployment and fluctuation
in the official rate of wages was most severe in the time-working
trades, the piece system was often associated with a more
insidious pressure on weakly organized trades.

The relative incidence of pauperism provides a useful comparative view of economic conditions; unlike standard wage-
rates it reflects the totality of economic experience, taking
account of the regularity of wages as well as their level. The
census of 1871 gives a table showing the 'Former or Present
Occupations of the Paupers in the County of Edinburgh' (i.e.
the county now known as Midlothian: 80 per cent of the population lived in Edinburgh and Leith in 1871). The table must
be interpreted with caution. The numbers in certain occupations (unskilled workers and those skilled trades diluted by

---

[1] T.C. Minutes, 15, 22 Feb. 1876.
[2] Ibid. The A.S.E. report to the Royal Commission on Labour (above, p. 47,
n. 5) indicated little piece-work in Edinburgh.   [3] Ibid., 15 Feb. 1876.
[4] According to one of Mayhew's informants: Thompson and Yeo (eds.), op.
cit., p. 186.
[5] T.C. Minutes, 15 Feb. 1876. The speaker's trade has not been identified.

unapprenticed labour) may be inflated by the fact that men originally in other occupations entered them immediately before going on poor relief. The age structure of different occupations may also have an effect; for example, the difference between masons and joiners may simply reflect the fact that masons' work was heavier and less healthy and men therefore had to leave the trade at an earlier age, whereas in the joiners' trade 'old men are often preferred'.[1] The table is nevertheless of some interest, if only for revealing that certain occupations may have been the second-to-last resort of the pauperized.

With the exception of carters (and possibly sawyers, whose level of skill is something of a borderline case, though they will be classified as semi-skilled for the purposes of this study), the

TABLE 4.4

Numbers of Paupers from Occupations, Edinburgh County, 1871,
as Percentage of Total in those Occupations
(Average of 1861 and 1871)

Over 1·5 per cent			1·0 to 1·5 per cent	
Building labourer	8·1		Cabinet-maker ⎫	
Messenger, porter	2·5		Baker ⎬ 1·4	
Shoemaker	2·4		Watchmaker ⎭	
Painter	2·2		Sawyer	
General labourer ⎫			Cooper	
Plumber ⎬ 2·1			Litho-printer ⎬ 1·3	
Tin-worker ⎫			Blacksmith	
Slater ⎬ 2·0			Brass-founder ⎭	
Iron manufactures*	1·9		Boilermaker ⎫	
Type-founder	1·8		Carter ⎬ 1·2	
Tailor ⎫			Joiner ⎫	
Printer† ⎬ 1·7			Bookbinder ⎬ 1·1	
			Tanner ⎭	
			Engineer	1·0

Less than 1·0 per cent	
Glass-worker ⎫	
Mason ⎬ 0·9	
Goldsmith etc.	0·6
Plasterer	0·4
Coachmaker	0·2

Source: *Census of Scotland, 1871,* vol. iii.

* Probably includes various other groups of foundry workers, as well as the skilled iron-moulders.

† Like all census figures, this regrettably fails to distinguish compositors and machinemen.

[1] *Edin. News,* 2 Oct., 1852; Gordon, *Handbook of Employments,* p. 177.

unskilled occupations fall near the top of the list; so do the painters and the shoemakers. While the masons, joiners, and engineers all fall towards the bottom. It was predominantly those trades marked by problems of casual and/or sweated labour (most notably the shoemakers and painters) that had the higher proportions of men obliged to turn to the last resort of the Victorian poor.

There were therefore considerable differences in economic standards, both between skilled and unskilled and within the skilled working class. The reasons for these differences are best approached from an examination of the experiences of particular trades. But it is first necessary to discuss in more general terms the economic relationships that affected the regularity, as well as the level, of workers' incomes.

It is now generally recognized that we must identify three cycles of investment and employment in order to chart the growth and fluctuations of the British economy: the cycles of building, home industry, and overseas investment.[1] All three types of movement had effects on the level of employment in Edinburgh.[2] There were also marked seasonal patterns in certain local industries. The cycles of building and the capital-goods industries in Edinburgh appear to follow well-charted national movements. The 1870s saw an exceptionally strong boom, based on the interaction of investment in building and in capital goods. The collapse of the boom was followed by a period of general depression in both sectors, with severe down-swings and only relatively weak up-swings until the mid-1890s. The years from 1894 or 1895 to the end of the decade were marked, again, by strong booms in both sectors, together con-stituting the 'home boom of the 1890s'.[3]

The building industry was also characterized by a marked seasonal variation in the level of activity. The wage in 1890 for a winter week was below that for summer by 17 per cent (for masons), 12 per cent (for joiners) and 33 per cent (for painters).

---

[1] See e.g. W. H. B. Court, *British Economic History, 1870–1914: commentary and documents* (1965), pp. 7–8.

[2] For an impressionistic picture of fluctuations, see references to the state of trade in Trades Council Minutes and *Reports, passim*.

[3] E. M. Sigsworth and J. Blackman, 'The Home Boom of the 1890s', *Yorkshire Bulletin of Economic and Social Research*, 17 (1965).

And this is leaving aside the numbers laid off altogether for all or part of the winter, as also fluctuations due to the weather, rather than simply to the hours of daylight.

The consumer-goods industries are less well charted. The nature of local society would suggest that these industries were oriented largely to middle- and upper-class markets. The tailors' delegate argued at the Trades Council that depression was due to: 'Minor Industries . . . being to a large extent only such as supplied the wants within itself. At present very much funded money upon the Dividends from which Edinburgh mainly depended were not paying, whence the stagnation.'[1] According to this diagnosis, effective demand in local consumer-goods industries depended on the level of investment incomes; in Edinburgh, such incomes probably had more to do with the cycles of overseas investment and building than of domestic industry. To substantiate this view is far beyond the scope of the present study. But there is some evidence for a pattern peculiar to the consumer-goods sector: in 1885, for instance, the shoemakers and the tailors were reported to be thriving, while the ironmoulders reported heavy expenditure on out-of-work benefit.[2]

Tailoring and shoemaking were susceptible to shorter-run fluctuations. Stedman Jones has explored this phenomenon in a seminal study of casual labour in London. The small amount of fixed capital in the consumer sector encouraged 'the regulation of manufacture according to consumer demand', rather than stockpiling.[3] The concomitant of this, in Edinburgh as in London, was the casualization and under-employment of a large part of the labour force. In tailoring, for example, it was normal to take on thirty or forty men in the busy season, of whom only half a dozen would still be employed in the slack season.[4] The shoemakers likewise suffered great variations in earnings, but had no distinct seasonal pattern.[5] Here, as in the building trades, the incidence of fluctuation is bound up with organization and bargaining power, the struggles of different trades to maintain their position in the face of cut-throat

---

[1] T.C. Minutes, 18 Nov. 1884.   [2] Ibid., 21 Apr., 2 June, 29 Dec. 1885.
[3] G. Stedman Jones, *Outcast London* (1971), pp. 33-4.
[4] *Edin. News*, 12 Mar. 1853.   [5] Ibid., 2 Apr. 1853.

competition, casual labour, and sweating. The well-organized cabinet-makers (like the shoemakers and tailors a piece-working trade producing for the local consumer market) enjoyed relatively stable earnings.[1] As Mayhew noted, 'wages depend as much on the distribution of labour as on the demand and supply of it';[2] violent short-run alternations of slack and busy trade would, by encouraging the growth of a casual and semi-employed work-force, drive down wages and conditions. The small amount of fixed capital and the fact that piece-workers were paid *entirely* by output meant that costs varied directly with the amount produced, rather than with the size of the work force; while at the same time employers had every reason to create a work force that was large, amorphous, and difficult to organize. This was so especially where the various systems of out-work and sub-contract, generically labelled 'sweating', exerted their influence.[3]

Both piece-work and a certain amount of sweating were features of tailoring and shoemaking in Edinburgh. The tailors told the Select Committee on Sweating (1889) that, because of the limited extent of the ready-made trade in the city, 'the very lowest class of sweating does not affect us directly';[4] but the system still existed, and was at one time resorted to by 'almost every employer in the clothing trade', bespoke as well as ready made.[5] Out-work prices were said to be 25 to 30 per cent lower.[6] The shoemakers worked entirely on an out-work basis until 'honourable' employers (i.e. those who recognized agreed wage-rates) provided workshops, apparently in the 1860s.[7] The short-term fluctuation in demand characteristic of the clothing

---

[1] *Edin. News*, 14 May 1853.

[2] Thompson and Yeo (eds.), op. cit., pp. 384–5.

[3] Contemporary social investigators got into endless confusion as to the definition of 'sweating'; it is perhaps most meaningfully defined, not simply as 'under-pay and over-work', but as those systems where the worker hired part of the fixed capital employed, either because he worked on his own premises, or because he was obliged to rent working (and often also living) accommodation from the employer.

[4] *Select Committee on Sweating*, P.P. 1889 XIV, pt. i, q. 26517 (N. M'Lean, Scottish Operative Tailors).

[5] Edin. Branch, Scottish National Association of Operative Tailors, *The Sweating System in Edinburgh* (n.d.).

[6] *Select Committee on Sweating*, loc. cit., q. 26520.

[7] *North Briton*, 18 Aug. 1863.

and shoe trades was compounded by the sweating system, casual
labour, weak organization, and a consequent downward pressure on wages and conditions.

The cyclical pattern of the printing industry appears to have
been relatively unaffected by the cycles of economic activity so
far considered. There was a period of dislocation, fierce competition, and rapid structural change, marked by such legal
changes as the abolition of monopolies in bible printing in the
1840s, and the better-known repeal of the 'taxes on knowledge'
in the fifties and sixties.[1] This was also the period of the capitalization of the industry, the emergence of Edinburgh as a printing centre with widespread markets, and the growing dominance
of certain leading firms (many of which are still in existence).
There is little evidence of cyclical movements in employment
after the period of structural change. There was, on the other
hand, a distinct seasonal pattern, though perhaps less sharp
than in building or tailoring. Again, this was compounded by a
problem of casual labour among piece-working compositors.

The foregoing discussion would lead us to expect recurrent
cyclical unemployment in engineering and building, seasonal
unemployment in building and printing, and casual labour and
under-employment in the clothing and shoe trades and among
compositors in printing. The only figures found for unemployment are shown in Table 4.5. They were collected from trade
unions during the depression of 1893, and are, as the author
points out, an under-estimate, since 'the members of the Union
are the best and steadiest workmen, and consequently the best
employed.'[2] Whatever their drawbacks, the figures show the
heavier incidence of the depression in engineering. The unemployment in building, on the other hand, is dispropor-
tionately due to the painters (other building trades, 3·5 per
cent). The figures hide a good deal of concealed unemployment
in the clothing and shoe trades: 'The condition of the Tailoring
and Shoemaking trades has not been so depressed for a number
of years, and although there are few men absolutely without
work there is a large number who are only half employed.'[3]

---

[1] S. Kinnear, *Reminiscences of an Aristocratic Edinburgh Printing Office* (1890), p. 31;
Scottish Typographical Circular, Nov. 1861.

[2] J. Mallinson, *Statistics Bearing on the State of Employment . . . in . . . Edinburgh,*
December, 1893.   [3] Ibid.

Similarly, the incidence of unemployment (as opposed to under-employment) was greater among the time-working machine-men than the piece-working compositors. Although the main figures regrettably are not broken down further than by industry, skilled workers registered as unemployed (in a procedure designed to supplement the trade-union information, mainly with regard to unskilled workers) included fifteen machinemen and only two compositors, whereas we know that compositors comprised three-quarters or more of the labour force in the two departments combined.[1]

TABLE 4.5
Percentage of Skilled Trades Unemployed, 1893
(based on estimates by union secretaries)

Printing	2·4	Clothing and Shoe	1·0
Building*	6·5	Cabinet and Furniture	7·1
Iron and Engineering	8·6	Miscellaneous	5·7

Source: Figures in J. Mallinson, Statistics Bearing on the State of Employment . . . in . . . Edinburgh, December, 1893.
* The figures are for winter.

Regularity of employment was as important as differences in the standard wage-rate. Thus the painters, who occupy the same wage bracket as the masons and joiners (Table 4.1), were more vulnerable to seasonal unemployment and pauperization (Table 4.4). It is customary to distinguish different sources of irregular employment. The most discussed of these is cyclical unemployment; this was certainly an important feature of working-class experience in the nineteenth century, especially in the capital-goods and building industries. It is, however, a mistake to dissociate the different types of unemployment too rigidly from each other. A particularly severe cyclical crisis might initiate the process of casualization and occupational decline; the collapse following the 'building mania' of the 1820s, for example, was said to have ended a 'golden age' for the Edinburgh painters.[2] With this important qualification, we can conclude that seasonal and other short-term movements had a more severe effect on relative economic standards than

[1] J. Mallinson, *Statistics Bearing on the State of Employment . . . in . . . Edinburgh, December, 1893.* See above, Table 3.2, for the structure of the labour force in printing.   [2] *Edin. News,* 27 Nov. 1852.

the movements of the trade cycle. Those trades vulnerable to cyclical fluctuations (engineering and building) were in general less precariously placed than those trades (such as shoemaking) characterized by a large permanent reserve army of casual workers with consequent chronic under-employment.

This casual-labour problem was not simply a reflection of unavoidable seasonal conditions, or of market fluctuations caused by the vagaries of 'fashion', the social 'season', etc. Casualization was a strategy to reduce wages, and its incidence varied with the capacity to resist, and especially to prevent detrimental changes in the division of labour. The painters, with their 'professional gradations' and dilution by unapprenticed labour,[1] complained that employers deliberately accentuated seasonality, allegedly even misleading their customers about the possibility of undertaking painting work at certain times of year.[2] The well-organized masons, on the other hand, were apparently 'time conscious', even a decade before the nine hours' movement. 'It is a custom of the trade that a mason with his mell in the air will let it descend without hitting the chisel when he hears the first sound in the signal [to stop work].'[3] This concern to uphold the standard working day no doubt arose partly from a belief that any variation in hours would accentuate irregularities of employment and encourage the growth of casual labour.[4]

II. OCCUPATIONAL EXPERIENCES

The foregoing discussion has been of a deliberately general character. The aim has been to identify patterns and variables, and thus to provide a framework for a more focused analysis of particular occupations. The general discussion has itself indicated the need for this more specific approach. The seasonal variation in earnings, for example, did not depend simply on the weather, but also on the employers' strategies and the shop-floor struggle to resist those strategies. This can be understood

---

[1] *Edin. News*, 27 Nov. 1852. [2] *Reformer*, 13 Feb. 1869. [3] *Edin. News*, 2 Oct. 1852
[4] Not only did the short Scottish winter days mean a particularly severe cutback, but the long summer evenings may also have facilitated systematic overtime.

only in specific industrial and occupational contexts. One important aspect of this, the differentiation within a particular trade, has been largely obscured at the level of generality. It is therefore necessary to consider the specific situations of a number of trades, which between them exemplify the range of variation within the skilled strata of the working class.

Compositors

The compositors, perhaps because of the educational requirements of their job, seem traditionally to have been considered a superior occupational group.[1] Recollections of the earlier nineteenth century give a picture of relative economic stability and recognized social status: compositors got 10s. weekly, and the balance of their piece earnings every third week; 'the almost used-up human material of the establishment' were kept employed, although 'their wages must have formed a considerable deduction from the profits of the concern'.[2]

With the expansion, capitalization, and growing scale of the industry the compositor's position became less secure. Printing, like other consumer industries, suffered the vicissitudes of seasonal production (an added seasonal factor being the stimulus to demand of the law courts, government work, and the annual Assemblies of the Church of Scotland).[3] Unlike most consumer trades, however, the printing industry contained a considerable amount of fixed capital, with the introduction of steam presses, and increasingly also of purpose-built factories. The fixed capital tied up in the machine room, and the bargaining power which accrued to the machineman from his high productivity and mastery of a rapidly changing technology, meant that the 'regulation of manufacture according to consumer demand'[4] bore most heavily on the labour-intensive composing room—an arrangement facilitated by the fact that most compositors were paid according to output.

The economic pressures affecting the compositor arose from the employer's attempts to cut wage costs in the labour-intensive part of the printing process, and adjust them as nearly

---

[1] Cannon, 'Social Situation of the Skilled Worker', p. 56.
[2] Kinnear, op. cit., pp. 17, 30.
[3] See reports on state of trade in *Scottish Typographical Circular, passim.*
[4] Stedman Jones, loc. cit.

as possible to fluctuations in the market for his product. This involved a decline in the compositor's position, relative to the skilled machineman (who largely replaced the old hand-pressman): 'the remuneration of pressmen and machinemen as a class is unquestionably higher than that of compositors', the conclusion being that this was because machinemen were on time-rates.[1] Several means of cutting wage costs were open to employers; these means are summarized by a Typographical Society document of 1891: 'The position of the Piece Compositor has for years been one of peculiar hardship. Subject to all the vicissitudes of a fluctuating trade, his precarious and uncertain earnings have been further endangered by the more general adoption of the 'Stab system, the large increase of Apprentices, and the introduction of Female Labour.'[2]

The dislike of the 'stab system relates to the problem of casualization. As the 'stab (or time-rate) was used more extensively (but still, apparently, only for a minority of favoured regular employees), so the fluctuations in trade bore more heavily on the piece-workers: 'the printing trade in Edinburgh has suffered very severely so far as regular employment is concerned to journeymen—those that are in piece work, at any rate.'[3] This tendency was accentuated by the effect of the 'stab system on work allocation—a matter of vital importance to the piece-working compositor. A complicated scale of prices, held in reverence by many union activists, was regarded as the piece-working compositor's charter of rights and privileges;[4] 'extras' for such things as footnotes, passages in foreign languages, and so on, were designed to ensure that the worker was adequately rewarded for the more demanding and time-consuming kinds of work. The advantage of the 'stab from the employer's point of view was that he could allocate the more lucrative items on the piece scale (the 'fat') to time-workers, thereby evading the spirit, if not the letter, of the scale. As a result, 'you will find one section of the men continually kept setting the "rubbish" of the

---

[1] *Scottish Typographical Circular*, Dec. 1860.
[2] Edin. Typographical Society, *To the Master Printers* (1891).
[3] *R.C. on Labour, group C*, P.P. 1893–4 XXXIV, q. 23175 (Secretary, Edin. Typographical Society).
[4] For the strong attachment to this scale see *Scottish Typographical Circular*, Jan. 1862, editorial.

house, while others, with perhaps less ability, are lolling in fat of all kinds; and beyond that, the same is true when slackness settles down, it is the poor victims of the rubbish-heap who are the first for the slate and are kept longest there.'[1] The *North Briton* drew the contrast, in a caustic comment on the dinner held to celebrate gains won in 1862: 'In the Rainbow Hotel we find fifty printers faring sumptuously, and in the Strangers' Friend Society we find other fifty printers fasting grievously.'[2] The casualization of a part of the labour force thus created a marked division within the trade.

The issue of work allocation also entered into the threat posed to the compositor's position by apprentice and female labour. The older apprentices might be used as cheap labour, and work allocation manipulated to this end.[3] More generally, unregulated recruitment to the trade might intensify the process of casualization. According to the Webbs, union apprenticeship rules for compositors were not effectively enforced.[4] It is hard to gauge exactly the extent of apprentice and other male juvenile labour, since the census never distinguishes compositors from machinemen: 36 per cent of males in the census category 'printer' were aged under twenty in 1861, falling to 29 per cent in 1881 and 1891, and 15 per cent in 1901. This is certainly somewhat higher than in the other skilled trades examined for the first three censuses; but it must be remembered that the figures include machine-room workers, some of whom were semi-skilled boys rather than apprentices. Women were employed in type-setting during and after the strike of 1872; although they did not displace men on any large scale (being confined to certain simpler kinds of work), they must certainly have taken work from the piece-working compositor, and their introduction figured, as we have seen, in his list of grievances.[5]

The compositor, then, worked at a trade marked by seasonal fluctuations, a pressure to minimize wage costs and to adjust them to the variable level of demand, casualization of an

[1] *Scottish Typographical Circular* Jan. 1898, editorial. 'The slate' is trade slang for being paid off.   [2] *North Briton*, 5 Apr. 1862.
[3] This led to a serious dispute at the *Scotsman* office: *Scottish Typographical Circular*, Sept. 1872.
[4] Webb Manuscript Notes, loc. cit.
[5] Macdonald (ed.), *Women in the Printing Trades*, pp. 45–8.

appreciable part of the labour force, and relatively ineffective control on the recruitment of additional labour. In the 1890s he also felt threatened by technical change. The last decade of the century saw the introduction of the first really viable type-setting machines, the linotype and monotype. 'Battle seems to be very near at hand—compositors *v.* machines of all sorts and sizes, headed by the linotype.'[1] The *Typographical Circular* noted the dangers of the 'iron compositor', and 'uneasiness and displacement of labour'.[2] Related to these fears was a sharp struggle over rates and conditions on the new machines, as the union sought to make them as expensive as possible, and to ensure that their operation would be the prerogative of time-served compositors. Although fears of widespread technological unemployment proved groundless—the machines were anyway at first confined mainly to news work—the impact of the new machines cannot be ignored, given the background of a casual labour market, weak controls on recruitment, and disadvantageous methods of work allocation.

Machinemen

The new expertise demanded by the steam-powered printing press, the great increase in productivity associated with its advent, and the relatively small numbers of skilled machinemen placed them in a strong bargaining position. The process of change was a continuing one, with the steady proliferation of more efficient and specialized types of machine. 'When a new class of machinery is introduced into an office one of the greatest difficulties the employer has is to get a careful man who is competent to take charge of it.'[3] In 1892 the machinemen claimed a rise on the ground of increasing productivity, the 'size and speed of machinery', and the high value of the plant for which they were responsible.[4]

As the machinemen took advantage of this strategic situation, their economic position compared more and more favourably with that of most compositors. Following the failure of the strike

---

[1] Kinnear, op. cit., p 32.
[2] *Scottish Typographical Circular*, Jan. 1896, May 1896.
[3] 'Old Machine Manager', *Printing Machine Manager's Handbook*, p. viii.
[4] Edin. Press and Machinemen's Society, *Memorial to the Master Printers of Edinburgh and District* (1892).

of 1872 a number of machinemen seceded from the Typographical Society, to form the Edinburgh Press and Machinemen's Society;[1] its *Annual Report* for 1893 referred to the higher
benefits paid—presumably a reflection of the greater prosperity
of the membership, relative to that of the Typographical
Society—and to the recent gain of a standard rate of 32*s*. for
a fifty-two-and-a-half-hour week.[2] There is little sign of that
uncontrolled acquisition of the skills of the trade from which
the compositors suffered. Boys were apparently taken on in the
first place as semi-skilled labour for machine feeding etc.,
apprentices being later selected from among these boys.[3] There
must have been some danger of a dilution of the trade with men
who had picked it up as boys, without serving the regular
apprenticeship. But various factors probably enabled the
machinemen to limit any such tendency. In the first place, as
the direct supervisors of the semi-skilled boys, they must have
had some influence on the selection of apprentices and the
process of training, as well as on the skills that non-apprentices
were permitted to acquire. Secondly, the context of rapid technical change, and the fact that training on the latest machines
was probably available only in the larger centres, meant that
the migration of men who had served apprenticeships in weakly
unionized country towns—from which the compositors, like
many other trades, suffered[4]—was a less serious problem. The
increasing replacement of boys by women in the semi-skilled
machine processes must have strengthened the position of the
skilled men, since there was clearly no danger of women picking
up the trade and passing themselves off as time-served skilled
men.[5]

The machinemen therefore enjoyed an advantageous, and
improving, position based on technical change and their monopoly of the scarce knowledge and skills needed to operate the
new types of machine. They seem to have been relatively

---

[1] *Scottish Typographical Circular*, Jan., Feb. 1874.
[2] Edin. Press and Machinemen's Society, *Annual Report*, 1892–3.
[3] Gordon, op. cit., p. 313.   [4] Ibid., p. 316.
[5] The secretary of the Lithographers' Society considered women preferable to
boys for these semi-skilled tasks: *R.C. on Labour, group C*, P.P. 1893–4 XXXIV,
q. 22699. The proportion of females rose from 2 per cent (1861) to 31 per cent
(1901) of all printers enumerated in Edinburgh; but these figures reflect female
employment as compositors as well as in machine rooms.

homogeneous in this respect; there is little evidence of the kind of variation in experience between different groups of workers, so important for compositors and many other skilled trades. We may therefore place the machinemen among the group of unusually advantaged skilled occupations.

Bookbinders

The old-established craft of bookbinding was marked by the impact of innovation and a far-reaching rationalization of production methods. With the growing scale of book production a series of machines were introduced, and many operations were simplified, so that they could be performed by semi-skilled labour; more than half of the total in bookbinding and folding were female in 1861, and this had risen to 67 per cent by 1901. The effect of this process was not, however, to displace skilled men, but to make more efficient and specialized use of them.

The concomitant of this was that the bookbinders were able to regulate their numbers, so as to take advantage of the more specialized use of their craft skills and the productivity gains from innovation. Males in bookbinding rose by 24 per cent from 1861 to 1901, compared to 55 per cent for all bookbinders, and 94 per cent for the total occupied population; the proportion of males under twenty fell from 30 per cent in 1861 to 23 per cent in 1881 and 26 per cent in 1901. There is some more direct evidence of the operation of apprenticeship controls in the union branch minutes, which record the inspection of new members' indentures.[1] The subdivision of processes and the introduction of semi-skilled labour meant that job demarcation, as well as entry to the trade, was of importance to the skilled bookbinder. A national delegate meeting (1895) expressed 'a great amount of surprise' at the extent of female labour in Edinburgh and the classes of work allocated to the women, and declared this state of affairs to be 'a great danger to the whole union'.[2] And there are a number of instances of small strikes over 'encroachments' by female labour.[3]

---

[1] Edin. Union Society of Bookbinders, Minutes, 1822–72; Edin. Branch, Bookbinders' Consolidated Union, Minutes, from 1869.

[2] Bookbinders' Consolidated Union, Minutes, 18 June 1895.

[3] e.g. ibid., 28 Nov. 1874.

Despite these threats the bookbinders seem to have succeeded in retaining a strong position. In 1853 the *Edinburgh News* described them as a 'comfortable looking class of workmen . . . everything about them seemed to indicate steadiness in the workshop and comfort at home'.[1] Statistics given in the union minutes for a later date bear out this impression, showing relatively high wage rates and—more important—relatively few men at very low rates. The average rate for union members in 1885 was 28s. 9d., while 57 per cent were reported to earn from 28s. to 36s.; in 1890 66 per cent of journeymen bookbinders (unionists and non-unionists combined) were above the minimum rate of 27s. (51 per cent at 30s. or more), and 15 per cent were below the minimum.[2] These figures suggest that the bookbinders were among the relatively prosperous trades.

Masons

The masons likewise appear to have enjoyed a strong and improving position during the period. (After its end, however, they were badly affected by the building depression of the 1900s and by the introduction of stone-cutting machines.)[3] There was little change in the technology of building during the period, and the skilled stonemason continued to play a key part in that technology. The exceptional strength, as well as the traditional craft skills, required for masons' work created a scarcity of labour during the up-swings of the construction cycle.

After 1860 the masons did not attempt to control entry to the trade: any man could join the union, 'as soon as he can leave first employer'.[4] Despite the absence of regulations, only between 9 and 12 per cent of masons were aged under twenty at the various censuses. Even in the absence of more formal arrangements, the physique needed for the work, and informal occupational socialization and selection in the work place may well have functioned as controls on recruitment. The pursuit of a closed-shop policy, reported to the Royal Commission on

---

[1] *Edin. News*, 30 July 1853.
[2] Bookbinders' Consolidated Union, Minutes, 28 Sept. 1885, 7 Oct. 1890.
[3] Gordon, op. cit., p. 165; *R.C. on the Poor Laws, appendix vol. viii*, P.P. 1910 XLVIII, q. 197181 (law agent to Edinburgh Distress Committee).
[4] Webb Manuscript Notes, loc. cit.

Labour, presumably also reflects a measure of control over labour recruitment.[1]

Like all the building trades, masons were affected by the movements of the building cycle, and by seasonal fluctuations. At times of depression a surplus of labour tended to appear. A union leaflet of 1885 complains that the masons are losing their leading position among the skilled trades.[2] The hourly rate fell from a peak of 9d. in 1876 to 6d. in 1880, rising again to 7d. in 1888, then to 9½d. in 1896, remaining at that level for the boom years of the later nineties.[3] The impact of these movements on the earnings for a full working week in summer is shown in Figure I. The masons thus enjoyed a position of unusual strength in the 1860s (when they led the way in gaining the nine-hour day),[4] early 1870s, and 1890s, but were more precariously placed in the later 1870s and 1880s. Masons were, of course, affected by the seasonal cycle of employment. The trade also suffered from a high rate of death and disability, partly because of the accidents occasioned by working on high buildings and handling heavy blocks of stone, partly because of industrial diseases contracted from stone dust and from working outdoors in rough weather.[5] Men therefore left the trade young; but their high earnings may have enabled masons to make relatively advantageous provision for this eventuality (for example, the purchase of a small shop or pub). This must, however, remain a matter of speculation.

Joiners

The joiners' position differed in certain important respects from that of the masons. Their employment was less seasonal, partly because joiner work could be done when outside work was not possible, and partly because some joiners were employed in wood-working shops, shipyards, etc.; the more skilled and versatile might even enter such trades as cabinet-making and pattern-making. The masons, on the other hand, were tied

---

[1] *R.C. on Labour, group C*, P.P. 1892 XXXVI, pt. ii q. 17916 (secretary, Glasgow Branch, Operative Masons; the reference is to Scotland generally, Edinburgh being among the 'most united' places: q. 17919).

[2] *To Lodge Members and Non-members* (n.d., c. 1885).

[3] See sources for Table 4.1.

[4] MacDougall, op. cit., p. xxxvii.   [5] *Edin. News*, 2 Oct. 1852.

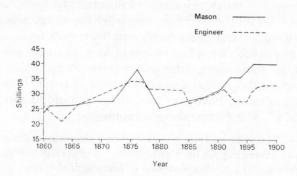

Figure I. Weekly Rate of Mason and Engineer, 1860–1900
Source: See Table 4.1

to the building industry. Joiners were 'naturally less subject to
fluctuation than masons'.[1] Their rates were less closely affected
by the building cycle, rising less in booms, but conversely falling
less in slumps. The joiner's rate reached 9½d. only in 1899, when
the mason's had been at that level since 1896; but, whereas the
mason's rate fell by 33 per cent from 1876 to 1880, the joiner's
fell by only 23 per cent.[2]

Controls on entry to the trade appear to have been weak.
According to the Webbs, controls broke down in the depression
of the 1870s:[3] a rise in the proportion of joiners aged under
twenty from 13 per cent in 1861 to 15 per cent in 1881 may
reflect this process. Even before then, the trade contained a
'numerous host of half-bred or indifferent hands', mainly recruited from the country.[4] This suggests the existence of divisions within the trade, and a penumbra of under-employed
casual labour. But if this problem affected joiners, it did not do
so on anything like the scale of the casual-labour problem facing
the painters.

Painters

The painters exemplify the syndrome of casual labour and
extreme seasonality which afflicted the more deprived skilled
trades. An old painter, quoted by the *Edinburgh News*, gives a

---

[1] *Edin. News,* 9 Oct. 1852.   [2] See sources for Table 4.1.
[3] Webb Manuscript Notes, loc. cit.   [4] *Edin. News,* 9 Oct. 1852.

vivid account of the deterioration of the craft; he looks back to
the period before the 'building mania' of the 1820s, when the
masters were 'perfect gentlemen', and 'there was no scramble
to execute a week's work in a couple of days, as we see now.' In
contrast to those days, 'the journeymen house painters of
Edinburgh at the present day are the most ill-requited and ill-
used class of men I have ever met with, or would like to meet
with again.'[1] The *Edinburgh News* comments:

We should like to know how it comes to pass that men with a cultivated taste exceeding all their compeers . . . generally possessed of
fine literary tastes . . . also possessed of fine musical tastes . . . who,
in fine, are no bellicose politicians, no furious Chartists, no un-
principled demagogues—we should like to know, we repeat, how it
came to pass that these men, who follow after this most artistic trade
in this most artistic city, are worse paid and less appointed, and in
every respect worse off than a common scavenger, a mason's
labourer, or a railway navvie?[2]

To understand 'how it came to pass' we must consider three
interrelated factors: extreme seasonality, uncontrolled competition by cheap, unapprenticed labour, and the growth of
the casual labour market. According to the *Edinburgh News*
two-thirds of the men were idle for four months of the year.[3] A
painter writing in the *Reformer* (1869) gives the same basic picture, quoting a figure of 370 out of 600 painters idle in winter.[4]
Little, if any, improvement is visible after the turn of the century; Gordon (1908) describes the trade as 'extremely seasonal',
with at least half unemployed in the slack season.[5] This seasonality was closely related to the problems of dilution with
unqualified labour, and casualization. The problem faced by
the skilled painters was not simply that of regulating apprenticeships (a problem faced by every skilled trade); the proportion
of painters under twenty is not notably higher than other trades.
The problem was rather one of *adults*—the 'off-scourings of
other trades'[6]—working at cheap rates, with no training whatsoever. A report in the *Reformer* about labourers doing painters'
work led to a long correspondence, mainly tending to the

---

[1] All the quotations in this paragraph are from the *Edin. News*, 27 Nov. 1852.
[2] Ibid.   [3] Ibid.   [4] *Reformer*, 6 Mar. 1869.
[5] Gordon, op. cit., pp. 285–9.   [6] Letter in *Reformer*, 6 Mar. 1869.

conclusion that labourers 'fill the places of legitimate tradesmen to their loss and injury'; one correspondent alleged that the labourers were kept on in winter in preference to tradesmen, only twenty-three out of 165 labourers, but over half the proper painters being laid off.[1] Here again, there is little change by the end of the period: in 1897 the Trades Council protested about the use of labourers to do painters' work on municipal contracts.[2] This dilution accentuated the seasonal pattern; the *Edinburgh News* reported that the number of painters in the city rose from 700 to 1,000 in the busy season, and that many painters worked as lamplighters, theatre scene-shifters, etc. during the winter, concluding that the problem was 'uneven demand', rather than over-supply of labour.[3]

The painters were almost certainly the worst placed of the trades under consideration. Although their *rates* of wages were comparable to those for other skilled workers, they suffered from chronic seasonality and casualization, and in many cases probably did not receive the standard rate, even for the hours they did work. A strong employers' association resisted the demand for a minimum rate in 1858, and subsequently retained a position of unusual power, even by the standards of Victorian labour relations.[4] The painting trade illustrates the importance of dilution and the casual-labour market, in accentuating fluctuations in employment, with a disastrous effect on the bargaining power and economic rewards of skilled labour.

Engineers

The engineers, according to a local reviewer of *Our New Masters*, 'are generally the élite of the working men, and so far removed from the operatives and labourers at the lower end of the scale that they have not many sympathies in common, and not much intercourse with them'.[5] The development of capital-goods industries as a leading sector, in both the domestic and export economies of the second half of the nineteenth century, created a heavy demand for the skills of the engineering trades.

---

[1] *Reformer* 31 Oct. 1868, 15 June 1870, 6 Mar. 1869.
[2] T.C. Minutes, 6 Apr. 1897.   [3] *Edin. News,* 27 Nov. 1852.
[4] Edin. Master Painters' Association, printed broadside (1858); G. Baird, *The Operative House Painters of Scotland* (1959).   [5] *Reformer,* 29 Mar. 1873.

Down to the 1890s technical change took the form of a series of improvements and refinements to the basic machine-tool innovations of the earlier nineteenth century, and their application to a wide range of tasks; production methods continued to rely on the knowledge and expertise of the skilled worker, rather than on the subdivision of mechanized tasks characteristic of the mass-production metal-working industries of the twentieth century. The effect of change was to create new, more specialized and demanding skills, rather than to displace skilled labour.

The engineer could offer the scarce skills needed by an expanding sector of industry, but there were elements of instability in his economic position. Engineering was affected by the trade cycle; as Table 4.5 indicates, unemployment in 1893 was heaviest in the engineering and metal trades. Engineering rates, like those of building workers, fluctuated with the level of activity in the industry. These movements are traced in Figure I, from which it is apparent that the fluctuations are less extreme, in both directions, than those in the mason's rate; the net effect is perhaps to place masons and engineers in the same broad 'income bracket'. The second element of instability was, as in every trade, that of uncontrolled entry. The Webbs reported no effective regulations in engineering.[1] The proportion under twenty appears to follow a cyclical pattern, falling in 1881 after the depression, and rising following the boom of the 1890s. The A.S.E. repeatedly complained of the large number of apprentices in Edinburgh and Leith, leading, as they claimed, to a greater labour surplus at times of depression.[2]

Technical change placed further pressure on the job monopolies of the skilled engineer. In a head-office questionnaire of 1876 the A.S.E. Edinburgh District reported that labourers 'sometimes' 'do the work of Mechanics' on planing and drilling machines;[3] and following the lock-out of 1897–8 men complained that they found labourers at their machines on returning to work.[4] New classes of work, the Webbs noted, were

---

[1] Webb Manuscript Notes, loc. cit.

[2] For example, A.S.E. *Quarterly Report*, May 1894; see also A.S.E. head-office questionnaire to Districts, 1876 (Manuscript at A.U.E.W. headquarters, London; photocopy supplied by G. Crossick). [3] A.S.E. head-office questionnaire, op. cit.

[4] A.S.E. *Monthly Journal*, Feb. 1898.

'learned largely by labourers and improvers'.[1] Large numbers of apprentices or boys could also be employed as semi-skilled machinists, presenting the familiar spectacle of half-trained men (or 'handymen') encroaching on parts of the work done by time-served craftsmen.[2] It is, however, important not to exaggerate the impact of these trends.[3] There was no massive downgrading of skilled labour (lathes, for example, remained the preserve of time-served men),[4] and the engineers retained a strong bargaining position based on the indispensability of their skills for kinds of work not as yet performable by semi-skilled workers.

Ironmoulders

Like the skills of engineers those of ironmoulders were placed in demand with the expansion of the metal-working industries. They were certainly well paid, their rates being sometimes slightly above, sometimes slightly below the engineers'. In some respects, however, their situation was less favourable. In the first place, there is some evidence of divisions within the trade. Apart from the foundry work undertaken in engineering firms, moulders were employed to produce large numbers of identical railings, gates, pipes, etc.[5] This work was apparently less skilled, and the element of product standardization made possible encroachments on the job monopolies of skilled moulders.[6] Apprentices or boys might become proficient only in certain branches of work, and this half-trained labour could then undercut the more versatile skilled men. The Webbs reported that apprenticeship controls collapsed in 1868, and this is confirmed by the Associated Ironmoulders' secretary.[7] In Edinburgh there was at least one case of a strike over the 'introduction of a Labourer to work as a Moulder'.[8] By 1908 mechanization was

---

[1] Webb Manuscript Notes, loc. cit.   [2] Gordon, op. cit., pp. 212–15.

[3] The Webbs were rather inclined to do this. Cf. S. and B. Webb, *Industrial Democracy* (1926 edn.), esp. pp. 470–2, 713–14 (this book was based on the Manuscript Notes from which I have quoted extensively).   [4] Gordon, op. cit., p. 214.

[5] *R.C. on Labour, group A*, P.P. 1893–4 XXXII, q. 23452 (secretary, Associated Ironmoulders).   [6] *Edin. News*, 20 Aug. 1853.

[7] Webb Manuscript Notes, loc. cit.; *R.C. on Labour*, loc. cit., q. 23459.

[8] T.C. Minutes, 5 Mar. 1895. The dispute was complicated by rivalries between the two unions at that time organizing ironmoulders, the newer and smaller Central Ironmoulders' Association claiming that the offending labourer had been taught by an Associated Ironmoulders' member.

leading to a more extensive use of unskilled men, and the trade
was said to be no longer attracting apprentices.[1]

Shoemakers

The shoemakers, in the words of the *Edinburgh News*, were
'systematically ground down to a greater extent than any class
without exception we have hitherto considered'.[2] Nineteen
years later the Operative Cordwainers (who represented the
more prosperous part of the trade) complained that they were
'the least paid of any skilled labour', estimating piece earnings
as on average equivalent to a time-rate of 4*d*. per hour.[3]

The Edinburgh shoemakers were divided into sections of the
trade similar to those Mayhew found in London.[4] In 1853 the
'first class' shops—those employing skilled labour in the production of high-quality goods to order—were said to employ
only fifty shoemakers (3 per cent of the total), 'second class'
shops employed another 500 (32 per cent), while the remaining
1,000 'journeymen, boys, everything' were in 'third class' shops
subject to no established rates of wages; informants estimated
that a 'second class' man could earn 12*s*. a week when fully
employed.[5] In 1868, the 'first class' rate was equivalent to 4*d*.
per hour, the 'second class' to 3¾*d*., and the 'third class' to 3*d*.[6]
In interpreting these figures it must be remembered that the
'third class' shaded into a vast penumbra of sweated and casual
workers, for whom—as Mayhew's investigations in London
revealed—hours might be extended and wages lowered almost
without limit.

Down to the 1860s all shoemakers worked at home, and the
Edinburgh News attributed their condition largely to this fact:
'This hereditary and deeply-rooted dislike to be called a servant
is then at the foundation of the shoemakers' misery. The sooner
they rid themselves of this ideology the better for themselves
and the better for society.'[7] It is certainly arguable that the
system of working, with the division of the process between
'closers' and 'makers', occasioned much waiting about and

[1] Gordon, op. cit., p. 241.   [2] *Edin. News*, 19 Mar. 1853.
[3] Operative Cordwainers' Society, *To the Master Boot and Shoemakers*.
[4] Thompson and Yeo (eds.), op. cit., pp. 232–5.   [5] *Edin. News*, 19 Mar. 1853.
[6] Scottish Amalgamated Union of Boot and Shoemakers, *Report*, Feb.–Aug. 1868.
[7] *Edin. News*, 2 Apr. 1853.

accentuated the irregularity of employment. Although shoe-making had no distinct seasonal pattern there were none the less great variations in employment and earnings.[1] As in the painters' case, these fluctuations were bound up with un-controlled recruitment and the growth of casual labour. Uncontrolled recruitment did not take the form of excessive numbers of apprentices, the proportion under twenty being generally less than for any other skilled trade. The influx was of adults, either from the country, or from town-dwellers who turned to shoemaking in the absence of other employment. An article in the *Typographical Circular* mentions mending shoes, together with such last-resort employments as lamplighting, leaflet distribution, etc., in a list of jobs open to the unemployed printer;[2] James Connolly, who certainly had no pretensions to be a skilled shoemaker, set up as a cobbler in 1894.[3]

There were important changes in the trade during the period. The advent of the sewing-machine in the 1860s led to the intro-duction of workshops. The *North Briton* commented on the improved condition of the shoemaking trade, whereas 'ten years ago the trade was proverbial for what appeared to be hopeless poverty.'[4] On the other hand, it is likely that home work per-sisted in the less-favoured part of the trade; the effect of the workshops may, indeed, have been to accentuate the difference between those working for regular employers and casual home workers. Even for the former, the workshop system had, they complained, reduced their piece earnings by shortening hours.[5] With further mechanization the sweated 'slop' trade gradually gave way to a mass-production factory industry, employing semi-skilled workers. The craft shoemaker, working for the bespoke market that was such a notable feature of the Edinburgh consumer trades, was less immediately threatened by the com-petition of cheap unqualified labour using a degenerated ver-sion of his skills, although he faced problems of demarcation, with the piecemeal introduction of new machinery. The in-creasing technical and occupational distinctiveness of the craft sector thus strengthened the position of the skilled shoemaker.

---

[1] *Edin. News*, 19 Mar. 1853.   [2] *Scottish Typographical Circular*, July 1869.
[3] C. Desmond Greaves, *The Life and Times of James Connolly* (1961), pp. 52–3.
[4] *North Briton*, 18 Aug. 1863.
[5] Operative Cordwainers' Society, *To the Master Boot and Shoemakers.*

'Young men who have been well taught in the country and come to the towns easily get work from some of the first class firms who make a speciality of hand-made goods; there is no surplus of labour in this line.'[1]

III. STATISTICAL EVIDENCE[2]

Although the reliability of the figures quoted above, and sometimes even their basic meaning, is in doubt, there are some sources that can be treated with a more systematic statistical methodology. Two such sources will be analysed, with a view to testing some of the conclusions presented above.

The first set of statistical data is based on company records—a rich, and oddly neglected, source for the researcher in this field.[3] Records were found for three printing firms in the city, and for firms in three other industries.[4] It was decided to use these sources for a comparative 'panel sample' analysis of earnings; an initial survey of the material suggested that such panel samples could be traced for one-year periods, before the problem of 'panel mortality' began to reach unmanageable proportions. For one firm (the *Scotsman*) three years in the 1850s and 1860s were chosen, while the other samples all fall in some or all of three years in the 1880s and 1890s; this choice of years being determined largely by the availability of simultaneous data for more than one firm. Random samples (generally of ten individuals)[5] were selected from the wage record for the first pay date of the year in question. The weekly earnings of the selected individuals were recorded throughout the year, and aggregated into monthly totals (or rather, totals for thirteen four-week periods); the data were then punched, each card including the thirteen monthly-income figures for one indi-

[1] Gordon, op. cit., p. 155.
[2] I am indebted to Mr. A. Fielding and Mr. R. Bland for indispensable advice and assistance with the statistical study of earnings discussed below.
[3] Cf. Neale, op. cit.; A. Slaven, 'Earnings and Productivity in the Scottish Coal-mining Industry during the Nineteenth Century', in P. L. Payne (ed.), *Studies in Scottish Business History* (1967).
[4] These business archives were surveyed by Professor P. L. Payne and by the National Register of Archives (Scotland), for whose assistance I am grateful.
[5] Those samples larger than ten were selected at an early, partly experimental, stage of the study.

vidual worker. It is on this data set of 13 × N observations of earnings that the statistical analysis reported below was carried out. (In future, the individual randomly selected workers are referred to as *cases*, their monthly earnings as *observations*, and cases excluded from the analysis for lack of sufficient observations as *panel mortality*.[1] Details of the samples are summarized in Table 4.6.) As always in social research, methodological decisions were made under constraints of time and resources— and, in this case, of inexperience and an absence of relevant precedents in the work of others. The decisions made are thus open to question, but the interest of the study lies partly in its exploratory character; and, whatever its shortcomings, it does give a more accurate view of workers' actual earnings than is otherwise obtainable.

The study includes two samples of compositors (from the *Scotsman* newspaper in the 1850s and 1860s and Constable, the publisher, in the eighties and nineties) and three samples from printing machine-rooms. Another sample from the third printing firm, Bartholomew the map-makers, covers a variety of highly skilled lithographic preparatory processes (litho artists, engravers, etc.), referred to here as 'litho trades'.[2] The fourth firm, MacKenzie & Moncur, employed various building trades in the manufacture and erection of greenhouses, conservatories, etc.[3] It is not possible to identify specific trades from the surviving

---

[1] The treatment of weeks when one or more cases do not appear in the wage record was a major problem. It was eventually decided to treat the first week when a name could not be found as a weekly income of zero for that individual; subsequent weeks were treated as missing data. In aggregating weekly earnings into months, months with one or more weeks missing were recorded as missing observations for that case. Each observation of monthly earnings is therefore based on *four complete figures* for weekly earnings, of which one, but not more than one, may be zero. Cases that disappear temporarily are treated in the same way on their reappearance in the wage book. The only exceptions to these rules are a few cases whose names do appear in the book, but with no wage shown against them, or with annotations such as 'ill', 'holiday', etc.; it seemed legitimate to treat all such instances as weekly earnings of zero. All cases with five or more (out of thirteen) monthly observations missing were dropped from the sample altogether. This procedure almost certainly under-estimates fluctuations in income, but it seemed better to avoid overloading the analysis with imponderables.

[2] P. Bartholomew, 'House of Bartholomew' (unpublished typescript). I am indebted to Mr. Bartholomew for the loan of this work, and for answering my questions.

[3] Information from Mr. I. MacKenzie, former Director. The firm also had a foundry, which made manhole covers, pipes, etc., as well as the metal work for the

records, so that my sample has to be regarded simply as one
of building workers.[1] The shoemaking firm included, Allan,

TABLE 4.6
Details of Samples of Workers' Earnings

Firm/Group	Panel mortality: % of cases dropped (insufficient observations)	Included in Analysis: N: Cases	N: observations	Years* covered by samples
Scotsman				
Compositors	7	42	555	1858, 65, 68
Machine-room	10	18	208	1865, 68
Constable				
Compositors	3	29	363	1887, 90, 99
Machine-room	10	27	345	1887, 90, 99
Bartholomew				
Litho trades	7	28	324	1887, 90, 99
Machine-room	10	18	225	1890, 99
MacKenzie & Moncur				
Building trades	20	20	243	1887, 90
Allan				
Shoemakers	15	17	210	1887, 99
Hamilton & Inches				
Silversmiths etc.	0	10	130	1899

Notes: * No wage records were available for the *Scotsman* after 1868, for the
Scotsman machine-room in 1858, for MacKenzie & Moncur in 1899, or for Hamilton & Inches before 1899. The samples for Bartholomew's machine-room, 1887,
and for Allan, 1890, were abandoned because of excessively high 'panel mortality'
(50 per cent and 60 per cent of cases dropped respectively).

See p. 73, n.1, for details of treatment of missing observations and panel
mortality.

belonged to the high-quality bespoke sector of the trade, while
the last firm, Hamilton & Inches, made silverware. (All the
firms sampled outside the printing industry were distinguished
by their orientation to a 'luxury' market.) Among the skilled
trades the most important omission from the available business
records are the engineering and metal trades. Semi- and unskilled labour, on the other hand, is not represented at all (apart

frames of prefabricated buildings; but the surviving wage books refer only to the
building trades employed.

[1] It is, however, safe to assume that not many labourers are included: the wage
books include some men taken on for very short periods, who can readily be
distinguished by the fact that they are not given pay numbers; these are almost
certainly labourers hired on the spot for particular jobs. In view of the very high
turnover of this group it was excluded from the sampling frame.

from a few apprentices and the boys and women employed in the three printing machine-rooms).

Before discussing the data, we must assess how the experience of workers in the firms sampled is likely to have compared with that of other firms. The *Scotsman* was unique among local employers, as a leading national newspaper, but sufficiently important in its own right to justify inclusion; Bartholomew were engaged in a highly skilled and specialized branch of the industry; Constable, however, may well be representative of a number of local firms of comparable size—though it is dangerous to assume this to be so. The remaining firms all belonged to that sector of local industry engaged in the production of high-quality goods to order. It is probable that employment at MacKenzie & Moncur was exceptionally stable for the building trades; while the silversmiths' earnings show no seasonal variation whatsoever, which clearly reflects the privileged position of highly skilled labour in the 'luxury trades'. The general bias—and, indeed, the bias implied in the very survival of appropriate company archives—is almost certainly to the more prosperous, expanding, and economically secure sectors of industry. For this reason, the following statistical inferences must be understood to refer only to the problem of generalization from my samples to the limited populations from which they are drawn, *not* to the larger population of workers in the occupation outside the particular firms; any inference to this more general level involves problems of a substantive, not statistical, character. Even within the population, as just defined, the panel-sample method implies a bias to the more regularly employed. On the other hand, the figures in Table 4.6 for panel mortality suggest that the majority of workers in the firms were employed with sufficient regularity to give the minimum of nine out of thirteen monthly observations which was the criterion of retention in the sample.[1] If the population studied had included large numbers employed for very short periods only, an entirely different statistical design would have been needed.

Table 4.7 shows the <u>mean</u> earnings of the samples, given in the form of earnings (shillings) per week. There was of course, some variation between years, the greatest (10·56s. difference

---

[1] See above, p. 73, n. 1.

between the highest and lowest yearly figure) being for the *Scotsman* compositors, the smallest (only 0·53s. difference) for the shoemakers. This factor may bias the results shown in the table; however, the figures for individual years make little difference to the rank order of the groups, so that combining years seems a valid procedure for descriptive purposes. The most notable trends over the years are an improvement in the earnings of the *Scotsman* compositors (rising from 19·74s. in 1858 to 30·30s. in 1865 and 29·36s. in 1868), and of the Constable and Bartholomew machine-rooms. The Constable compositors, on the other hand, show a steady decline, from 26·40s. in 1887 to 21·67s. in 1899. If this is at all typical of the trade, it certainly gives statistical support to the impression of relative economic decline, especially as compared to the machine-room workers.

Despite the possible distortions from the yearly differences a statistical test of the variation between firms seemed worth while. (Ideally, this test should have been performed on data adjusted[1] for inter-year differences. But the relevant data file had been inadvertently erased, and practical constraints prevented its reconstitution.) With this important qualification, analysis of variance indicated a statistically significant difference ($p < 0.001$) between the five firms (the machine-room samples and the silversmiths were excluded from the analysis; the former because their heterogeneous skill composition would bias the result, the latter because the absence of any monthly changes at all made computer processing unnecessary).

Further interpretation of the figures is complicated by the inclusion of apprentices (and, in the machine-room, of semi-skilled boys and women), as well as journeymen. There was no way of avoiding this, since one generally could not tell, *a priori*, which individuals were apprentices. In order to adjust the figures and give more satisfactory estimates of *journeymen's* earnings, the procedure adopted was to obtain personal means for every individual case, and then to recalculate sample means, excluding those cases whose mean earnings fell below a specified level. The second part of Table 4.7 gives maximum and minimum estimates obtained in this way. There is a danger

---

[1] See below, p. 78.

in this procedure of assuming what is, in fact, under investigation. Alternative estimates are given, in an attempt to steer a middle course between the two dangers that face us in estimating the real figure for journeymen's mean earnings: that of under-estimating by the inclusion of cases who are not really journeymen, and that of over-estimating by the exclusion of cases who are really journeymen. There is no real solution to the difficulty, and all that can be claimed for the figures is that they are probably closer approximations to the mean earnings of journeymen than either the unadjusted figures for my

TABLE 4.7
Mean Weekly Earnings of Samples (shillings)

All Cases

	Scotsman	Constable	Bartholomew
Compositors	26·41	24·34	Litho trades 30·87
Machine room	16·88	23·30	19·99
Building trades		34·77	
Shoemakers		23·74	
Silversmiths		32·00	

'Journeymen' only (estimated figures) *

	Scotsman		Constable		Bartholomew	
Adjustment	Min.	Max.	Min.	Max.	Min.	Max.
					Litho trades	
Compositors	28·38	31·74	25·60	28·48	36·52	37·21
†(N: observations)	(507)	(416)	(339)	(261)	(266)	(258)
Machine room	17·30	22·77	28·16	32·48	32·49‡	
(N)	(198)	(39)	(261)	(190)	(111)	
Building trades			34·77‡			
(N)			(243)			
Shoemakers			26·26‡			
(N)			(184)			
Silversmiths			32·00‡			
(N)			(130)			

Notes: * *Minimum estimate*: Mean recalculated excluding all individual cases with personal mean earnings of less than 10s. weekly.

Maximum estimate: excluding all cases with personal mean earnings of less than 20s. weekly.

† See Table 4.6 for N for unadjusted figures.

‡ No adjustment applicable, or only one adjustment applicable.

All figures are for all years sampled combined (see Table 4.6 for details of years).

samples, or the figures for standard wage-rates most often quoted by researchers. This is the sole purpose of the second part of Table 4.7. The statistical analysis presented below is based on the unadjusted figures, except when the contrary is specified.

The main difference made by the adjustment is, predictably, to reveal the relatively high earnings of the Constable and Bartholomew machinemen, previously concealed by their inclusion in samples of heterogeneous skill composition. The *Scotsman* machine-room, on the other hand, contained only three men with mean earnings of more than 20s. weekly. This may reflect differences between the newspaper and other sectors of the industry, or a strengthening of the position of skilled machinemen between the 1860s and 1880s, or both.[1] Apart from the *Scotsman* machinemen, these estimates are largely in accordance with predictions from the earlier account of occupational experiences, the Constable compositors and the shoemakers having lower earnings (on either estimate) than the other trades.

Monthly fluctuations within firms are of considerable interest in relation to the impressionistic discussion above.[2] A measure of monthly variation, and a picture of its seasonal patterning over the year, is obtainable by treating each of the thirteen months as 'dummy variables' (having the value One for observations falling in the month in question, and the value Zero for other observations), which can be correlated with the observations of earnings. Multiple correlation coefficients for all thirteen months will then indicate the over-all impact of monthly fluctuation, while the regression equations for each month show the seasonal form of variations in earnings. As a preliminary to this procedure, the data were standardized for the effect of yearly differences, each observation being adjusted by the difference between the mean for all years for the particular group, and that group's mean for the year in which the observation fell.

The purpose here is exploratory; monthly changes are only a part of the variation in earnings, and their relative importance in the different samples is of more interest than the magnitude of any single correlation taken in isolation. There is, however, reason to suspect that the correlation coefficients (shown in Table 4.8) may under-estimate the monthly fluctuation:

---

[1] Union controls in news machine-rooms were said to be weak. See letters in *Scottish Typographical Circular*, March 1887. News compositors, on the other hand, were always considered the best-paid section of the trade.   [2] See p. 55.

missing observations. When an individual does not appear in the wage book there is no way of knowing whether he has really disappeared from the population studied (because of death, migration, retirement, etc.), or whether he should still be treated as a member of the panel sample, with an income of zero for the weeks during which he is missing from the record (because of illness, unemployment, etc.). The rules adopted for such instances err on the side of under-estimating fluctuation.[1] That this does occur is suggested by the finding that, whereas under half of all months had one or more missing observations, at least two-thirds of months when earnings moved downwards had missing observations, except in three of the samples.[2]

From Table 4.8 it appears that the strongest monthly effects are in the Constable compositors, *Scotsman* machine-room, and building trades. The first- and last-mentioned results were expected, but that for the *Scotsman* machine-room was not (it

TABLE 4.8
Multiple Correlation Coefficient for Monthly Variation in Earnings

Compositors	Scotsman	0·10
	Constable	0·19
Machine-room	Scotsman	0·33
	Constable	0·12
	Bartholomew	0·12
Litho trades		0·16
Building trades		0·33
Shoemakers		0·16
Silversmiths		0·00

may reflect seasonal variations in the number of copies printed, but there is no evidence to confirm this suggestion). On the other hand, the smaller correlation for the other machine-room samples indicates that they were less affected by seasonal movements than the compositors.

Regression analysis can be used to trace the change in earnings for each month and to reconstruct the seasonal form of monthly variations. Figure II shows the beta coefficients for the thirteen months. Since the thirteen dummy variables in the

[1] See above, p. 73, n. 1.
[2] The exceptions are *Scotsman* compositors, Constable machine-room, and shoemakers; apart from the shoemakers these samples are among those with low correlations in Table 4.8.

equation have only two possible values, zero or one, the betas in fact show monthly fluctuations about the over-all average.)

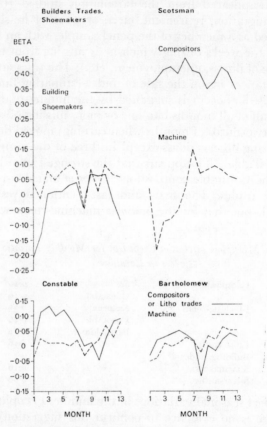

Figure II. Monthly Movements in Earnings

The pattern for Constable and Bartholomew bears out statements in other sources about the seasonal cycle in printing, with busy periods in the spring and towards the end of the year, and a slack period in summer;[1] although the pattern is shared by both departments, it is rather sharper for the compositors and litho trades than in the machine-rooms. The winter cut-back indicated by the curve for the building trades is likewise to be

[1] Stedman Jones, op. cit., pp. 34, 381.

expected.[1] Although the over-all correlation for the shoemakers
in Table 4.8 is quite large, the graph reveals that this reflects
changes from month to month, rather than any consistent
seasonal trend, and thus confirms the impression of considerable
short-run variation in earnings, without the clear-cut seasonal
pattern of the printing or building trades. The pattern for the
Scotsman is, once again, puzzling, with a considerable divergence
between the two departments in the form, as well as in the over-
all effect, of monthly variations. But, with this exception, the
data do confirm, with the 'harder' evidence of samples of
actual earnings, the impression given by other sources.

Finally, the earnings data throw light on a further dimension
of variation: that of intra-occupational divisions. The figures
for the personal mean earnings of individual cases can be used
to illuminate such divisions. In Table 4.9 individual cases
(excluding those with mean earnings less than 20s. per week)
are classified by their personal mean earnings for the whole
year. The *Scotsman* compositors, litho trades, Constable and
Bartholomew machinemen, building trades and silversmiths
have well over half with mean earnings of 30s. and over; whereas the Constable compositors and shoemakers have less than
half in this category. This distribution is to some extent pre-
dictable from the figures for mean earnings (Table 4.7). But
there also seem to be differences in the internal heterogeneity of
the samples, with a wider scatter of individual mean earnings
in the less-well-paid trades. Whereas most of the samples have
majorities of cases in the same earnings bracket as the maximum
estimate of journeymen's mean earnings (see Table 4.7), the
Constable compositors and shoemakers have majorities in the
categories above and below that containing the estimated
mean.

The second part of Table 4.9 indicates that this scatter has
some relationship to the incidence of fluctuation on the individual worker. The range of earnings over the year (lowest
monthly observation as a proportion of highest) appears to be
greater for cases with lower mean earnings. This is confirmed
by a further measure, the coefficient of variation, which is

---

[1] The troughs in month 8 for all firms, except the *Scotsman*, appear, from annotations in the wage books, to be holidays.

based on the standard deviation of the individual's earnings, rather than merely on the two extreme observations. This analysis confirms the conclusion that the compositors and shoemakers (especially the latter) had marked internal divisions, with a large low-paid 'tail'; and it was precisely the low-paid group that suffered the most severe fluctuations in income. The small number of cases, and various practical constraints on the data analysis make it impossible to test this in any rigorous fashion. But the findings do support the widely held views about the earnings structure of the occupations mentioned; and data from employment records are a rather 'harder' source than the impressionistic remarks about 'average' wages, on which we are otherwise forced to rely.

TABLE 4.9
Individual Variations in Earnings

Cases with mean earnings	20s.–24s.	25s.–29s.	30s. and over	Total cases
Compositors				
Scotsman	7	5	19	31
Constable	6	5	9	20
Machine-room*				
Constable	1	3	11	15
Bartholomew	0	1	8	9
Litho trades	3	2	16	21
Building trades	2	3	15	20
Shoemakers	9	2	4	15
Silversmiths	2	2	6	10

Cases† with mean earnings
Lowest monthly earnings as proportion of highest

	Under 30s.		30s. and over		Total
	three-quarters or more	less than three-quarters	three-quarters or more	less than three-quarters	
Compositors					
Scotsman	1	11	7	12	31
Constable	0	11	4	5	20
Shoemakers	4	7	3	1	15

Coefficient of variation:

	0·09 or less	More than 0·09	0·09 or less	More than 0·09	
Compositors					
Scotsman	2	10	8	11	31
Constable	0	11	4	5	20
Shoemakers	3	8	3	1	15

* *Scotsman* machine-room omitted (only three cases fell in relevant categories).
† Based on cases with mean earnings of 20s. and over only.

The earnings data have the important advantage that they reflect the observed employment incomes of individuals over periods of fifty-two weeks. But they still reflect only a part of the economic experience of the worker and his family. The panel-sampling method is viable for no more than one year for each set of cases; and even within this period the treatment of missing observations is, as we have seen, a serious problem. Nor do the records analysed reveal anything about family circumstances and those supplementary sources of income so critically important to nineteenth-century wage-earning families. The data to which I now turn complement those so far discussed, in that they reflect the total economic situation of manual working-class families, and its *cumulative* effect over several years.

In 1906 the local Charity Organisation Society published a *Report on the Physical Condition of Fourteen Hundred Schoolchildren*.[1] As the title implies, this work contains details of the heights, weights, and general health of the children studied; it also contains various pieces of information (based on interviews by the 'lady visitors' of the C.O.S.) about the family backgrounds of the children. The information for every family is reproduced separately in the published report, and can thus be reanalysed by occupation of household head. The population studied is defined by the children attending a particular school (North Canongate School); located in the old, central working-class area, this school is characterized as serving the poorest parts of the city, 'yet it has also an admixture of the children of the substantially comfortable and thoroughly respectable working-class'.[2] In my reanalysis of material relating to this population I have included all survey families in selected skilled occupations, and a 10-per-cent random sample of the remaining families divided into 'miscellaneous skilled' and 'semi- and unskilled' categories.[3] The less prosperous sections of the working class

[1] City of Edin. Charity Organisation Society, *Report on the Physical Condition of Fourteen Hundred Schoolchildren in the City* (1906). It would seem that the investigation was conducted during the winter of 1904–5.

[2] Ibid., p. 2. For identification of the school, see reference to the investigation in the printed *Minutes* of Edinburgh School Board, 6 Dec. 1904.

[3] Households were classified by occupations of father, or in a few cases of the oldest adult male wage-earner. Thirteen households headed by widows etc. and

are almost certainly heavily represented among these families; apart from the shoemakers, all the selected skilled trades are under-represented, compared to the industrial population of the city generally at the 1901 census. As so often in historical research, the problem of generalizing is substantive, rather than purely statistical in nature. It was decided, then, to treat the selected skilled trades as a population, rather than as representative of any wider population; the 10-per-cent random sample is one drawn from the same limited population of families served by North Canongate School. Despite the necessarily limited scope of generalizations based on the survey, the data are none the less of considerable interest—not least because the likely bias is a conservative one with regard to hypothesized occupational differences (especially those between skilled and unskilled labour).

The heights of the children were taken as an indicator of family standard of living. As such, they have the unique advantage of reflecting the *cumulative* incidence of the family's economic condition over the children's lifetime. Any difference in living standards must, moreover, be quite large to produce differences in height—such differences have, for example, diminished during the twentieth century, although economic inequalities have by no means disappeared.[1] Numbers are unfortunately too small to make direct comparisons of the age-specific heights of children in the different occupations. I have therefore used a measure based on the difference of each child's height from the appropriate mean age- and sex-specific height for all children at a school studied by the C.O.S. for comparative purposes, described as 'attended by children of small

six households headed by non-manual workers and manual workers of unclassifiable skill grade were dropped from the random sample. In assigning occupations from the random sample the same classification was used as for the studies of marriage and the social composition of voluntary organizations reported in a later chapter and discussed in Appendix II. The commonest occupations in the miscellaneous skilled group (total seventeen households) were plumbers and bakers (three each); the commonest semi- and unskilled occupations (total twenty-seven households) were not unexpectedly labourers (sixteen) and transport (mainly carters) (eight).

[1] J. B. de V. Weir, 'The Assessment of the Growth of Schoolchildren', *British Journal of Nutrition*, 6 (1952). I am indebted to Dr. R. Passmore for his guidance on the findings of recent physiological research.

shopkeepers, of skilled artisans, and of clerks'.[1] If this characterization of Broughton School is correct, it gives an index of differentials in height from the children of the lower-middle class—and
possibly of the most prosperous elements of the working class.
If it is not correct, the comparative figures may still be used to
construct an index of differentials from a school whose mean
age-specific heights are from one to three inches greater than
those of all children at North Canongate School.

TABLE 4.10

*Differences in Height from Broughton School of
Children Studied by C.O.S., 1904:
by occupation of household head*

Occupation	N (children)	Mean difference (inches)	S.D.	Coefficient of variation
Printers*	43	1·88	2·29	1·22
Bookbinders	15	1·96	2·20	1·12
Masons	27	2·15	2·72	1·27
Joiners	22	2·33	1·73	0·74
Painters	64	2·40	2·60	1·08
Engineers	17	0·93	3·12	3·35
Metal trades†	25	2·06	2·44	1·18
Shoemakers	32	1·76	2·48	1·41
Miscellaneous skilled	30	1·74	2·19	1·26
Semi- and unskilled	40	3·29	2·80	0·85

* Compositors, 'printers' (sic); these are combined since it is not clear that the
authors of the report made a systematic distinction between compositors and
machinemen.

† Ironmoulders, other iron workers, brass finishers.

Table 4.10 shows occupational mean scores on this index. A
certain amount of caution is called for in interpreting these
figures. Living standards are not the sole determinant of height;
nor is family income the sole determinant of living standards.
The extremely high coefficients of variation presumably reflect
the effect of genetic factors. It is, however, noticeable that the
coefficients are generally larger for those occupations with
the smaller differences from Broughton School (that is, with
the *tallest* children); this may well reflect the fuller operation of

[1] Edin. C.O.S., loc. cit. Preliminary analysis revealed little bias from different
age and sex distributions of children in the various occupations; this was relevant
since differentials in height vary with age. I have assumed that the ages given refer
to age last birthday, and have therefore not been able to follow the now standard
practice (Weir, op cit., p. 22) of subtracting date of birth from date of
measurement.

genetic variables among more prosperous groups, whose children
are more likely to attain their genetically determined potential
heights. The family's place of origin may be another source of
variation: children in rural areas were generally taller, and this
would presumably be reflected among recent migrants to the
city.[1] Despite these complicating factors, the figures are a useful
source of evidence. In particular, the wide difference between
the engineers' children and their school-fellows supports the
notion that engineers belonged to 'the élite of the working men'.
The figure for the painters' children is likewise to be expected
from the earlier discussion. The children of the semi- and unskilled sample have the largest mean difference of all from
Broughton School. The engineers and the semi- and unskilled
workers are thus both sharply distinguished from a central
group comprising most of the skilled trades. The figure for the
engineers is 0·81 inches smaller than that for the miscellaneous
skilled sample, while that for the semi- and unskilled is 0·89 inches
larger than that for the painters; the remaining occupations
are far more closely bunched. It must, of course, be remembered
that the semi- and unskilled figure is based on a sample, whereas the selected skilled trades have been treated as populations;
a 95-per-cent confidence interval gives a minimum value for the
unskilled workers' mean of 2·53 inches—still larger than the
figure for any skilled trade.

Some of the figures, however, fit less easily into the framework
of the earlier analysis. The figures for the masons and joiners—
both of which I placed in the group of relatively advantaged
skilled trades—are the second and third largest among the
skilled trades; the figure for the shoemakers, on the other hand,
is the third smallest—although both the sample data for workers'
earnings and other evidence suggest that they were far from
prosperous. The two building trades may have been affected by
the severe building depression of the 1900s, while the masons
also suffered technological unemployment with the spread of
mechanization.[2] With regard to the shoemakers, the survey
material suggests a polarization within the trade, so that the
mean may conceal a wide range of variation in economic conditions. Although they rank next to the engineers in the

---

[1] Edin. C.O.S., op. cit., p. 22.   [2] See above, p. 63 and footnote.

proportion of children actually *taller* than the mean for the 'lower middle class' school, the shoemakers rank next to the painters and masons in the proportion of children three inches and more shorter.[1] The factor of migration may also be especially important in their case: 33 per cent of households, more than in any other occupation, were described as 'not always' resident in the city.[2] The most skilled, and therefore best-paid, shoemakers were said to come from the country, where a thorough craft apprenticeship was still obtainable.[3] Further analysis of the survey material points to an association between migration and economic condition. Although no relationship was found between the children's heights and migration, nearly half (four out of nine) of 'migrant' shoemakers, but only four out of eighteen 'non-migrants' paid 3s. 6d. and more weekly rent. The same pattern may be inferred from the fact that only 14 per cent of shoemakers described as in 'casual' employment,[4] but half those not so described paid 3s. 6d. and more rent; in no other trade was there such a systematic association between rent and 'casual' work. The figure for the shoemakers, then, conceals a variation in economic conditions perhaps greater than in any other trade. Shoemakers' families in the survey include, at one extreme, a case earning no more than 16s. weekly, in 'casual' employment, paying 2s. rent; this family was described as living in a 'very low stair', and the man indulged in 'bouts of drinking'. At the other end of the scale are men earning 30s. and more weekly, in 'regular' employment; one such family (described as 'decent, industrious') paid as much as 5s. 5d. rent, the husband played the harmonium at a Mission Hall and the wife was learning the piano.[5]

Like the earnings study, the survey data refer to a rather limited sub-population, rather than to the whole population of skilled manual workers. Yet the two sub-populations are defined in different ways—by the employment records of firms at

---

[1] Children taller than at Broughton School: engineers 29 per cent, shoemakers 28 per cent; children 3 inches and more shorter than at Broughton School: painters 42 per cent, masons 41 per cent, shoemakers 37 per cent.

[2] The relevant question reads: 'have the family always lived in Town?': Edin. C.O.S., op. cit., p. 5. Information from these interviews must be treated with great caution. [3] Gordon, loc. cit.

[4] 'Whether work regular or casual?': Edin. C.O.S., loc. cit.

[5] Ibid., Cases 573, 647.

particular dates, and by the families of pupils at a school in central Edinburgh. And the two sub-populations may have been biased in different directions: whereas the nature of the business archives available, and the statistical design used, imply a bias to the more regularly employed men on the pay-rolls of successful and expanding firms, the bias of the C.O.S. survey is towards unskilled labour, and the less-prosperous sections of skilled labour resident in the old, central working-class area of the city. The fact that the findings from these two sub-populations are broadly consistent with each other, and with predictions on the basis of other sources, strengthens the conclusions that can be drawn.

IV. CONCLUSION

While the statistical data are by no means comprehensive in their coverage, they do in general confirm the conclusions drawn from more impressionistic kinds of analysis. Both documentary and statistical approaches underline the point that economic differentiation within the working class is more complex than a simple skilled/unskilled, or even an occupational, classification will allow. It is, however, possible to draw some more general conclusions, and Table 4.11 attempts a summary of these. As this summary indicates, more detailed analysis confirms the suggestion that casual labour is the key factor distinguishing the prosperous from the poverty-stricken occupations.

The evidence considered indicates marked economic differences within the skilled strata, as well as between artisans and labourers. Such differences must be seen in relation to the organization of production and work-roles. It is likely that the growth of new forms of division of labour, hierarchies of specialization, and a distribution of authority and responsibility, was linked to differences in income and security. The better-paid and more regularly employed were no doubt those whom the employer 'trusted', and on whom responsibility devolved; the man who could be trusted to look after a new machine 'has his situation secure, and his wages best'.[1] The labour aristocracy did not arise simply from differences in

---

[1] 'Old Machine Manager', op. cit., p. vii.

income and living standards, but from the way those differences were linked to industrial structures characteristic of later-nineteenth-century British capitalism.

To demonstrate the existence of this structural configuration does not exhaust the questions posed at the beginning of this study. It remains to investigate the much more difficult problem

TABLE 4.11

Summary of Economic Situations of Selected Skilled Trades

	Fluctuations		Casual	Technical
	Cyclical	Seasonal	Labour	Change
Advantaged Trades				
Machinemen		×		×
Bookbinders		×		×
Masons	×	×		(From 1900s)
Joiners	×	×		
Engineers	×			×
Intermediate Trades				
Compositors		×	×	(From 1890s)
Ironmoulders	×			(From 1900s)
Deprived Trades				
Painters	×	×	×	
Shoemakers			×	×

of how these conditions were ideologically mediated, 'the way in which these experiences were handled in cultural terms'.[1] The summary in Table 4.11 may provide a convenient reference point for such an investigation. We should expect the 'advantaged' trades to be well represented in the ideological formation of the labour aristocracy; but not all privileged workers came from these occupations, nor were all workers in these occupations privileged. The classification has to do with the *relative proportions* in different trades of 'advantaged' and 'deprived' workers. The relationship of inter-occupational and intra-occupational differences is important here. The trades towards the lower end of the scale have a greater *internal* range of variation, and a higher proportion of men at the bottom of that range. The various trades may be visualized as pyramids of

[1] E. P. Thompson, *The Making of the English Working Class* (Pelican edn., 1968), p. 10.

varying shapes and sizes, all contained within the bigger pyramid representing manual labour as a whole. At the top of this bigger pyramid would be foremen and other workers whose irreplaceable skills and special responsibilities earned exceptionally high wages and secure employment; below them would be the well-paid and relatively secure 'superior artisans'; below them, the general run of skilled labour; and so on. Towards the bottom would be large numbers of sweated and other casual workers in the 'deprived' trades, together with a certain proportion from more prosperous trades, as well as semi- and unskilled workers. Every trade had some men who lived at the economic level of the upper strata, but also some men who lived at very low levels; it is the varying proportions of these groups that determine the over-all position of a trade in the hierarchy of skilled labour. Perhaps somewhere between the economic extremes was the standard which many artisans perceived, albeit dimly, as the 'fair day's wage' to which their labour should entitle them; and it was in terms of this conception that, however weak their organization, they struggled to preserve their wages and conditions.

5   The Community and Social Status

THE ideology of the artisan strata, and the emergence of 'labour aristocratic' forms of social consciousness, may be seen partly in terms of the impact on older, inherited values and modes of behaviour of industrial and urban capitalist development. Thus the values of 'respectability', which, in varying interpretations, were so pervasive in Victorian society, derived in part from the culture of eighteenth-century small farmers, self-employed artisans, and small masters: God-fearing, self-reliant, assertive of their moral independence, struggling to remain at a social level just above that of the 'labouring poor'.[1] By the mid-nineteenth century, at least in big cities, the artisan's class position had become quite unambiguously that of a wage-labourer, and, by the same, token, the capitalist class was more clearly defined; there was a transition, 'from the old outlook of "the Trade" to the duality of the masters' organizations, on the one hand, and the trade unions on the other'.[2] Yet many of the values of the pre-industrial tradespeople were perpetuated, in a modified form, as they were interpreted and diffused by new agencies, and implanted within the upper strata of the industrial proletariat.

The earlier popular culture of old-established urban centres like Edinburgh was marked by a series of occupational subcultures. This way of life was still, at the mid-nineteenth century, within living memory. Memories of the turn-outs of the Edinburgh trades in their craft regalia, for the royal visit to the city in 1822, and again at the Reform demonstration in 1832, were handed down to younger generations of journeymen.[3] At a less formal, but more pervasive, level, the daily contacts of the workshop carried over into non-working time. Alexander

---

[1] See Smout, *History of the Scottish People*, pp. 282–7, 338–9.
[2] Thompson, *Making of the Working Class*, p. 466.
[3] L. Fleming, *An Octogenarian Printer's Reminiscences* (1893), p. 21; *Scottish Typographical Circular*, Oct. 1881.

Somerville and Hugh Miller both describe the drinking customs
of the Edinburgh trades.[1] The very distinction between 'work'
and 'leisure' was less marked than it has since become, if only
because of the long working hours and the tendency to cook,
eat, and drink in the workshop; flowers and birds were kept in
the printing office where Samuel Kinnear served his apprenticeship.[2]

A strong sense of occupational identity thus helped to form
the social consciousness of the Victorian artisan. The craft pride
of the occupational subculture, and its emphasis on the value of
manual labour, distinguished the artisans as a social group, and
ultimately contributed to a wider consciousness of class. Craft
tradition provided a social imagery of class identification. The
Reform demonstration of 1866 affords an example of this. 'The
Various Trades of the City walked in Procession. The Bookbinders turned out to the Number of One Hundred and Twenty
four, they carried some fine specimens of Binding, along with a
Flag and several Banners with Mottos appropriate to the
Occasion the Day was enjoyed by all who took a Part in the
Proceedings.'[3] In this procession the display of artisan skills, and
the use of metaphor based on occupation supported the claim
of working men, as 'the producers of wealth',[4] to political rights.
The printing trades had a compositor at work on the back of a
lorry and lithographers with a machine in operation, running
off copies of an appropriate political cartoon. The smiths, 'the
very types of the honest blacksmith Longfellow has immortal-
ised', had an anvil; the masons were each dressed in, a white
apron trimmed with blue, and masonic emblems'; the plumbers
carried a 'shower bath, with a most uncomfortable looking
inmate, represented to be "Bob Lowe bathing" '; the coopers
had 'two automata . . . hammering a cask, their work being
described as "Down with the Tories" '; and so on. Many of the
slogans drew on occupation as a source of metaphor. The
masons, for example, had the slogan 'justice to the line and

---

[1] Somerville, *Autobiography*, p. 59; H. Miller, *My Schools and Schoolmasters* (1854)
pp. 320–3.

[2] Kinnear, *Reminiscences*, pp. 20, 27.

[3] Bookbinders' Union Society, Minutes, 17 Nov. 1866.

[4] This phrase was used in one of the speeches: *North Briton*, 21 Nov. 1866. The
information and quotations that follow all come from this report.

equity to plummet', the shoemakers, inevitably, 'true to the last', the tobacco workers, 'may the designs of our enemies vanish in smoke'.[1] The popular politics of urban-industrial society seem here to be in process of emergence from the craft pageantry of an earlier period. As the *Scotsman* commented: 'In 1832 it was thought important to defend the Edinburgh demonstrations from imputations that the working men would not join in them. On Saturday the processionists were artisans exclusively.'[2]

Occupational sub-cultures played an important part in the growth of political radicalism—as well as of trade unionism—in the 1860s. And these sub-cultures remained a distinguishing feature of artisan life; many of the new leisure pursuits of the later nineteenth century, for example, were carried on by work- or occupation-based organizations.[3] But it is likely that there was a relative decline in the importance of the occupational community. A number of considerations lead to the conclusion that the life of the craft was becoming less self-contained than it had been. In the first place, changes in occupational structure point to a relative—and sometimes absolute—decline of many old-established crafts, and the emergence of new skilled occupations—such as engineers or printing machinemen—without the long history that figures in the occupational consciousness of the older trades. In the older crafts themselves, various structural changes undermined the all-pervasive, face-to-face occupational community. The increase in scale, both of the urban settlement and of industrial enterprises, surely had this effect. In the more important skilled trades it was already, by the mid-nineteenth century, impossible for a man to know personally and be known to all his fellow-craftsmen;[4] and there was almost certainly an increase in the mobility of labour. The location of new industries around the railways and the Union Canal, and the growth of large new tracts of working-class housing, contrasted with the typical setting of the old artisan

---

[1] *North Briton*, 21 Nov. 1866; cf. J. Gorman, *Banner Bright* (1973), pp. 66–90, see also introduction by G. A. Williams, pp. 9–11. [2] *Scotsman*, 19 Nov. 1866.

[3] The printers had an inter-firm football league: *Scottish Typographical Circular*, July 1895.

[4] Tades with more than 1,000 males aged twenty and over at the 1861 census include printers, masons, joiners, shoemakers, tailors, and cabinet-makers.

sub-cultures—a town-centre back-street mixture of craft work-shops and the dwellings of shopkeepers, artisans, and the various other strata of the common people.

The most fundamental change was in productive organiza-tion and the structure of industry. The growing scale of industry and the concentration of ownership in the hands of a socially distant class emphasized the worker's position as a wage-labourer, as opposed to the distinctiveness of his craft. The demand for shorter hours was no doubt in part a response to such structural changes; but the shorter working day may itself have contributed to the separation of 'work' from 'leisure' and 'home',[1] and thus to the erosion of occupational com-munities. This is not to deny the continuing significance of craft-based attitudes among skilled workers; but it is equally misleading to overlook the weakening of such attitudes and the growth of other kinds of social identity. Moreover, the skilled manual labour force itself became less homogeneous, with the emergence of more elaborate divisions of labour, and hierarchic specialization of work roles (see above, Chapters 3 and 4). If the industrial and economic structures are associated with the ideological patterns implied by the labour-aristocracy thesis,[2] these patterns are not to be found simply in craft sectionalism (which is by no means peculiar to this period), but also in other kinds of life-style and social imagery emerging from the mid-nineteenth century.

Thus, although the occupational culture remained an im-portant element in the social identity of the artisan, it became less self-contained; the milieu of 'the trade' became one of a range of contexts in which the worker lived his daily life. The change is noted in the reminiscences of a hatter, published in 1861: 'the great part of the labouring classes may be said to have vegetated in their circles. Tradesmen, in the bustling life of industry, although they were sharpened by intercommunion, their ideas wanted breadth as well as tolerance.'[3] The writer relates this to the growth of new types of leisure pursuit. In the past, there were 'no lectures soirées or concerts for the unwashed'; but 'amusements are now of a refining and elevating nature'.[4]

---

[1] E. P. Thompson, 'Time, Work-discipline, and Industrial Capitalism', *Past and Present*, no. 38 (1967).   [2] See above, Ch. 1, especially pp. 1–3.
[3] *North Briton*, 27 Apr. 1861.   [4] Ibid.

This implies that the break-up of the old occupational sub-cultures was not simply a matter of the negative effect of structural changes; there was also the positive attraction of new styles of life and sources of social identity. A syndrome of attitudes and behaviour patterns, linked to the values of 'respectability', contributed to the cultural formation of an upper-artisan stratum. This process had a dual significance. On the one hand, it broke down the traditional fragmentation of the working class into a series of occupational communities. But in doing so it fostered new, 'horizontal' divisions between working-class strata. The life-style of the 'respectable' artisan tended to project a sense of social superiority, a self-conscious cultural exclusion of less-favoured working-class groups. This process will be examined, first, in the context of housing and residential segregation.

A number of sources comment on the social mixture to be found in the tenements of the Old Town during the early to mid-nineteenth century, the 'different grades in the social scale (for even among the working classes there are many gradations) overlying each other with nearly all the regularity of geological strata.'[1] Proximity to work, the location of the craft workshops among the tenements of the Old Town and in the back streets of the New Town, was an important feature of this urban scene. The location of many newer and larger-scale industrial enterprises in newly developing areas away from the town centres contributed to the changes of the period. The effect of the early slum clearances (beginning in Edinburgh with Chambers's Improvement of the 1860s) and of the acquisition of urban land for railways and other town-centre developments is also well known; whereas the more prosperous of the former slum dwellers were able to move to new and superior housing, the effect on the poorer, and probably more numerous, group was to aggravate the over-all housing shortage.[2]

The houses that were erected were too good for the class of tenants

---

[1] J. Symington, 'The Working Man's Home', in J. Begg, D.D., *Happy Homes fo Working Men and How to Get Them* (1866), p. 161.
[2] For other cities see: C. M. Allan, 'The Genesis of British Urban Re-development with Special Reference to Glasgow', *Economic History Review*, 2nd ser., 18 (1965); Best, *Mid-Victorian Britain*, pp. 60–1; Stedman Jones, *Outcast London*, pp. 160–78.

that we displaced in the lower part of the town; and the consequence was that the houses were never let; but they were exposed for sale they were very eagerly looked after by artizans of a superior class, who acquired them with the little savings they had of their own, or with the assistance of loans from investment companies.[1]

In one case improved housing was built by a 'Building Association' composed of working men.[2]

From the Royal Commission on Housing (1884–5) we get a picture of well-marked and well-understood gradations in types of working-class housing in the city. Those living in one room only were 'labourers and people of the poorer class';[3] at the upper end of the scale a 'growing demand' was reported for self-contained flats, built in two storeys with outside stairs and separate street doors.[4] Housing of this type had been erected by the Co-operative Building Company; founded at the end of the masons' nine-hours strike in 1861, it catered, according to its manager, for the 'better class of working man'.[5] The President of Edinburgh Trades Council reported a 'general desire among our artizans to be laird of their own house, as the saying is'.[6] The trend to owner occupation no doubt involved only a minority, even of the 'superior' artisans; most manual workers of all occupational groups continued to live in rented flats of the tenement style. But among these there was a wide range, from district to district, street to street, even block to block or stair to stair. 'Improved' blocks might be found interspersed among dwellings of a distinctly poor class.

Some statistical evidence, for the families surveyed by the C.O.S. in 1904, is given in Table 5.1. Thirty-two per cent of the semi- and unskilled, but only 14 per cent of the skilled were reported as living in one room; conversely, 40 per cent of the skilled, but only 20 per cent of the semi- and unskilled were reported as paying 3s. 6d. or more weekly rent.

In view of the difficulty posed by the regrettably small numbers in some of the occupations, we should avoid reading too much into the *size* of percentage difference, but focus

[1] *R.C. on Housing*, q. 18738 (clerk to City Improvement Trustees).
[2] Commemorative plaque on building in Blackfriars Street.
[3] *R.C. on Housing*, q. 19250 (president of Edinburgh Trades Council).
[4] Ibid., q. 18688 (City Valuer and Assessor).   [5] Ibid., q. 19071.
[6] Ibid., q. 19185.

TABLE 5.1

Housing of Families in C.O.S. Survey, 1904

	*N** (*households*)	*Mean weekly rent* (*shillings*)	*Percentage in houses with:* *Rent 3s. 6d. or more*	*Three or more rooms*	*One room only*
Engineers	9	3·78	67 (6)	55·5 (5)	11 (1)
Joiners	10	3·70	60 (6)	50 (5)	20 (2)
Printers	30	3·53	60 (18)	27 (8)	3 (1)
Shoemakers	16	3·38	44 (7)	31 (5)	– (–)
Bookbinders	9	3·30	44 (4)	11 (1)	11 (1)
Miscellaneous skilled	17	3·19	41 (7)	12 (2)	12 (2)
Painters	31	2·95	23 (7)	19 (6)	23 (7)
Masons	13	2·90	15 (2)	38·5 (5)	23 (3)
Metal trades	18	2·76	22 (4)	28 (5)	22 (4)
Skilled total	153	3·22	40 (61)	27 (42)	14 (21)
Semi- and unskilled	25	2·69	20 (5)	20 (5)	32 (8)
Total	178	3·15	37 (66)	26 (47)	16 (29)

Notes: * Eight households in furnished lodgings, renting shops as well as homes, or for whom no housing information is given, have been omitted.
Figures in brackets indicate raw numbers in categories.

instead on the *direction* of differences, similarities in the distribution of different variables, and the rank order of occupations. The important point to emerge from this approach is that the differences are broadly consistent with the occupational analysis of economic conditions in Chapter 4. The printers, joiners, and engineers have 60 per cent and more in the 'high rent' group. This suggests that differences in housing marked off a 'superior' stratum of skilled workers, drawn from certain favoured trades, and from the best-placed workers in other trades.

How do the gradations in housing and neighbourhood relate to particular social attitudes? What were the meanings to working people of movement to a different sort of housing? A good deal of caution is necessary here. The written evidence is hard to interpret, since it relates to a minority of exceptional, articulate working men, or to comment by journalists, philanthropists, and other interested observers. Accordingly the intention is not to argue that cultural factors were a *cause* of the emergence of new housing patterns, independent of demographic and economic variables, but rather to show that residential segregation, whatever its causes, had a cultural *meaning*, at any rate for the tiny minority of artisans who have left some documentary record of their personal views. Given this vital qualification, it is possible to delineate certain attitudes and aspirations which had begun to emerge before the slum clearances of the sixties, so that the construction of improved dwellings at higher rents in place of the slums helped to meet a pre-existing demand for better housing. And this demand did not simply reflect a desire to spend improved incomes on improved housing; it was associated with particular values and ways of perceiving the urban neighbourhood and its inhabitants. A common theme is the desire to escape identification with the inhabitants of the old central working-class area. A typical comment is that of the 'Old Journeyman Hatter' in his published reminiscences: 'In a moral point of view these localities will never contain a well conditioned population.'[1] The winner of Dr. Begg's essay prize on 'The Working Man's Home' (a compositor by trade) complained of the difficulty of maintaining 'respectable' standards in the old tenements, with their social mixture, gregarious street (or court or close) life, and lack of privacy.[2] The proprietor of one superior block, who had managed to let only twelve out of fifty flats, attributed this to a stigmatization effect from the low reputation of the neighbourhood.[3] The *North Briton*—a local radical paper with a working-class orientation—advocated the provision of running water in dwellings, on the grounds that: 'It is grievous to find a decent woman, perhaps in feeble health, standing at a public well for an hour, waiting for a supply of water—perhaps in the midst of prostitutes and viragos.'[4]

Aspirations with regard to housing conditions and the urban neighbourhood reflect cultural divisions between strata of the working class. The movement to better housing was also an escape from the stigma of association with the poorer sections of the working population, and which must often have been reinforced by racial and religious prejudice against the Irish. Asked whether the slum dwellers resented their poor conditions, A. C. Telfer, the President of the Trades Council (a joiner by trade), told the Royal Commission on Housing: 'Properly speaking it is generally the Irish element, labourers and what

---

[1] *North Briton*, 27 Apr. 1861.   [2] Symington, in Begg, op. cit., p. 162.
[3] *R.C. on Housing*, q. 19154.   [4] *North Briton*, 25 May 1859.

not who live in that locality, and I must confess that I do not come into communication with them as a rule, so as to feel as it were the touch of their inner feelings in that respect.'[1]

This desire to escape the stigma of proximity to the 'Irish element, labourers and what not' had a more positive counterpart, in the values of domesticity and the home. The Reverend Dr. Begg articulated these values, from the standpoint of the Free Church social conscience: 'Man must not only have a covering, but a HOME. It is upon the right ordering of these little kingdoms that the peace and social order of all the great kingdoms of the world depends.'[2] Like the stigmatization of the disreputable poor, this valuation of family life is an important feature of Victorian middle-class ideology; like the social imagery of stigmatization, it found an echo in the 'respectable' working class. Telfer complained to the Royal Commission that the cost of decent housing forced artisans to take lodgers, and that consequently 'the home is not the home it ought to be.'[3] The prize essayist already quoted even had reservations about any extra-familial leisure pursuits at all, on the ground that they 'must draw the head of the household away from his family at the time when he is most required, and give him a taste for engagements and companionships which can only be gratified beyond the pale of the domestic hearth.'[4] The author is not referring, as one might imagine, to brothels, nor even to pubs—but to reading rooms! No doubt this is an extreme statement of the values of domesticity; those groups most likely to have high aspirations with regard to housing were also characterized by high levels of participation in various voluntary organizations. But there seems equally little doubt that, in milder forms, the positive evaluation of home and family life was quite widely diffused.

There is, then, a certain amount of evidence to support the hypothesis that residential patterns were related to particular kinds of value and aspirations, and to marked cultural divisions within the working class. Popular recreation, and participation in various voluntary organizations, seem likewise to have been bound up with the projection of a sense of social superiority.

---

[1] *R.C. on Housing*, q. 19273.
[2] Begg, op. cit., p. iv.
[3] *R.C. on Housing*, q. 19198.
[4] Symington, in Begg, op. cit., p. 178.

Best has commented that in the 1850s and 1860s we can detect the beginnings of 'the leisure patterns of modern industrial urban mass society'.[1] The specialized organizations emerging in place of older ways of spending free time tended, however, to take the form of voluntary organizations, rather than of the business investment in leisure facilities more often associated with 'mass society'. The newer leisure organizations provided in the first instance, not for an undifferentiated 'mass', but for more clearly identified social groups. Social identities were, indeed, partly created through the construction of particular styles of life, as the 'superior' artisan sought to distinguish himself from the test of the working class.

The new leisure patterns are associated with a rejection of certain aspects of the older popular culture, especially its drinking customs. This is reflected in 'those evening entertainments called soirées so common among the sub-middle and working classes of society'.[2] The entertainment on such occasions was generally an eclectic mixture of popular songs (sentimental and humorous), recitations (Burns being a great favourite), humorous sketches, perhaps some painless adult education, and so on, together with (non-alcoholic) refreshments. There was nothing of a risqué character, for one feature of the soirée was that wives and 'sweethearts' could safely be invited. For example, 'upwards of a thousand' printers and their womenfolk gathered at the invitation of William Nelson, the publisher, to hear a lecture on the 'noble art' of printing and then 'enjoy the humour and pathos of some of Scotland's choicest national songs, including Burns's proud protest, which could there be appreciated without any thought of social wrong—"A man's a man for a' that" '.[3] The Typographical Circular, a journal owned by the union, struck the note of working-class respectability in its comment on the occasion: 'Here were a thousand men, nearly all in superfine black coats and spotless shirt-fronts; a thousand women in tasteful dresses and bonnets of the latest mode . . . and in all this great mass of the 'lower orders' not a word out of joint; not a gesture of impatience; no crowding, jostling . . . nothing but courtesy and . . . perfect good breeding.'[4] The

[1] Best, op. cit., p. 199.
[2] J. S. Blackie, Notes of a Life, ed. A. S. Walker (1908), p. 228.
[3] Wilson, William Nelson, p. 82.   [4] Quoted ibid.

soirée was likewise the stock-in-trade of the Workingmen's Club and Institute, formed in 1864 to provide 'healthy recreation combined with mental improvement';[1] of benevolent employers (like Nelson); trade unions; or any body desirous of holding a respectable social gathering.

The content of the cultural programme on such occasions is of some relevance to my theme. To assess the quality of that culture is a difficult, and possibly dangerous enterprise. One must none the less note a sense of its eclectic and undemanding character. It is in some respects a watered-down version of the literature and art of the middle class, adapted for lower-middle and upper-working-class audiences, diffused as the badge of 'respectability' and 'self improvement'. There are some more authentically popular elements: recitations and humorous sketches in broad Scots were favourite items on any programme. Even the desire for the trappings of the established culture might be inspired by egalitarian values, a stress on the independence and human dignity of the worker, and his needs as a 'whole man'. The acquisition of visible signs of refinement reflected the working man's demand for access to a cultural life from which he had hitherto felt shut out. As Smiles (whose writing affords one point of approach to the problem) argued: 'The chief disadvantage attached to the calling of the laborious classes is, not that they are employed in physical work, but that they are too exclusively so employed, often to the neglect of their moral and intellectual faculties.'[2] We find the same stress on the cultural needs of the 'whole man' in Lord Gifford's address at the prize-giving of the Edinburgh Workingman's Flower Show:

He had very great pleasure in taking part in the proceedings of that day, for he had sometimes thought and felt that some of their practical philanthropic movements were just perhaps a little too narrow and restricted in their influence. (Hear, hear). It was quite right and necessary that the wants of the body should be supplied. . . . But they seemed to forget that they had implanted in them by Him who made them tastes and aesthetic faculties which, if cultivated a little, would produce the highest, purest, and most elevating pleasure,

---

[1] *Scottish Typographical Circular*, Oct. 1864, according to which the committee were 'principally printers'.
[2] S. Smiles, *Self Help* (Sphere Books edn., 1968), p. 206.

and which served as a shield to protect their whole nature from what would otherwise defile it. (Applause).[1]

In interpreting this syndrome of cultural aspiration one is confronted, as so often in the analysis of Victorian attitudes, with the ambiguous nature of 'respectability'. One one hand, 'it entailed a healthy self-respect, an assertion of personal worth over external condition'; but on the other hand, it tended to be defined in practice by 'precisely that acquisition of external characteristics' condemned by Burns.[2] The ambiguity is nicely brought out by the Edinburgh printers, assembling in their 'superfine black coats', to hear declaimed from the platform: 'The man o' independent mind, He looks and laughs at a' that.'

The social identity of the 'respectable' working man was created through a commitment to sobriety and propriety and consequent rejection of traditional drinking habits, and of that *demi-monde* which continued to attract 'a curious throng . . . a kind of hybrid, between the gent and the pickpocket'.[3] More positively, the growth of those voluntary associations favoured by skilled workers was linked to their claim to be brought within the pale of civic respectability—a claim which played a part in the Reform agitation of 1866–7. Those associations connected with thrift—co-ops, savings banks, and so on—are a familiar theme of the social comment literature of the period; the emergence of certain kinds of organized leisure pursuit can be viewed in a similar light.

The best example of this is perhaps the Volunteer movement.[4] The initial conception was a force of 'men of the classes having means of their own'.[5] But there was a remarkable response from skilled workers, demonstrating, one prominent Volunteer wrote, 'even a higher public spirit than the professional Volunteers'.[6] Two artisan companies were among the eight companies originally raised in the city in 1859 (the others being

---

[1] *Reformer*, 13 Aug. 1870.

[2] F. Reid, 'Keir Hardie's Conversion to Socialism', in A. Briggs and J. Saville (eds.), *Essays in Labour History, 1886–1923* (1971), p. 22.

[3] *North Briton*, 30 Apr. 1862; cf. D. A. Jamieson, *Powderhall and Pedestrianism* (1943), p. 13.

[4] See Dr. H. Cunningham's forthcoming book on this topic; I am indebted to Dr. Cunningham for guidance.

[5] J. H. A. Macdonald, *Fifty Years of It: the experiences and struggles of a Volunteer of 1859* (1909), p. 3.   [6] Ibid., p. 24.

occupational companies catering for the university, accountants, lawyers, etc.), and were said to be 'the first genuine artisan companies in the kingdom'.[1] By 1868 there were eight artisan companies, whose 712 men together made up 37 per cent of the effective strength of the Edinburgh Rifle Volunteer Brigade; seven companies based on middle-class occupations; and seven Highland companies (two of these were said to consist mainly of artisans).[2]

The artisans proved, moreover, to be the most consistent supporters of the movement; the business and professional elements tended to drop away when the war scare had passed, and 'if it had not been for the zeal and energy of the working classes the Volunteer Force might have dwindled'.[3] This picture is borne out by an analysis of membership figures (in view of special factors affecting the Highland companies, these are excluded from the discussion). Whereas the other companies reach their peak of effective strength in the international crises of 1870–1 and 1877–9, the artisan companies are not affected by these events, and their proportion of the total strength of the force consequently falls from 51 per cent in 1870 to 46 per cent in 1871.[4] It seems reasonable to infer from this difference in recruitment patterns the distinctive nature of the skilled workers' attachment to the movement.

A part of the meaning of Volunteering lay in the embodiment of values of patriotism and citizenship—values perhaps reinforced by the occasional Garibaldian overtones of the movement. It also had a relation to the growing enthusiasm for 'healthy' recreation.

The youths are enthusiastically in favour of it—some chance now of drill, or cricket or outdoor play in general after 'supper' . . . short

---

[1] W. Stephen, *Queen's City of Edinburgh Rifle Volunteer Brigade*, p. 61.
[2] Based on information about the various companies in Stephen, op. cit., *passim*.
[3] Macdonald, op. cit., p. 92.
[4] Calculated from membership figures in Stephen, op. cit. Highland companies were excluded because of the special effects on recruitment of the clan associations, to which many Highlanders resident in the city belonged (Stephen, p. 336). The proportion of effective strength in artisan companies did not recover after the Franco-Prussian war (perhaps because of the slump of the later 1870s), while middle-class recruitment rose again with the Balkan crisis: the figures do not, however, cover a long enough time span to establish fully the effect of slumps or other factors on artisan participation.

space is wanted to bring the whole trade within the social pale . . .
to allow the husband and father to have the fellowship with his
family heretofore denied him—to enable the young to share the
advantages of bodily recreation and culture enjoyed by the great
bulk of the artisan class—to give the employers full return of nerve
or brain force for which they pay at a uniform rate throughout the
day; and, in short, to allow printers as a class to live, and move,
and have their being like other rational people.[1]

Thus the *Typographical Circular*, greeting the shorter hours gained
in 1868. Swimming, golf, walking, excursions and seaside
holidays, cricket, football, were all growing pastimes in this
period.[2] Above all, football. Like the other sports mentioned,
this seems at first to have been based on voluntary organizations
(whether self-governing or under religious or other sponsor-
ship). Football was thus initially part of the pattern of 'healthy
recreation', distinguishing the respectable skilled worker with
the ability and inclination to participate in voluntary organizations.

That such differences continued to be important is indicated
by Table 5.2, which is based on the 'comments' on each family
by the 'lady visitors' who conducted the C.O.S. investigation.
It seemed best to treat these comments as a measure of the perception of working-class families in different occupational and
other circumstances by middle-class observers.[3] We are therefore concerned with the *saliency* of the activities mentioned in the
middle-class investigators' perception or recollection of the
various families. The pattern of variation is similar to that
in housing conditions (as is indicated by repeating figures for
mean rent from Table 5.1). The semi- and unskilled sample falls
below the figure for all skilled occupations combined, on all
three categories of activity; the printers, bookbinders, engineers,
and miscellaneous skilled are above that figure on at least two
out of three; and the painters and masons are below on all
three. The association between housing conditions and reported
participation is borne out by analysis at the level of the individual families. Taking all occupations together, 64 per cent of

[1] *Scottish Typographical Circular*, May 1868.
[2] See A. G. Docherty, 'Urban Working Class Recreation before 1914' (unpublished undergraduate dissertation, Edinburgh University, Department of Economic
History).   [3] Cf. below, p. 137.

TABLE 5.2

Organizational and Leisure Affiliations of Families
in C.O.S. Survey, 1904

	$N*$	Mean Rent (shillings)	Savings Institution		Religious, Temperance, etc.		Voluntary Organizations, Sports, and Hobbies	
			Percentage recorded as participants in					
Engineers	9	3·78	33	(3)	78	(7)	11	(1)
Joiners	11*	3·70	27	(3)	18	(2)	18	(2)
Printers	30	3·53	33	(10)	20	(6)	23	(7)
Shoemakers	18*	3·38	17	(3)	28	(5)	28	(5)
Bookbinders	9	3·30	55·5	(5)	33	(3)	22	(2)
Miscellaneous skilled	17	3·19	35	(6)	41	(7)	18	(3)
Painters	33*	2·95	18	(6)	27	(9)	9	(3)
Masons	14*	2·90	21	(3)	7	(1)	7	(1)
Metal trades	18	2·76	33	(6)	22	(4)	17	(3)
Skilled total	159*	3·22	28	(45)	28	(44)	17	(27)
Semi- and unskilled	27*	2·69	18·5	(5)	22	(6)	11	(3)
Total	186*	3·15	27	(50)	27	(50)	16	(30)

Notes: * Includes households in furnished lodgings, etc., omitted from Table 5.1. Figures in brackets indicate raw numbers.

Savings Institution: savings banks, friendly societies, co-op, thrift clubs, etc.; not trade unions.

Religious, Temperance, etc.: All activities and facilities under religious or temperance auspices, as well as membership of churches, temperance organizations, Salvation Army, etc.

Other Voluntary Organizations, Sports, and Hobbies: Participation in any other sort of voluntary organization (working men's club, political parties, etc.) or any specific type of recreation, inside or outside the home; reported attendance at meetings, office-bearing, etc. in friendly societies is counted here, but simple membership of friendly societies is counted only under 'Savings'.

Participation by any family member in these activities is counted; but no family is counted more than once for the same category of activity.

families paying 3s. 6d. or more, but only 41 per cent of those paying less than 3s., are recorded as participants in one or more type of activity. Living in the higher-rent houses, and being perceived as participants in the various activities are both part of a style of life, distinguishing in cultural terms the different strata of the working class.

Further evidence of the differentiation in leisure activities is provided by the social composition of four voluntary organizations (Table 5.3). These organizations cannot be claimed to be a representative cross-section of popular leisure in the city.

Moreover the nature of the four activities—their demands on money, time, and other resources—perhaps contains a built-in bias to the more prosperous sections of the working class. (Many of the classes in the Flower Show, however, were for window boxes, indoor plants, etc., and some were specifically for dwellers in central tenement areas.) Activities of a less demanding and less formally organized kind—of which no records

TABLE 5.3
Social Composition of Four Voluntary Organizations

Percentage of	Officers, Mechanics Library 1840–1858		Members, Bruntsfield Links Allied Golf Club, 1869		Prizewinners, Working Men's Flower Show 1870		Officers, Bowling Clubs 1890–1892	
Professions	5	(2)	6	(2)	–	(–)	20	(7)
Business	15	(6)	12	(4)	14	(11)	28	(10)
White-collar I	19·5	(8)	9	(3)	3	(2)	31	(11)
White-collar II	19·5	(8)	6	(2)	6	(5)	3	(1)
Retail, warehouse	–	(–)	–	(–)	6	(4)	3	(1)
Manual—skilled	37	(15)	62*	(21)	59	(46)	6	(2)
Manual—semi- and unskilled	2	(1)	–	(–)	8	(6)	–	(–)
Manual—skill unclassifiable	2	(1)	3	(1)	1	(1)	–	(–)
Domestic service	–	(–)	–	(–)	3	(2)	–	(–)
Miscellaneous services	–	(–)	3	(1)	1	(1)	9	(3)
N traced (= 100 per cent)	41		34		78		35	
Not traced	–		7		25		10	

Source: List of officers' names and occupations in Edin. Mechanics' Subscription Library, *Laws and Catalogue,* (1859); Tracing of names and addresses from census schedules: list of members, 1869, Minutes of Bruntsfield Links Allied Golf Club, 1869–80; list of prizewinners, Edin. Working Man's Flower Show, *Reformer,* 13 Aug. 1870; officers of bowling clubs in J. Prestell (ed.), *Edinburgh Bowling Annuals,* 1890–2. I am indebted to the Registrar General for Scotland for allowing me to consult census schedules.

Notes: For occupational classification see Appendix II. No cases occurred in categories mentioned in Appendix II missing from the table. Women and children Flower Show prizewinners classified by occupation of household head (untraced cases included six households headed by widows etc.). Families with more than one prize are counted only once, as are Library and Bowling Club officers serving for more than one year.

* Nine cases (five printers, three furniture trades, one shoemaker) assigned by work-place address to appropriate skilled trade (three cases with both work-place and home address were skilled workers). Skilled manual = 36 per cent, white-collar (I and II) = 41 per cent if cases with work-place address only are treated as white-collar rather than skilled-manual employees.

Figures in brackets indicate raw numbers.

survive—may well have involved a greater degree of social contact between working-class strata. The figures in Table 5.3 are, none the less, the only ones found for voluntary-organization membership; and their interest relates partly to the contacts they reveal between the artisan membership and non-manual groups.

The skilled-manual category accounts for a majority of the Golf Club and Flower Show, and for the largest single category among the Mechanics' Library committeemen. The Bowling Club committees, on the other hand, have a preponderance of middle-class groups.[1] Semi- and unskilled workers are under-represented in the Library and Flower Show, while they do not appear at all in the other two organizations.[2] And the occupational breakdown of the skilled-manual category shows a concentration of occupations which we might expect, from other evidence, to find represented in the 'superior' stratum: printers are by far the largest group in the Library, with seven out of the fifteen skilled workers, while bookbinders, engineers, and brass-founders have two each; printers and furniture trades are the largest occupations in the Golf Club; masons, joiners, smiths, and shoemakers[3] in the Flower Show. It is also worth noting the concentration of transport workers among the few semi- and unskilled workers belonging to these organizations. The one Library officer in this category was a carter; railwaymen account for two of the semi- and unskilled Flower Show prizewinners, road transport for another two, while the remaining one was a post-office worker. Transport workers appear to be distinguished from other semi- and unskilled

---

[1] It may be misleading to compare committee composition with total membership composition, but the only available membership details for an individual Bowling Club show a similar pattern, with only one skilled worker among eighteen new members: Minutes of Edinburgh Bowling Club, 1890–1.

[2] If all the untraceable cases (other than six households headed by widows etc. among the Flower Show prizewinners) were in fact semi- and unskilled workers, the relevant percentages would be:

	Golf Club	Flower Show	Bowling Clubs
Skilled	51	47	4
Unskilled	17	26	22

[3] Unlike those in the other trades mentioned, the shoemakers did not enjoy an advantageous economic position. On the other hand, they were by far the most numerous of the skilled trades at this period.

occupations by somewhat more contact with the artisan social world.

As well as differences between activities favoured by various social strata we sometimes also find differences in the social composition of organizations catering for the same activity. Certain golf clubs drew their membership from professional and superior business groups, in contrast to the artisan and white-collar membership of the Bruntsfield Links Allied Club.[1] Similarly, the university and professional-based Grange Cricket Club was clearly of a more exalted social tone than the cricket clubs playing on the Meadows, which on one occasion sought the aid of the Trades Council in preserving their ground.[2] The occupational distinction between different Volunteer companies exemplifies the same tendency.

This evidence suggests that certain voluntary organizations in the city had a distinctively artisan character, combining high participation by skilled workers with low participation by less skilled groups of the working class and—as Table 5.3 indicates—considerable participation by business and white-collar groups. Business and the two white-collar groups together account for an actual majority (53 per cent) of the Library committees, for 27 per cent of the Golf Club, and for 23 per cent of the Flower Show. Taken together with the low unskilled-manual participation in these organizations, this would seem to bear out the assertion of Hobsbawm and other writers that the social gulf above the 'labour aristocrat' was narrower than that below him.[3]

But to determine the social significance of this pattern it is necessary to examine more closely the nature of these non-manual strata. Business, in particular, is a heterogeneous category, ranging from large local employers, who belong most properly with the professions in the upper-middle class, to self-employed shopkeepers and tradesmen of manual-working-class origins and affiliations.[4] To find reliable social indicators of these differences would entail a separate programme of research

---

[1] T. S. Aitchison and G. Lorimer, *Reminiscences of the Old Bruntsfield Links Golf Club* (privately printed, 1904).

[2] *Reminiscences of the Grange Cricket Club, Edinburgh* (1891); T. C. Minutes, 9 Feb. 1886.

[3] Hobsbawm, *Labouring Men*, p. 274.   [4] See below, Appendix II.

into the structure and life-styles of the middle class; here, I can only draw attention to the strong probability that those businessmen with whom artisans came into social contact belonged predominantly to the small-business sector. With regard to the white-collar groups, more rigorous occupational distinctions can be drawn. Whereas the white-collar I category (clerks, book-keepers, etc., more or less equivalent to Lockwood's *Blackcoated Worker*)[1] are the largest category in the Bowling Clubs, in the other organizations they are more evenly balanced by white-collar II—comprising a wide range of teachers, minor officials, managerial, supervisory (above foreman level) and technical employees, and other miscellaneous non-manual employees distinguished by special skills or responsibilities. The distinction between these two white-collar groups is suggested by the fact that the preponderance of white-collar I (clerks, etc.) in the Bowling Club is combined with high proportions in the professional and business categories, and only one case (= 3 per cent) in white-collar II. Although the difference in date between the sets of figures—and the likely changes in occupational structure between those dates—dictate great caution in drawing inferences, this pattern does suggest that the 'blackcoated workers' in white-collar I justify their reputation for 'status climbing', by their association on the Bowling Club committee with professional and business groups; whereas the more heterogeneous white-collar II category have a higher level of participation in those organizations with a large artisan membership.

It is therefore arguable that skilled workers' social contacts with non-manual strata were mainly with a relatively unformed, fluid, and transitional petty bourgeoisie of small businessmen, managerial and supervisory grades, etc. As the introduction to the Mechanics' Library *Catalogue* commented: 'it may be confidently affirmed, that during the whole of its history the great proportion of those who have directed its movements have either been mechanics, or very slightly raised above them in the social scale.'[2] In the light of this comment,

---

[1] D. Lockwood, *The Blackcoated Worker* (1958).
[2] Edin. Mechanics' Subscription Library, *Laws and Catalogue* (6th edn., 1859), p.v.

the list of non-manual occupations among the Library officers for 1840–59 may be taken as a guide to the composition of the strata considered to occupy this position in 'the social scale'. Apart from two professional men (a doctor and a solicitor), the officers include a clothier, a cheesemonger, a house agent, a corn merchant, a spirit merchant, a bookseller, eight clerks etc., four teachers, two reporters, a surveyor, and a collector.[1] This range of occupations was probably often recruited from skilled workers, or their children. With regard to elementary-school teachers, the official regulation of the recruitment, training, salaries, and general social behaviour of the teacher in grant-aided schools provides some documentation for this. It was generally assumed that pupil teachers were recruited from the children of 'respectable' skilled workers, and the framers of educational policy appear to have designed a niche for the qualified teacher slightly above the level of the 'superior' artisan.[2]

The leisure activities of some artisans therefore brought them into contact with certain petty-bourgeois groups; this is, moreover, in striking contrast to the paucity of contacts with less skilled groups of manual workers. But in stressing the 'shading over of the aristocracy of labour into other strata'[3] there is a danger of missing the other side of the coin; one should perhaps equally stress the marginal position of these non-manual groups, *vis à vis* the remainder of the middle class. Rather than the familiar 'ladder' image of the social order—with small business-men, teachers, and white-collar employees spread over the rungs above the upper working class and below the larger businessmen, professions, etc.—it may be more appropriate to think of culturally differentiated social worlds within the setting of the Victorian city. In this perspective, certain lower-middle-

---

[1] Mechanics' Library, *Laws and Catalogue*.

[2] See R. Johnson, 'Educational Policy and Social Control in Early Victorian England', *Past and Present*, no. 49 (1970), pp. 113–15; G. Sutherland, *Elementary Education in the Nineteenth Century*, (1971); and cf. Hobsbawm, loc. cit. Despite the important difference in educational tradition, elementary education in large cities, and the workings of the pupil-teacher system seem to have paralleled the English developments analysed in the works cited. For Scotland, see J. Scotland, *The History of Scottish Education*, vol. i (1969), pt. III, which suggests that the traditionally high standing of Scottish teachers was not shared by college-trained elementary-school teachers, who were recruited from the pupil teachers (see esp. p. 309).   [3] Hobsbawm, loc. cit.

class strata inhabit the fringes of a social world dominated by the 'superior' artisan.[1]

Occupational data from marriage certificates throw further light on patterns of contact between different social strata. Table 5.4 is based on the marriage certificates for all grooms in selected skilled trades and in two unskilled occupations (building labourers and carters) marrying in the Registration District of Edinburgh during 1865–9.[2] In all the skilled trades but one (the ironmoulders) a third or more married the daughters of other skilled workers; similarly, the daughters of semi- and unskilled workers account for the largest single category of the brides of building labourers and carters. The carters, however, have a rather larger proportion in the skilled-manual category, which bears out the impression, from voluntary-organization membership, that transport workers had rather more contact than other unskilled workers with the social world of the artisan. The figures for the business and white-collar categories combined are more than double those for both unskilled occupations, in every skilled trade. One further general point must be made about the figures: the occupations with the higher proportions marrying the daughters of agricultural workers, farmers, or crofters—the masons, joiners, engineers, and the two unskilled occupations—are, on the whole, those in which we should expect to find considerable numbers of migrants from rural areas (including Ireland and Highland Scotland).[3] These figures suggest that migration was an important source of cultural differentiation in the urban working class at this period;

---

[1] But see below, Ch. 7, for an analysis of certain critically important links between these social worlds.

[2] I am indebted to the Registrar General for Scotland for access to these certificates, and to Mr. P. Morse for assistance with computing work. Strictly speaking, the data are for marriages solemnized in the city, not for men resident there; this may contribute to the figures for 'rural' groups. An analysis based only on grooms gives only a part of the picture; its rationale is that a man's chances of marrying a woman from a particular social group is a critical test of social barriers.

[3] The 'agricultural, fishing, seaman' category consists overwhelmingly of agricultural workers, a further breakdown making little difference to the overall picture. For the rural origins of carters see A. Tuckett, *The Scottish Carter* (1967), pp. 22–3. The figures for the building labourers probably reflect the influence of Irish immigration; whereas the carters had a higher propensity to marry the daughters of farm *workers*, the building labourers married the daughters of farmers or crofters.

TABLE 5.4

Marriage: Distribution of Fathers-in-law of Grooms in Selected Occupations, 1865–1869

Percentage Marrying Daughters of:

N (Grooms)		Professions	Business	White-collar I	White-collar II	Retail, warehouse	Manual—skilled	Manual—semi- and unskilled	Manual—skill unclassifiable	Domestic service	Miscellaneous services	Police	Armed forces	Agriculture, fishing, seaman	Farmer, crofter	Other, miscellaneous		Summary			
																		Business/white collar§	Manual—skilled	Manual—semi- and unskilled	Rural**
Printer*	135	1·5	13·3	0·7	3·7	2·2	54·8	7·4	3·7	3·7	1·5	—	0·7	3·7	3·0	—		17·7	54·8	7·4	6·7
Bookbinder	31	—	9·7	—	9·7	—	58·1	3·2	9·7	3·2	—	—	—	—	6·5	—		19·4	58·1	3·2	6·5
Mason	188	—	9·0	1·1	4·8	—	37·8	14·4	4·8	5·9	—	—	—	10·6	11·7	—		14·9	37·8	14·4	22·3
Joiner	216	0·5	15·3	1·9	4·6	0·5	36·6	8·8	4·2	8·3	—	—	1·9	8·3	9·3	—		21·8	36·6	8·8	17·6
Painter	77	5·2	9·1	1·0	7·8	1·0	37·7	20·8	5·2	2·6	2·6	—	1·3	6·5	1·3	—		16·9	37·7	20·8	7·8
Engineer†	100	—	10·0	—	—	—	48·0	13·0	2·0	6·0	—	—	—	13·0	3·0	—		14·0	48·0	13·0	16·0
Ironmoulder	23	—	21·7	—	8·7	—	30·4	21·7	8·7	—	—	—	—	4·3	4·3	—		30·4	30·4	21·7	8·6
Shoemaker	116	1·7	9·5	—	0·9	2·6	47·4	12·9	4·3	6·0	—	0·9	—	4·3	6·9	2·6		10·4	47·4	12·9	11·2
Building labourer‡	114	—	—	—	1·8	—	13·2	51·8	2·6	7·0	—	—	0·9	5·3	13·2	1·8		4·4	13·2	51·8	18·5
Carter	81	—	1·2	—	2·5	1·2	28·4	38·3	2·5	2·5	1·2	—	1·2	14·8	4·9	1·2		3·7	28·4	38·3	19·7

Notes: See Appendix II for occupational classification.

* All grooms described as 'compositor', 'press and machineman', 'printer'.
‡ Building labourers in all trades.
** Agriculture, fishing, seaman, farmer, and crofter combined.
† All described as 'engineer', 'fitter', 'turner'.
§ Business, white-collar I, white-collar II combined.

for it would seem that men in occupations recruited from rural areas maintained contacts, either with other people of rural origin, or possibly with people still resident in their place of origin. And this is true, not only of unskilled labourers of Irish descent, but also of such skilled trades as the masons and joiners.[1]

Some other differences among the skilled trades are less easily explained. Although the high proportion of painters marrying the daughters of semi- and unskilled workers was predicted from their economic condition, the ironmoulders have a still higher proportion, while the shoemakers, despite their precarious economic position, do not have an unusually large proportion of unskilled fathers-in-law.[2] These figures become less 'anomalous', in the light of the more detailed occupational composition of the unskilled fathers-in-law. While painter grooms have an unusually high proportion of building-labourer fathers-in-law, the semi- and unskilled fathers-in-law of ironmoulders are accounted for by high proportions of carters and miners, and the shoemaker grooms have the highest proportion among the skilled trades of marriages to the daughters of men described simply as 'labourer'.[3] Whereas the ironmoulders marry differentially the daughters of carters and miners, the painters marry differentially the daughters of building labourers; variations in the occupational composition of unskilled fathers-in-law, as well as in their over-all proportion, can thus be related to the differences in the class situation of the various skilled trades. An occupational breakdown of the fathers-in-law of building labourer and carter grooms throws a similar light on the differences between unskilled occupations. Whereas the skilled fathers-in-law of building labourers are confined to the

---

[1] The two 'rural' groups of farm workers and farmers and crofters are fairly evenly balanced in these trades, which may reflect their contact with a rather higher stratum of Lowland rural society, and/or a high concentration of men of Highland origin, tending to marry the daughters of crofters.

[2] The figure for ironmoulders may be partly an effect of small fluctuations on the rather small total of cases for this trade. The shoemakers have the smallest total in business and the two white-collar groups combined.

[3] This, and subsequent references to specific occupations of fathers-in-law concerns only occupations each accounting for at least 1 per cent (= nine cases) of the fathers-in-law for all skilled grooms combined. The miners' skill grade is something of a borderline case; and they were in any case resident outside the city.

building trades and to three other large skilled occupations (smiths, shoemakers, and talors), those of carters include a wider range.[1] Of unskilled occupations, 22 per cent of building labourers, compared to 1 per cent of carters, married the daughters of building labourers; no building labourers, compared to 15 per cent of carters married the daughters of carters; and 26 per cent of building labourers, compared to 11 per cent of carters, married the daughters of general labourers.[2] These differences are of considerable interest, in the light of the finding that transport workers largely account for the unskilled participation, such as it was, in voluntary organizations with a high artisan membership.

The evidence of participation in voluntary organizations and marriage points to the existence of considerable social segregation within the manual working class of the 1850s to 1870s, and to associated differences in the degree of mixing with non-manual strata. The trades distinguished by superior housing standards, high levels of participation in voluntary organizations, and, to a lesser extent, by distinctive patterns of marriage are, broadly speaking, those that we would expect, from variations in economic situation, to find forming an upper stratum of the working class. But it would be misleading to postulate any simple, one-for-one correlation, implying a mechanistic economic determinism. It is fairly clear that there were independent sources of variation in styles of life and patterns of aspiration, related partly to the traditions, expectations, and value systems inculcated by particular occupational cultures. The high participation of printers in voluntary organizations, taken together with the somewhat insecure economic position of compositors, suggests the importance of this factor.[3] And the shoemakers, unlike the painters, are not distinguished by an especially high rate of marriage to the daughters of unskilled workers, although the economic position of the two trades was fairly comparable.

---

[1] This refers to the existence of *any* marriages at all to daughters of the trades mentioned, not to differential tendencies of intermarriage.

[2] That is 'labourers', not otherwise described.

[3] The machinemen had a more favourable economic position, but the occupational titles used rarely distinguish the two printing trades; it is, however, unlikely that machinemen accounted for all the printers' participation in voluntary organizations.

It is important to bear in mind the complexity of the link between class situation and the life-style of the 'superior' artisan. The values of the upper stratum exerted a wider influence, as less-favoured groups of artisans—and even some groups of semi- and unskilled workers—sought to emulate its behaviour patterns, within the limits set by economic circumstances. The *Edinburgh News* gives a vivid picture of the vestiges of the life-styles of the 'educated working man' in the home of a decayed craftsman (a painter); despite his dilapidated surroundings this man still owned a treatise on Helvetius, and his conversation is described as highly cultured.[1] The analysis of occupational differences in culture and life-style has therefore to be of a probabilistic type: men in such 'superior' trades as the joiners and engineers were *more likely* to manifest the patterns of behaviour in residence, leisure and intermarriage that have been described as those of working-class 'respectability'. This is really the most that can safely be said, in the absence of data enabling us to correlate class situation and cultural patterns at an individual level; one can merely point to the emergence of certain trends of social demarcation in the urban community, and to their likely connection with the structural differentiation within the working class. Given this vital qualification, we can conclude that the working class of the mid-decades of the century was marked by very wide cultural differences, which had some discernible connection with the formation of a socially distinct upper-artisan stratum.

It remains to ask whether this cultural pattern underwent any change during the last two decades of the century. These decades saw important changes in trade unionism and labour politics, and it may well be that the origins of these changes must be sought in the urban community, as well as in the more often discussed economic and industrial changes of the period. That marked differences in life-styles—at least as perceived by middle-class observers—remained important, has already been noted from Table 5.2. But there are signs of a shift towards the turn of the century, away from the exclusiveness of the 'superior' artisan towards more broadly based and open kinds of extra-work social activity.

---

[1] *Edin. News*, 27 Nov. 1852.

In the first place, although money-wage differentials did not narrow, and possibly widened, in the 1880s and 1890s, the fall in food prices and improvement to real wages may well have given some unskilled workers, and the less-favoured sections of skilled labour access to goods and services hitherto reserved to the 'superior' artisan. Changes in occupational structure may also have been important. Transport was one of the fastest-growing sectors of employment: the number of rail servants rose from 368 in 1861 to 1,051 in 1901, and carters increased from 698 to 3,090. This trend may have had some social and cultural impact, in view of the higher degree of contact between transport workers and the artisan social world.

The strongest evidence for changes in leisure patterns is that relating to the development of football. The modern form of the game appears to have grown up in the 1860s, when it was one of those forms of 'healthy recreation' which were part of the way of life of the 'respectable' artisan. Football teams were often ancillary activities for such bodies as the Volunteers; the Third Edinburgh Rifle Volunteers are described as among 'the pioneers of the game in the Scottish capital'.[1] One veteran player recalled teetotal gatherings at Buchanan's Temperance Hotel at this early period—a clear enough indication of the place of football in the range of 'respectable' leisure activities.[2] On the other hand, the association of some teams (in Edinburgh, Hibernian) with the community organizations of the Catholic Irish presumably brought with it some element of unskilled participation in the sport. By the later 1870s there was some form of organized cup contest between the various teams in the city: 'It is incontestable that the East Meadows was the first real nursery of the Association game in Edinburgh: the Heart of Midlothian and Hibernian clubs had their origin there, and they were still public parks' clubs when they met in the final round of the Edinburgh Football Association's Cup competition in the early spring of 1878.'[3] It is from this local cup final that the historian of Hearts dates widespread public interest in the game: although 'the game itself made no appeal to him' a

---

[1] W. Reid, *The Story of the Hearts* (n.d., c. 1924), p. 12.
[2] 'Twenty One Years Ago', *Edinburgh Athletic Times*, 23 Sept. 1895.
[3] Reid, op. cit., pp. 14–15.

reporter who was present became convinced of its importance 'when he saw the members of the winning team run for their lives from the enraged followers of the Hibernians and witnessed the partial wreckage of a cab'.[1] The development of football as a mass spectator sport, with the emergence of a few leading clubs, dates from the 1880s. By 1881 the Hearts had their own ground.[2] By the 1890s the pattern of organized championships, with a large spectator element, and a substructure of talent spotting, boys' clubs, etc., underpinning the main local teams, had emerged.[3]

There is little doubt that, whereas the artisan leisure pursuits of the third quarter of the century tended to separate various strata of the working class, the development of football as a mass spectator sport made for a more homogeneous urban working-class culture.[4] Unlike, for example, those artisan pursuits included in Table 5.3—library membership, golf, and gardening —soccer could be followed and played on fairly limited financial resources, and 'does not call for great expense of time in which to enjoy oneself'.[5] There is certainly a considerable volume of comment, from various points of view, on the widespread appeal of the game. According to the *Typographical Circular* (1894), football was 'the favourite amusement of a large number of printers';[6] in the same year the 'Scottish notes' in *Justice* commented sadly: 'Twas a cold, wet Saturday afternoon as he stood inside the barricade, he had not got his dinner, his feet were wet and he shivered all over. Where was this and who was he? This was a foot-ball match and he was a wage-slave enjoying his half holiday!'[7] Some years later the complaint is echoed, but from rather different assumptions: 'A very large number of employers complain of the lack of interest shown by the men and lads in their work, and say that football and sports absorb any intelligent attention they have to give. This complaint is by no means confined to the employers of unskilled labour, but is made also by master plumbers, builders, sawyers, plasterers and

---

[1] W. Reid, *The Story of the Hearts* pp. 15–16.   [2] Ibid., p. 24.
[3] This is clear from the *Edinburgh Athletic Times* (1895–6).
[4] Cf. I. R. Taylor, 'Soccer Consciousness and Soccer Hooliganism', in S. Cohen (ed.), *Images of Deviance* (1971), pp. 141–3.
[5] *Edin. Athletic Times*, 23 Sept. 1895.
[6] *Scottish Typographical Circular*, Jan. 1894.   [7] *Justice*, 31 Mar. 1894.

others.'[1] It is arguable that, with the emergence of football as a mass spectator sport, popular leisure became less closely linked to a pattern of stratification within the working class; although it must be emphasized that cultural divisions were still very strong.

The evidence of marriage certificates also suggests a greater degree of social homogeneity. Table 5.5 gives the same information as Table 5.4, for grooms marrying during the years 1895–7, and Table 5.6 summarizes the changes between the two periods. Many of the differences visible in the 1860s have diminished. Thus, the proportion marrying daughters of business and white-collar groups shows a fall in some trades and only small increases in others, while it rises in both the unskilled occupations. The engineers, on the other hand, have a large increase in this category. Thus, there was a general narrowing of occupational differences, with increases in the proportion of unskilled men marrying daughters of the lower-middle-class groups and decreases, or only small increases, in the equivalent proportions for the skilled trades, but the engineers are a notable exception to this trend. Another trend suggesting greater social homogeneity is a decrease in the proportion marrying daughters of the 'rural' groups, in those occupations with exceptionally high proportions at the earlier period. Along with the decline in the proportion of grooms marrying the daughters of non-manual and rural groups went a general increase in the proportion marrying the daughters of other manual workers. In most of the skilled trades the unskilled category shows an increase, while there is a considerable increase in the proportion of building labourers with fathers-in-law in the skilled category, and a smaller one in the proportion of carters. Here again, the figures suggest a general trend towards greater social homogeneity. The detailed breakdown of the occupations of the manual fathers-in-law confirms this impression. Nineteen per cent of building labourers and 5 per cent of carters married the daughters of building labourers (compared to 22 per cent and 1 per cent in 1865–9), and 6 per cent of building labourers and 7 per cent of carters married the daughters of carters (compared to none and 15 per cent in 1865–9).

---

[1] Gordon, *Handbook of Employments*, p. 2.

TABLE 5.5

Marriage: Distribution of Fathers-in-law of Grooms in Selected Occupations, 1895–1897

	N (Grooms)	Professions	Business	White-collar I	White-collar II	Retail, warehouse	Manual—skilled	Manual—semi- and unskilled	Manual—skill unclassifiable	Domestic service	Miscellaneous services	Police	Armed forces	Agriculture, fishing, seaman	Farmer, crofter	Other miscellaneous	Business/white collar	Manual—skilled	Manual—semi- and unskilled	Rural
																	Summary			
Printer	127	—	9·4	3·9	3·1	1·6	54·3	10·2	3·9	7·1	—	—	0·8	3·1	2·4	—	16·4	54·3	10·2	5·5
Bookbinder	27	—	7·4	3·7	3·7	3·7	59·3	7·4	3·7	—	—	3·7	3·7	3·7	—	—	14·8	59·3	7·4	3·7
Mason	168	—	10·7	0·6	4·8	1·8	42·9	17·3	2·4	4·2	—	0·6	2·4	10·1	2·4	—	16·1	42·9	17·3	12·5
Joiner	178	—	8·4	5·6	5·6	1·1	38·2	12·4	5·1	7·3	0·6	—	0·6	6·2	9·0	—	19·6	38·2	12·4	15·2
Painter	82	—	2·4	2·4	—	1·2	51·2	22·0	2·4	3·7	1·2	1·2	2·4	4·9	4·9	—	4·8	51·2	22·0	9·8
Engineer	99	1·0	9·1	1·0	10·1	2·0	43·4	9·1	8·1	5·1	—	2·0	2·0	4·0	5·1	—	20·2	43·4	9·1	9·1
Ironmoulder	29	—	6·9	—	6·9	—	51·7	17·2	3·4	3·4	—	—	—	3·4	6·9	—	13·8	51·7	17·2	10·3
Shoemaker	64	1·6	3·1	1·6	6·2	1·6	53·1	12·5	4·7	1·6	—	—	1·6	4·7	7·8	—	10·9	53·1	12·5	12·5
Building labourer	108	—	1·9	0·9	2·8	—	28·7	51·9	2·8	0·9	—	—	—	4·6	5·6	—	5·6	28·7	51·9	10·2
Carter	127	—	1·6	3·1	3·1	2·4	31·5	37·8	3·9	6·3	—	—	—	5·5	4·7	—	7·8	31·5	37·8	10·2

Notes: See Table 5.4.

Analysis of intermarriage confirms the impression of a weakening of social segregation and cultural distinctions within the working class. Whereas the earlier part of the period saw the emergence of a distinctive upper artisan stratum, its second half saw a blurring—albeit on a limited scale—of the distinctions between working-class strata.

TABLE 5.6

Differences in Marriage Patterns, 1865–1869 and 1895–1897

| | Difference in percentage of Brides' Fathers: | | | |
	Business/ white-collar	*Manual— skilled*	*Manual—semi- and unskilled*	*Rural*
Printers	− 1·3	− 0·5	+2·8	−1·2
Bookbinders	− 4·6	+ 1·2	+4·2	−2·8
Masons	+ 1·2	+ 5·1	+2·9	−9·8
Joiners	− 2·2	+ 1·6	+3·6	−2·4
Painters	−12·1	+13·5	+1·2	+2·0
Engineers	+ 6·2	− 4·6	−3·9	−6·9
Ironmoulders	−16·6	+21·3	−4·5	+1·7
Shoemakers	+ 0·5	+ 5·7	−0·4	+1·3
Building labourers	+ 1·2	+15·5	+0·1	−8·3
Carters	+ 4·1	+ 3·1	−0·5	−9·5

6   Opportunities and Aspirations

THE value of 'thrift' was a pervasive one in mid-Victorian Britain, and formed part of the cluster of 'respectable' behaviour patterns. 'Respectability', as Best has pointed out, was closely linked in the minds of the mid-Victorian generation to 'independence'—reliance on one's own resources and the ability to make personal provision for oneself and one's dependents.[1] Any account of the culture of the artisan must consider the extent to which he attempted to solve the pressing problems of economic survival by the individual exercise of thrift, restraint, economic prudence in personal and family decision-making.

There seems little doubt of the special appeal to the artisan stratum of a range of institutions catering for those who wished to save small amounts from limited incomes. Spokesmen for friendly-society lodges in Edinburgh all gave the same picture to the Royal Commission of 1872; in the words of the Free Gardeners' secretary, the members were 'generally speaking artizans'.[2] Similarly, shareholders in the Co-operative Building Society consisted of 'masons, joiners, plasterers, plumbers, printers, and every trade in Edinburgh'; and local mortgage companies catered mainly, though not exclusively, for working men.[3] The historian of St. Cuthbert's Co-operative Association —by far the most successful of several attempts at consumer co-operation in the city—traces its origin to the fact that: 'The cabinet works of Messrs. J. & T. Scott almost adjoined the railway works, so that, at Haymarket alone, there was a large number of intelligent workmen to whom co-operation would naturally appeal.'[4] Founder members included three cabinet-makers, a wood turner, two blacksmiths, an engine-driver,

---

[1] Best, *Mid-Victorian Britain*, pp. 257–60.
[2] *R.C. on Friendly Societies, Second Report*, pt. ii, P.P. 1872 XXVI, q. 9655; and see also qq. 9877, 10032.   [3] Ibid., qq. 9013, 9073.
[4] W. Maxwell (ed.), *First Fifty Years of St. Cuthbert's Co-operative Association Ltd., 1859–1909* (1909), p. 24.

three joiners, a warehouseman, and a foundry manager; the joiners and cabinet-makers, 'throughout the long history of the society . . . have been well represented on the board.'[1]

Table 6.1 gives figures based on the few records available of the occupational composition of organizations catering for the

TABLE 6.1

Social Composition of Savings Institutions

| | | Percentage of | |
| | Oddfellows,* | Savings Bank: | |
	1850s to 1870s	*1865–1869*	*1895–1899*
Professions	1	2	8
Business	8	9	8
White-collar I	2	11	13
White-collar II	1	2	4
Retail, warehouse	1	3	2
Manual—skilled	71	52	37
Manual—semi- and unskilled	1·5	10	12
Manual—skill unclassifiable	3·5	2	1
Domestic service	4	5	8
Miscellaneous services	3·5	1	2
Police	0·5	0·9	1
Armed forces	–	0·1	0·3
Agriculture, fishing, seaman	0·5	1	2
Other, miscellaneous	2·5	1	0·8
N	202	1,420	772

Source: List of members' occupations, *City of Edinburgh Lodge, No. 1 Branch of the Scottish Order of Oddfellows* (n.d., *c.* 1940, duplicated); occupations from 10 per cent samples of 'declaration forms' completed by new clients of Edinburgh Savings Bank (excluding females and schoolboys). I am indebted to Mr. T. Donoghue, Secretary of the Lodge, for lending me the otherwise unobtainable material on the Oddfellows, and to the staff of the Bank for allowing me to consult their archives.

Notes: See Appendix II for occupational classification.

* The list of members' occupations is said to refer to the '1850s to 1870s', but no precise dates are given. The figures are based on estimates, skilled trades said to have 'several' members being counted as five each; excluding altogether these trades with unknown numbers, skilled manual = 67 per cent.

small saver. (The reader is also referred to the figures in Table 5.2 for reported participation in savings institutions.) The figures for the Oddfellows, and for the Savings Bank in the 1860s show a pattern broadly similar to that found for some local recreational organizations, with a preponderance of skilled workers, a certain amount of participation by business and white-collar groups, and under-representation of unskilled-

---

[1] W. Maxwell (ed.), *First Fifty Years of St. Cuthberts Cooperative Association Ltd., 1859–1909* (1909), p. 24.

manual labour. 'The savings bank was still mainly the bank of
the skilled worker, the domestic servant, widows and children,
and the small middle-class man and woman.'[1] However, the
proportion of unskilled workers is rather higher for the Savings
Bank than for either the Oddfellows, or any of the voluntary
organizations analysed in Table 5.3.

There were thus differences between different sorts of savings
institution. Membership of a friendly society entailed payment
of a regular subscription, whereas simply to open a bank account
implied no such commitment; friendly societies were also
distinguished from bodies like savings banks by their social life
and recruitment and initiation procedures, which no doubt
made for a more socially homogeneous membership.[2] The
importance of the distinction is also suggested by more detailed
occupational analysis. Most of the five trades said to have
'several' members in the Oddfellows—masons, joiners,
engineers, shoemakers, and gold-beaters—belong to a now
familiar list of 'superior' occupations. But among the skilled-
manual Savings Bank clients—although the masons and
joiners do appear to be over-represented—there is far less of a
clear-cut occupational concentration. The figures for the
Savings Bank at the later period indicate three main trends: a
decline in the proportion of skilled workers, an increase in the
unskilled category, and a marked increase in the professional
category. The dramatic increase in the professional category
may be explicable by the raising in 1893 of the maximum permitted deposit.[3] The rather less-marked increase in the proportion of unskilled clients may reflect rising real wages (although
both manual categories fell in absolute numbers compared to
the 1860s; this increase is therefore a relative one). The decline
in the proportion of skilled workers—and in the total number
of new accounts opened—is probably an effect of the establishment of other forms of provision; for example, the People's
Bank, an offshoot of the co-operative movement, was founded

[1] H. O. Horne, *A History of Savings Banks* (1947), p. 232. Female clients and males
described as 'schoolboy' etc. were not sampled for Table 6.1, though students and
apprentices were.
[2] See *City of Edinburgh Lodge, No. 1 Branch of the Scottish Order of Oddfellows*
(duplicated, n.d. *c.* 1940).
[3] Horne, op. cit., p. 265; A. W. Kerr, *History of Banking in Scotland* (2nd edn.,
1908), p. 162.

in 1889.[1] The figures refer to only one of a number of friendly-society lodges in the city, and to only one of the rather smaller number of banks catering for the small saver. With this quali-fication, they do bear out the impression of high artisan parti-cipation in savings organizations, especially in the third quarter of the century.

Evidence regarding the use made of facilities for the small saver suggests that artisans were especially likely to behave in ways congruent with the norms of thrift. It remains to discuss the meanings attached to this behaviour, and the part which saving might play in the lives of working people. There is a fairly clear connection, not only in the ideology of middle-class observers but also in that of skilled workers themselves, between those claims to a 'respectable' social status—which, it has been argued, conditioned much of the activity of the upper-working-class strata in the community and in recreational pursuits—and the ability to provide, by setting aside part of a limited income, for the future needs of oneself and one's dependents. Once again, there is the familiar insistence on the special identity of the 'respectable artisan': 'Generally speaking, should you say that your society included the poor?—No; the members of our lodge are rather of a respectable class,—what are called respectable artizans.'[2] In this emphasis on 'respectability' a moralistic perspective is often in evidence:

He met the objections of those who looked upon the Co-operative movement as a mere matter of £ s.d., as though the members had no higher aim than the gaining of a few shillings per year in the shape of dividend, losing sight altogether of the grand moral prin-ciples which lay at the basis of the movement, as it must be patent to every right-minded and thoughtful man that, if the Co-operative element were to pervade society more generally than it did at the present time, a vast amount of the misery and crime, consequent upon intemperance and improvidence, would be altogether unknown.[3]

The imposition of 'temperate' and 'provident' standards of conduct seems to have occasioned a good deal of tension during

[1] Kerr, op. cit., pp. 324–5.
[2] *R.C. on Friendly Societies*, q. 9659 (secretary, Free Gardeners).
[3] Maxwell, op. cit., pp. 46–7.

the early history of St. Cuthbert's. In one instance, some members took exception to another group adjourning to a nearby pub after meetings:

While these men were known to be sober and respectable, this habit of adjournment was very unpalatable to other members of the committee ... At last the matter was raised at a quarterly meeting, and, of course, provoked a storm. Mr. James Veitch led the attack; and, although not a teetotaler himself, he condemned the officials and those associated with them in no unmeasured terms for showing such a poor example while being leaders of social reform.[1]

This striking passage suggests that the ground for complaint was not an allegation of heavy drinking, nor was it teetotal opposition to all drink; but rather an objection to the style of life identified with the public house. The implication that the task of a 'leader of social reform' was to 'set a good example' certainly points to a pervasive value system of mid-Victorian 'respectability'. Credit was another bone of contention at quarterly meetings of the Association; although the banning of credit was repeatedly rejected, it is clear from Maxwell's account that those occupying strategic positions in the organization consistently opposed it, and restricted it as far as they could.[2]

The differences in membership of savings organizations, and in related patterns of behaviour seem to be part of more general cultural distinctions within the working class. It would, of course, be quite wrong to suppose that less skilled workers did not set aside part of their income for future contingencies; the available evidence suggests that they did this whenever possible (though the types of contingency to which they gave priority may have differed somewhat).[3] But the institutions catering for working-class savers were differentiated, in a way that reflects the stratification and the cultural divisions within the working class; those institutions that offered the largest benefits,[4] with correspondingly higher payments from current income, catered for the upper artisan stratum. Alongside the local lodges of the

---

[1] Maxwell, op. cit., p. 91; cf. pp. 49, 78 for other incidents concerning drink.
[2] Ibid., pp. 32–3, 88–90, 116–17.
[3] See family budgets in D. N. Paton et al., *A Study of the Diet of the Labouring Classes in Edinburgh* (n.d., c. 1900).
[4] The benefits may include a rate of interest, home ownership, etc., as well as friendly-society social-security provision.

big friendly societies—which tended, as we have seen, to draw their membership from skilled workers and some lower-middle-class elements—were a number of small, local, and often 'unsound' societies;[1] these, as well as work- or neighbourhood-based savings arrangements of an informal kind, might cater for unskilled workers. The demands of financial soundness often enough coincided with those of 'respectable' conduct, a socially homogeneous membership, and cultural exclusiveness. According to the district secretary of the Oddfellows, a 'better class' had entered the Order since the introduction of higher rates on actuarial principles; the 'poorest class' were excluded.[2]

The vexed question of credit in St. Cuthbert's may have had a similar significance, especially when seen in relation to the other great difficulty of the early years: that of persuading members to give their custom to the store.[3] Despite the decision to extend credit, it is probable—given the attitude of members in key positions—that this was on a less generous scale than private traders' credit. Working people in need of credit would be obliged to use private shops; and even if their need for credit was occasional, private shopkeepers would no doubt make it available only in return for consistent loyalty.[4] For St. Cuthbert's to offer credit on a comparable scale would—as opponents of credit pointed out—deplete the capital and make it more and more difficult to pay any dividend. Membership of the Association, from this point of view, was one of the various forms of saving adapted to the circumstances of the artisan, the interest accruing in the form of dividend being the return on credit foregone as well as on the initial cost of a share. The problems of economic viability facing any organization catering for the working class thus reinforced the social distinctions implied by the norms of 'provident' conduct.

The most general reason for saving was to provide for various kinds of personal social security. This might, as in the friendly

[1] The *North Briton* warned readers of the dangers of the 'yearly' type of society: e.g., the editorial of 21 May 1860.

[2] *R.C. on Friendly Societies*, qq. 9302–3; expulsions for arrears in the 1840s mentioned in *City of Edinburgh Lodge*, op. cit., may reflect this process.

[3] Maxwell, op. cit., e.g. pp. 34, 92.

[4] Cf. F. Bechhofer and B. Elliot, 'An Approach to a Study of Small Shopkeepers and the Class Structure', *European Journal of Sociology* 9 (1968), 194; R. Roberts, *The Classic Slum* (1971), pp. 60–2.

societies and trade unions, take the form of regular payments, for which specific benefits were provided, but which could not be 'cashed' unless the claimant came within the relevant category of need; or it might take the form of general saving for the proverbial 'rainy day'. In either, or both, of these forms saving against unemployment, sickness, old age, and death was very widespread. It is, however, likely that the ability to commit regular sums from current income for specific social-security purposes—rather than to a fund of liquid assets—distinguished the more prosperous sections of the working class. On the other hand, benefits (whether from friendly societies or trade unions) could rarely do more than tide a family over short-term losses of income; those who wished to guard against longer-term need would require also to have a pool of savings of the general 'rainy day' type.[1]

A less widespread need for saving related to the cost of tools in certain skilled trades. According to the *Edinburgh News* (1852), a set of mason's tools cost £2 to £2. 10s. 0d., while joiners' tools might cost as much as £10 to £25.[2] 'But it is not difficult to perceive that in this case what appears to be a heavy affliction is in reality a social blessing; and that the habits of saving early acquired, and the possession of property gradually increased are of . . . advantage to the progress and elevation of their possessor.'[3] In a brewery labourer's family studied by Paton et al. (c. 1900) the son, an apprentice joiner, gave 5s. of his 6s. wage to his mother, who 'can count on 37s. a-week but she saves out of this to buy the more expensive joiners' tools for her son.'[4] The masons and joiners do appear to be overrepresented among the Savings Bank clients.

A third type of saving related to the system of rent payment. According to the President of Edinburgh Trades Council, only the 'very poor class' paid weekly; yearly tenancies and half-yearly payment was the rule.[5] It was no doubt fairly common for those who could manage it to put money aside for the rent; Paton et al. report two cases where the Co-op dividend was earmarked for this purpose.[6]

[1] For the short-term nature of the support given by friendly societies see *R.C. on Friendly Societies*, qq. 9708–29 (assistant inspector of parochial board, St. Cuthbert's, Edinburgh).   [2] *Edin. News*, 2, 9 Oct. 1852.   [3] Ibid.
[4] Paton, *et al.*, op. cit., pp. 30–1.   [5] *R.C. on Housing*, qq. 19176–7.
[6] Paton *et al.*, op. cit., pp. 23, 26.

These purposes of saving—social security, tools, rent—were of a relatively modest character, related to the exigencies of day-to-day existence in working-class communities (though, as we have seen, the level of provision, for example the standard and cost of housing, varied widely within the working class). But there are also some indications of the accumulation of savings, and sometimes of property, on a rather more ambitious scale. St. Cuthbert's was almost crippled in its first year when the opponents of credit, who were able to muster no more than nine votes against thirty at the quarterly meeting, could none the less withdraw between them about half the working capital in protest; twenty-three years later, in 1883, the committee held £1,000 of capital, 10 per cent of the total.[1] The larger accumulations of savings were doubtless connected with the trend to house ownership. In 1885 St. Cuthbert's started giving loans to members for house purchase;[2] and the upper-artisan composition of purchasers of the Co-operative Building Co. houses, and of borrowers from finance companies, has already been noted.[3] The accumulation of savings was thus often linked to the hopes of moving to superior housing, and the associated evaluations of the home. A further use for accumulated personal savings may be mentioned. For skilled men in certain trades the possibility of setting up in business on their own was a real one. The founder of Messrs. Hunter & Foulis, bookbinders, purchased the business with savings accumulated (by 'an epic of Scottish frugality') from his earnings as a journeyman, 'a small legacy, and a loan of £75'.[4]

The habit of saving was sometimes seen in the context of what the *Edinburgh News* called the 'progress and elevation' of the skilled worker.[5] The aspects of this 'elevation' so far considered have reference mainly to the artisan's life outside his work, in the local community. To interpret fully such decidedly ambiguous phrases as 'progress and elevation', 'rising in the social scale', and so on, we have also to examine the possibility of movement to a superior occupational position. Although there are few rigorous data for any of the kinds of mobility discussed below, some general points may be made.

---

[1] Maxwell, op. cit., pp. 33, 125.   [2] Ibid., p. 139.   [3] Above, p. 121.
[4] *A Hundred Years of Publishers' Bookbinding*, pp. 9–10.
[5] *Edin. News*, 9 Oct. 1852.

It is important to set those types of mobility to which subsequent analyses of class structure have drawn attention—the
crossing of the line between manual and non-manual labour,
or between employee and employer—in the context of mobility
within the skilled manual working class. This is probably one of
those commonplace facets of working life so obvious to contemporaries that it has been ignored by historians. But, as the discussion of economic position in Chapter 4 indicated, there was
in every trade a more or less wide range of variation, from those
in casual employment who could perhaps hope to average little
more, if not less, than a labourer's earnings, to those whose key
contribution to the production process encouraged their employers to offer special inducements, and to 'hoard' them, even
in periods of depression. Quite apart from variations in the
incidence of unemployment, there was almost certainly a wide
spread of individual and company wage-rates, below, and more
rarely above, the standard union rate. The bookbinders, a
prosperous trade, none the less complained that men were
receiving an 'improver's' wage, instead of the full rate, at the
end of their apprenticeships.[1] Given this industrial structure, it
is likely that the characteristic ambition of the skilled worker
was to enter the more desirable jobs in his trade. Conversely,
for those already in the favoured sections, there was the fear of
falling—through some loss of efficiency from a long period of
illness or unemployment, accident, or ageing—into the depressed and casually employed low-paid 'tail' of the trade.[2]
The position of the skilled worker would depend on his efficiency and sometimes on his versatility, rather than simply on
his occupation. Here the quality of apprenticeship training
might be important.[3] The man's ability to keep abreast of
technical change throughout his working life also affected his
prospects. Thus, smiths sought experience in the 'more exact
working-shop of an engineer', after serving a traditional
apprenticeship.[4]

---

[1] Bookbinders' Consolidated Union Minutes, 16 June 1887, 10 Sept. 1894.
[2] 'Journeyman Engineer', *The Great Unwashed* (1868), pp. 282–3, discusses the
loss of efficiency following a period out of work.
[3] Artisans often complained about the inadequate training given to apprentices: e.g. reader's letter in *Scottish Typographical Circular*, March 1896.
[4] *Edin. News*, 13 Aug. 1853.

Mobility within the working class was linked to the whole cluster of 'respectable' behaviour patterns, as well as to the technical proficiency of the worker in a narrow sense. The ability to withstand sickness or unemployment without detriment to longer-term career prospects was, for example, a function partly of how much the worker had managed to save. Education was also an important dimension of differential opportunities, in a society where many workers were only minimally literate, and some were still illiterate. The desire to keep abreast of technical developments was one reason for interest in adult education; but it is also likely that the extent to which a man appeared to be generally educated—for example, to be capable of following drawings and written instructions—affected his standing in the eyes of employers. The artisan's chances were thus conditioned by his total life-style, his ability to project a general image of intelligence and self-discipline. It was claimed for the Volunteer movement that it inculcated work discipline: 'Employers who have had, or still have, any connection with the service fully comprehend and appreciate its advantages; and their favour in many cases is extended to the man who can show himself to be imbued with the real spirit of a Volunteer.'[1] The ideology of thrift and respectability was thus linked to the structural differentiation of the skilled labour force; like any ideology, it was powerful because it offered a plausible way of looking at social experience.

It therefore seems likely that the ideology of 'progress and elevation' had reference mainly to the struggle for survival and promotion within the skilled working class. Many of the white-collar and managerial positions recruited from skilled labour—and there can be little doubt that such promotion was far more common in the nineteenth century than in the twentieth, although we have no rigorous data—could be seen simply as minor extensions of the 'artisan career'. Printing overseers (works managers) were appointed from compositors;[2] a joiner, as the 'comptroller general' of building work, might become a clerk of works, a surveyor, even (in the 1850s) an architect.[3] There is less information for other trades, but the general

---

[1] Stephen, *Queen's City of Edinburgh Rifle Volunteer Brigade*, p. 219.
[2] Gordon, *Handbook of Employments*, p. 316.
[3] *Edin. News*, 9 Oct., 1852.

importance, in all industries, of craft skills and experience presumably favoured the appointment of ex-journeymen to managerial and white-collar posts.

A second form of mobility which may likewise have been a relatively small extension of the skilled-worker 'career ladder' was the traditional move from the status of journeyman to that of small master. Movement of this kind was still, in the mid-nineteenth century, of some relevance. There were, however, important variations between different sectors of industry. The prospect of setting up in business with the resources in the reach of the artisan clearly depended on such factors as the amount of fixed capital, and the average size of firm in the industry. The not altogether reliable census figures for employment status (Table 6.2) give some indication that the proportion of employers and self-employed was higher in the labour-intensive industries.[1]

The tracing of samples of names taken from the trades section of *Post Office Directories* gives a further indirect indication of chances of mobility, on the assumption that a relatively high

TABLE 6.2

Percentage classified as 'Employer' and 'Working on own Account' in Selected Occupations, 1891 and 1901

| | Percentage classified as | | | |
| | 1891 | | 1901 | |
	Employer	Self-employed	Employer	Self-employed
Printing*	2	0·3	1	0·2
Masons†	9	0·4	7	0·2
Joiners†	11	2·6	10	2·2
Painters†	15	2·2	12	0·9
Engineering‡	4	0·8	2	0·65
Shoemaker	13	12	10	12

Source: Calculated from census occupation tables.
* Printers, lithographers, bookbinders, and paper rulers combined.
† 'Builders' classified as employers added to employers in each specific trade.
‡ All occupations included under 'Engineering' in part A of Table 2.4: see Appendix I.

rate of mobility of this type would also imply a high turnover of businesses (Table 6.3). These data have many defects, of which the likely exclusion from *Directories* of the smaller and

---

[1] For industrial structure, see above, Table 3.1.

more ephemeral concerns—as well as possible variations over time in this respect—are only the most obvious. Other defects include the fact that the disappearance of a name does not necessarily mean the end of the business; and many new names may reflect the purchase of highly expensive plant by men of some wealth, rather than the launching of a new enterprise by an ex-wage-earner. But the figures do indicate some interesting tendencies. There is a marked difference between the building trades and shoemakers and the printers, bookbinders, and engineers. Thus the more labour-intensive industries have more turnover. There would appear to be marked variations within the skilled working class in the extent of opportunities to establish a new business.

It is true that we cannot assume that 'new' owners were in fact ex-journeymen. But, taking the turnover data together with known structural features of the industries, it is reasonable to argue that those trades with the higher turnover rates were those in which wage-earners would be most likely to acquire property in the means of production. To assess the significance of this it must be remembered that there was also a good deal of movement in the other direction. As the Registrar General for Scotland told the Committee on the Census (1890), 'people who are employers one day and employed the next' were common 'in all small trades';[1] men setting up in business sometimes retained their union membership.[2] In all industries, even the labour-intensive 'small trades', the small-firm sector existed alongside a number of larger and more stable firms. Thus the smaller kind of engineering business—which might be little more than a back-street smithy equipped with a few second-hand machine-tools—contrasted with large local firms like Bertram's, which were among the world leaders in the production of particular kinds of machinery. The owners of the small businesses, particularly those who were self-employed, were closer socially to skilled workers than to the owners of the larger firms.

We may conclude—although we lack the kind of biographical case-studies that would prove this—that acquiring his own

---

[1] *Report of the Committee . . . to Enquire into . . . the Census,* P.P. 1890 LVIII, q. 2030.   [2] Hobsbawm, *Labouring Men,* p. 296.

TABLE 6.3
Turnover of Business Names in Post Office Directories

| | *1860–1869* | | *1890–1899* | |
	N	Percentage surviving ten years or more	N	Percentage surviving ten years or more
Printers	63	68 (43)	63	70 (44)
Bookbinders	34	74 (25)	50	74 (37)
Masons/builders	108*	53 (57)	70	47 (33)
Joiners	104	59 (61)	78	56 (44)
Painters	74	61 (45)	80	61 (49)
Engineers/ ironfounders†	42	69 (29)	40	70 (28)
Shoemakers	91	58 (53)	76	54 (41)

Source: Random samples from *Post Office Directories*, trades section; samples are 10 per cent, except shoemakers in both decades (5 per cent), joiners in the 1890s (5 per cent), and bookbinders in the 1890s (25 per cent). Figures in brackets indicate raw numbers.

* Very few firms are listed as 'masons' in the 1860s; the sample therefore includes firms listed as 'builders'.

† Excludes civil, consulting, etc. engineers, offices of firms manufacturing outside Edinburgh and Leith, and heating, domestic, etc. engineers.

business was unlikely to take the ex-journeyman far from the √ social world with which he was familiar. Like promotion to managerial positions, it was a relatively small extension of the 'career ladder' within the skilled working class. There were, however, various kinds of employment opportunity—especially in public services—that involved moving outside the industry, if not far outside the artisan stratum. A range of white-collar posts in the public services, as well as in industry, were probably filled by skilled workers or their children; the pupil-teaching √ system provides the best documentation for this pattern.[1] For other, socially similar, kinds of white-collar occupation there is no comparable evidence, beyond that of the possibly atypical cases of individuals whose biographies are recorded because they became in some way public figures (mainly through activity in the labour movement). Thus William Paterson, ex-secretary of the Associated Joiners, became fire master of Glasgow;[2] two other prominent Edinburgh trade unionists (a shoemaker and a cabinet-maker) became respectively a superintending school-attendance officer and registrar for the

[1] See above, p. 110 and footnote.
[2] MacDougall (ed.), *Minutes of Edinburgh Trades Council*, p. xxiv.

Canongate.[1] These cases serve to draw attention to the fact that trade-union and political activity was becoming, from the mid-nineteenth century, a means of movement into non-manual positions. This does not mean that men embarked on labour activity with an 'official' career in mind;[2] it was rather the unanticipated result of the development of the movement. St. Cuthbert's decided in 1873 to discontinue the policy of hiring men from the ordinary retail trade, and to appoint store managers from the membership; while the first manager of the Scottish Co-operative Wholesale Society was the son of a prominent Edinburgh trade unionist and founder of St. Cuthbert's.[3] Apart from employment in the institutions of the labour movement itself, it is likely that the growing role of its representatives on local and national bodies gave access to jobs in the public services.

As to trends over time in the various types of white-collar employment, little more than informed guessing is possible. Those positions associated with the growth of the labour movement undoubtedly expanded. The expansion of other sectors of white-collar employment in the late nineteenth century may, however, have been offset, so far as the artisan stratum were concerned, by the growing importance of formal educational qualifications, the establishment of longer, more rigidly institutionalized, white-collar 'career ladders', and growing competition from children of the expanding clerical groups for access to white-collar posts of all kinds.[4] The disappearance of the fluid and often informal patterns of recruitment to responsible and qualified white-collar posts characteristic of the earlier period may have narrowed the possibility of movement outside the ranks of manual wage-earners.

It is unlikely that any of the jobs recruited from artisans were far removed from the upper strata of the manual working class. This has already been implied by the argument that the small-business and white-collar groups with whom artisans might associate in voluntary organizations are correctly seen as

---

[1] MacDougall (ed.), *Minutes of Edinburgh Trades Council*, p. xxiv; W. H. Marwick, 'Municipal Politics in Victorian Edinburgh', *Book of the Old Edinburgh Club* (1969).   [2] As Michels, for example, assumed: R. Michels, *Political Parties* (Dover edn., 1959), esp. pp. 272–5, 289.   [3] Maxwell, op. cit., pp. 106–7, 27–8, 94.   [4] Cf. Hobsbawm, op. cit., pp. 274–5, 297.

inhabiting the fringes of an artisan social world, rather than the intermediate rungs of a societal ladder of occupational statuses. The career of William Paterson may again be cited to illustrate the haziness at this period of boundaries which, in the twentieth century, have become far more clearly marked. The son of a small master joiner in Elgin, Paterson worked in various white-collar jobs after leaving school, then served an apprenticeship in his father's business; coming to Edinburgh at the age of twenty (in 1863), he became first branch, then general secretary of the union, and ended his life as fire master of Glasgow.[1]

I would therefore interpret the movement of skilled workers into small-business or white-collar occupations as a move within the artisan social world, rather than as a foothold on the lower reaches of the bourgeois world. Nevertheless the artisan's social experience—especially in the third quarter of the century —might well have disposed him to think in terms of individual ascent on a 'ladder' of occupational opportunities, and to seek a relatively long-term improvement in his personal situation by practising the virtues of thrifty behaviour. But his ladder was clearly separate from that of the middle class, and its most important rungs may well have been those *below* the line between manual labour and what, for want of an alternative, must be rather loosely called the 'lower-middle class'.

---

[1] Biographical sketch, *Reformer*, 6 May 1872.

7   The Meanings of 'Respectability'

THE aspects of social behaviour analysed in the preceding chapters suggest the importance of particular styles of life and patterns of aspiration in distinguishing a 'superior' stratum of skilled workers. It is therefore valid to talk of the cultural formation of an upper stratum, or labour aristocracy. The connection of this process with values of 'respectability', 'provident' conduct, 'progress and elevation', etc., has been an interpretative thread running through the whole analysis. In this sense, it is possible to identify the formation of the labour aristocracy with the implantation of bourgeois ideologies and norms of conduct. But this statement needs some qualification, to avoid oversimplifying a complex pattern of social relations and values —in particular, to account also for the formation of specifically working-class institutions. We have to consider the possibility that the meanings of the common language of 'respectability' may have varied, in ways that gave rise to important social tensions.

To assess the wider significance of the aspirations of the 'superior' artisan stratum, we must begin by discussing briefly the perspective of those elements of the middle class—in Edinburgh, especially the professional intelligentsia—particularly concerned to foster 'respectable' patterns of behaviour among the working class. The attitude of these groups is relevant, since they often appear in 'patronage' roles within what may be described as the institutional framework of working-class 'self improvement'. Middle-class observers commonly interpreted the behaviour patterns under discussion, in terms of a model of the 'respectable', 'temperate', 'self-improving' working man. Dr. Begg evokes the image nicely, in his description of the houses erected by the Co-operative Building Company: 'When he enters—which, of course, he will do very respectfully —he will be greatly pleased with the clean and tidy interior of the dwellings, the carpets, arm-chairs, libraries, family Bibles, and, in a word, every appliance by which a man can make his

home comfortable and happy.' And the inevitable moral
follows: 'What necessity have such men for other engagements,
during the comparatively short hours of leisure, beyond the
range of their own families? Here is the true antidote to the
public-house! What a struggle will such men make before they
dream of applying for poors'-rates!'[1]

There were, no doubt, many variations on the theme. The
existence of a social imagery which structured middle-class
social action is perhaps indicated by one finding from the
C.O.S. survey: 71 per cent of those families described in terms
of general approval (i.e. such epithets as 'decent', 'sober',
'respectable', and so on), but only 46 per cent of those not so
described are also reported to participate in one or more of the
activities analysed in Table 5.2.

The terms of the middle-class social imagery are often enough
reproduced by spokesmen for the institutions of the artisan
world, but values of this kind co-existed with alternative modes
of conduct, sharply divergent from those of the middle class.
The ideological defence of trade unionism was the most articulate expression of this, involving as it did a critique of certain
basic individualistic assumptions about the economic order.
This dimension of artisan life, which has so far been neglected,
is explored in the remaining chapters of this study. More
generally, it is important not to allow the *relative* economic prosperity of the aristocrat of labour to obscure the fact that he was
closely enmeshed in the realities of working-class existence in a
violently cyclical low-wage economy. The deep-rooted habits of
solidarity and mutual aid which developed in response to these
realities were never completely obliterated by the rhetoric of
'self help'—that rhetoric might, indeed, be reinterpreted, in a
collective rather than purely individual sense.[2] Thus Thomas
Wright, the 'journeyman engineer', in his evocation of the
experience of tramping and the solidarity of the trade, at one
point articulates a practical ethic in marked contrast to that of
bodies like the Charity Organization Society: 'it is better to be
"had" sometimes than from over-suspicion to refuse such help

[1] Begg, *Happy Homes for Working Men*, pp. 46–7.
[2] See R. Harrison 'Afterword', in Smiles, *Self Help* (Sphere Books edn.), pp.
268–9.

as it is in your power to give to a case that may be one of real distress.'[1]

In organizations closely associated with the image of the thrifty 'respectable artisan' solidaristic values played some part. The ritual of certain friendly-society lodges gave membership a meaning beyond its purely economic functions. The Odd-fellows' City of Edinburgh Lodge resolved, 'each Brother shall furnish himself with an apron . . . be it understood that they shall be all of one pattern', and held regular social gatherings.[2] And the survival of the Co-op, against the opposition of vested interests and other difficulties, probably owed something to 'solidaristic' behaviour by members; on one occasion it was decided to continue an uneconomic van service in recognition of the loyalty of members who had been evicted, rather than stop using the store at the behest of their landlord, a local grocer.[3]

The co-existence of solidaristic values and practices with aspirations expressed in the language of hegemonic individu-alism made for a certain ambivalence in the ideology of the artisan. This ambivalence is perhaps reflected in an old member's comments on the beginning of St. Cuthbert's: 'We were all yet working-men, but we began to have the feeling that we were something more, and would soon be business men, reaping benefits we had for long been sowing for others.'[4] As so often in statements of this kind, the precise meaning of the hope of becoming 'something more' is ambiguous; it might mean either the hope of rising individually from the ranks of the manual working class, or the desire to change the position of the working class (or at least its more 'respectable' sections), to obtain a corporate stake in the community and social recog-nition, through the building of powerful working-class insti-tutions: 'some of us found a new relish in our butter, ham and meal, in that it was turned over to us from our own shop, through our own committee.'[5] Thomas Wright emphasized that the 'intelligent artisan', the man who looked to an improve-ment in the position of his class, was altogether commoner and more influential in working-class institutions than the 'educated

---

[1] 'Journeyman Engineer', *The Great Unwashed*, p. 160.
[2] *City of Edinburgh Lodge.*   [3] Maxwell, *First Fifty Years of St. Cuthbert's*, p. 125.
[4] Ibid, p. 27.   [5] Ibid.

working man', the man striving to climb out of the working class.[1]

One meaning of the extremely ambiguous language in which skilled workers often expressed their aspirations is the claim to social recognition of the 'respectability' of the artisan, which, although expressed in terms of the hegemonic ideology, nevertheless contains a dimension of class-conscious assertion. As Wright remarks, his term the *Great Unwashed*, 'exactly embodies the working class idea of themselves, excluding, as it does, not only the "counter-skipper" class, whom the great unwashed regard (unjustly perhaps) as their inferiors, but also professional men, merchants, M.P.'s and others.'[2] Feelings of this sort indicate the existence of social groups which have *alternative criteria* for allocating prestige. Whereas the clerk emphasizes his clean hands and educational attainments, the skilled worker emphasizes his skill and strength, the indispensability of manual labour—dirty hands are the sign that one does useful work. Status claims cannot be assumed to reflect an unequivocal acceptance of the values of the dominant group in society; they may, on the contrary, reflect a certain social tension between groups with alternative value systems.

The claim to 'respectability' must be set in the context of a strong sense of class pride. I would argue that it is properly interpreted as a claim to status recognition and citizenship on behalf of skilled workers as a corporate group. In some ways that claim was met by the 1867 Reform Bill. But at the local level the tensions were harder to resolve. Partly this was a matter of the economic circumstances of skilled workers, and the consequently high visibility of their class position. The artisan Volunteers, for example, were without rifles, 'while lawyers and merchants and civil servants swaggered with their short Enfields', until the War Office was bludgeoned into subsidizing the movement.[3] Members of St. Cuthbert's complained that assistants used to the private trade treated them with contempt; presumably this reflects the social difference between co-operators and the middle-class customers of the large private grocers.[4]

---

[1] 'Journeyman Engineer', op. cit., pp. 6–20.   [2] Ibid., p. viii.
[3] Macdonald, *Fifty Years of It*, p. 31.   [4] Maxwell, op. cit., pp. 47–8.

A series of apparently trivial incidents illuminate the local meanings of class and status. The *North Briton* commented on the Burns centenary: 'It is the people alone who can truly keep the birthday of Robert Burns, for they best of all understand him and claim him as one of themselves. Do not, then, ye workingmen of Edinburgh, give him up to the higher classes of the city.'[1] In the Minutes of the Trades Council we find a record of reiterated protest about community issues: against a proposed road through the Meadows 'for the convenience of a comparatively small number of citizens'; an imputed slight to the working classes in the allocation of tickets for the Volunteer Review of 1881, 'especially as they had contributed so much to the success of the Volunteer Movement'; restrictions on football, again in the Meadows.[2] There is certainly no lack of evidence for the resistance to any hint of patronage or social subordination. The *Typographical Circular* commented on proposals for a printers' Volunteer company: 'If the present movement fail it will be from the way in which it is managed, and from the very old-fashioned notion that if the thing be patronised by the "master" the man will of course "fall in".'[3] At a meeting to discuss the formation of the Working Men's Club, the secretary of the Edinburgh Typographical Society protested against 'a kind of demi-charitable affair, a hybrid between a soup kitchen and a penny reading room with in all probability interesting old women in black mittens to talk in a goody-goody strain to the recipients of their bounty'.[4]

How, then, did this insistence on the social independence of the working man relate to bourgeois leadership in the urban community? This question is perhaps best answered by a rather impressionistic, and therefore tentative, analysis of the organizational framework within which the life-style of working-class 'respectability' was formed and projected. Voluntary organizations concerned with the provision of leisure ranged from

[1] *North Briton*, 1 Dec. 1858.
[2] T.C. Minutes, 11 Aug. 1874, 2 Aug. 1881, 25 Oct. 1881.
[3] *Scottish Typographical Circular*, Jan. 1860.
[4] *North Briton*, 13 Apr. 1864; the speaker was identified as secretary of the Typographical Society from T.C. Minutes, 9 Oct. 1860. Cf. R. N. Price, 'The Working Men's Club Movement and Victorian Social Reform Ideology', *Victorian Studies* 15 (1971).

facilities run entirely by and for working people, to those provided by philanthropic employers, churches, and other middle-class bodies, on a charitable or 'patronage' basis. Organizations with a fairly clear-cut middle-class central leadership, but also with relatively autonomous sub-units, of varying social composition, comprise a further category. The loose-knit coalitions of Liberal politics exemplify this third type, as perhaps does the 'spirit of emulation, and the friendly rivalry that existed between the various sectional bodies' of the Volunteers.[1] We should expect the nature of skilled workers' attachments to vary with the form of organization. Attachments to bodies of the 'patronage' type are likely to have been limited, with a considerable 'calculative' component—one fairly well-documented case being the connection of working people with facilities (especially educational) offered by churches and Sunday schools.[2] Given the resistance to patronage and deference, we should expect the fullest working-class participation in those organizations (or sub-units of organizations) less directly controlled by bourgeois groups.

There is, however, a sense in which this whole range of organizations, facilities, and activities were knit together, under middle-class hegemony; the distinctive institutions of the artisan stratum were contained within a social world dominated by the middle class. This process is perhaps best seen as one of implicitly negotiated accommodation between bourgeois leadership and working-class resistance to the more direct form of social subordination. Working men eager for 'self improvement', but loath to accept patronage could perceive this situation as one of bargaining, rather than of social subordination. The peculiarities of the local class structure are also important here: the diversity of the middle class and the rivalries between middle-class groups made for a degree of pluralism in the leadership of local institutions.

Certain categories of public figure seem to have played key roles in linking the world of the 'respectable' working class to that of the middle class. Voluntary organizations of all kinds

---

[1] Stephen, *Queen's City of Edinburgh Brigade*, p. 62.
[2] See A. A. MacLaren, *Religion and Social Class: the Disruption Years in Aberdeen* (1974), Ch. 7; H. Pelling, *Popular Politics and Society in Late Victorian Britain* (1968), pp. 30–1.

were linked up into a network, largely through the overlapping activities of these individuals. The Free Gardeners, for example, gave honorary membership to 'gentlemen of means who wish to encourage the society'.[1] Liberal-Radical politicians (especially Town Councillors) were responsible for one set of links, often reaching working arrangements with the Trades Council.[2] Other identifiable categories include some philanthropists and social reformers (such as Dr. Begg), professional men who would deliver lectures in the cause of 'self culture', and so on. Sometimes the categories overlap, as in the person of Lord Gifford, who addressed the Flower Show exhibitors in 1870; a lawyer, associated with voluntary work in Dr. Guthrie's Ragged Schools, an 'advanced politician', he 'often lectured to literary and philosophical societies'.[3] We frequently find Volunteer officers in similar roles. John Gorrie, a lawyer, was involved in the raising of the first artisan companies, lectured for the Trades Council on 'diggings into the city records', and judged the Working Man's Flower Show;[4] another Volunteer officer chaired a Trades Council public meeting, and later used the machinery of the Trades Council to appeal for recruits to the Volunteers; an Ensign of Volunteers marshalled the reform demonstration of 1866.[5] Middle-class public figures graced the platforms even of the more independent type of working-class institution. This form of social recognition can be related to the status claims of the 'superior' artisan. A characteristic note was struck by Lord Gifford at the Flower Show, who 'in addressing the assemblage before him as "ladies and gentlemen" said he never used the word with more confidence than he did at that time because he believed that every working-man who loved and tended a plant was a gentleman, and every workingman's wife or daughter who loved and tended a plant was a lady.'[6] The desire for this kind of social approval reflects a degree of acceptance of the established order, but the consciousness

---

[1] *R.C. on Friendly Societies*, q. 9648.

[2] MacDougall, op. cit., pp. xxviii–xxx, p. 235, footnote.

[3] *Dictionary of National Biography*.

[4] Stephen, op. cit., p. 221; MacDougall, op. cit., p. 72, footnote; T.C. Minutes, 30 Nov. 1861; *Reformer*, 13 Aug. 1870.

[5] T.C. Minutes, 20 Feb., 26 Mar. 1861; *Scotsman*, 19 Nov. 1866.

[6] *Reformer*, 13 Aug. 1870.

involved is, at the same time, not precisely deferential. It is rather a kind of demagogic flattery: the notion of the gentleman appearing as a bizarre surrogate for the 'citizen' of more rapidly democratized nations. Thomas Wright comments on this sort of rhetoric, with perhaps a hint of cynicism: 'I am a working man—what a gentleman wanting my vote (if I had one) at election time, or the chairman at the prize-distribution meeting of an industrial exhibition, would probably call "an intelligent artisan".'[1]

The class relationships involved in the pursuit of 'respectability' were complex, and certainly not adequately described by terms such as 'deference'. The more direct forms of patronage and control from above were typically resisted by artisans, who insisted on the autonomy of their institutions. Yet the aspirations and norms of conduct of such institutions were frequently stated in a language adopted from the dominant middle class. Thus the style of life created by the upper artisan strata may be seen, from one point of view, as a transmission of middle-class values—certainly as an assertion of social superiority, a self-conscious cultural exclusion of less-favoured working-class groups. On the other hand, the very pursuit of 'respectability', especially in so far as it involved claims to status recognition and participation in local institutions, was a source of social tension, a focal point in the growth of a sense of class identity. This, and the fact that the dominant bourgeois ideology always co-existed with other modes of thought and behaviour made the outlook of the labour aristocracy an ambivalent and unstable one.

---

[1] 'Journeyman Engineer', op. cit., p. 126.

8 The Mid-Victorian Working-Class Movement

THE transmission of the hegemonic value system of Victorian Britain by the labour aristocracy involved a process which was problematic for all concerned. The upper-artisan outlook was in some respects sharply distinguished from that of the bourgeoisie, and even those modes of thought adopted 'from above' could undergo significant transformations, as they were reinterpreted at the social level of the labour aristocracy. It is thus necessary to guard against one-sided emphasis on the aspirant, individualistic, socially conformist, and collaborationist character of the labour aristocracy.[1] Another side of the historical significance of the stratum lies in its role in the development of working-class defensive institutions, notably trade unions, relatively independent of direct control from above. It is because it played this role that the labour aristocracy had such far-reaching effects on the development of the British working class. Conversely, the forms of class hegemony in the more stable capitalist society of the 1850s and 1860s rest on a *de facto* acceptance of working-class claims to social independence. The 'liberalization' of these decades reflected a socio-economic equilibrium, resting essentially on the historical changes of an earlier period of sharper class confrontation;[2] there could be no return to older, more direct forms of subordination and control.[3]

The social position of the labour aristocracy was not freely conceded, but had to be fought for, and maintained against the pressure to cut living standards. The worker's position in society depended fundamentally on the sale of his labour power, and the growth of trade unions reflects the labour aristocracy's

---

[1] Foster, *Class Struggle and the Industrial Revolution*, Ch. 7; and MacLaren, *Religion and Social Class*, pp. 158–62, seem open to this criticism.

[2] Such confrontation was certainly less marked in Edinburgh than, e.g. Oldham (Foster, op. cit.); but the widespread public attention fastened on the social crisis of the textile districts meant that the resolution of that crisis led to a *general* shift in ruling-class attitudes. [3] Foster, op. cit., pp. 213–23.

conviction that employers would buy that labour power as cheaply as possible. Hence, the view that 'so long as a man worked for wages his interests were exclusively determined by that fact'[1] was deeply embedded in the social consciousness of the stratum. This may seem paradoxical, given the labour aristocracy's strategic role in the stabilization of Victorian capitalism. Yet if the surval of the stratum was in the interests of the ruling class as a whole, it was not necessarily in the immediate interest of the employers of particular groups of 'aristocratic' workers. An emphasis on the role of the labour aristocracy in implanting accommodative responses to industrial capitalism should not, therefore, be taken to imply some 'conspiracy theory' of a monolithic ruling class. The labour aristocracy's position arose from the way in which the ruling class came to terms with particular working-class responses to industrial capitalism, under the economic conditions of the mid-nineteenth century.

The engagement of the labour aristocracy in class conflict must be kept firmly in view. Particular economic circumstances were not translated into higher wages, and the life-styles that depended on such wages, without organized industrial struggle. Wage-rates and conditions were maintained by vigilance and militancy in those trades with a high proportion of aristocratic workers, while other trades were engulfed by casual labour, or displaced by new techniques. (The given industrial structure certainly made strong craft unions possible; but it did not make them inevitable.) When, in the 1890s, some skilled workers felt threatened by the growing scale and organization of capital, new techniques, and the drive to cut costs by overthrowing established conditions and practices, the result was the widening of a trade-union class-consciousness which always existed, however latent it may have been at certain periods.

The labour movement in mid-Victorian Edinburgh was dominated by the craft unions of skilled workers, although there are some occasional signs of organization among less-skilled groups.[2] Many of the Edinburgh trades had histories of local organization, at least from the early nineteenth century; from the 1850s these local bodies tended, as MacDougall points

---

[1] Hobsbawm, *Labouring Men*, p. 323.
[2] MacDougall, *Minutes of Edinburgh Trades Council*, pp. xviii–xxi.

out, to become branches of Scottish or British unions.[1] The
Edinburgh Typographical Society was one of the bodies that
federated in 1852 to form the Scottish Typographical Association, and the local organization of bookbinders merged in 1872
with the hitherto much smaller branch of the national Bookbinders' Consolidated Union.[2] This was only one aspect of a
tendency to increasingly formal and elaborate union organization, which was no doubt a response to the growing scale of
industry, mobility of labour, and organization among the
employers. The decline of the face-to-face occupational community may well have created the need for more formal
methods of collective regulation of wages and conditions.

Fifty years ago, the means or mechanism by which anything useful
was accomplished was exceedingly strong, and readily and effectively used . . . if a question was raised affecting the well being of
any one man or any body of men in any trade, every individual
member of that branch of industry felt and spoke upon the matter
as if his own honour was at stake and his own personal interests were
involved . . .[3]

The growth of large, elaborately organized craft unions was a
notable feature of British working-class history from the 1840s.
Under the guise of the Webbs' 'new spirit' and 'new model',[4]
this trend is often seen as linked to the accommodative attitudes
of the labour aristocracy. It is certainly possible to show the
pervasive influence of the labour aristocracy on trade unionism
at this period. But that influence cannot be identified simply
with unions conforming to the Webbs' 'new model', nor always
with industrial pacifism. The relationship is at a deeper structural level, identifiable in the ideological forms of class-
consciousness and the limited character of working-class
aspirations.

Although unions were becoming larger, more formal, and

---

[1] MacDougall, *Minutes of Edinburgh Trades Council*, pp. xviii–xxi.
[2] Ibid.; Scottish Typographical Association, *Rules* (1852). Most unions in Edinburgh between 1850 and 1900 were branches of Scottish unions; the most important
British unions were the A.S.E., Bookbinders' Consolidated Union, and (from the
1880s) the Boot and Shoe Operatives; the most important purely local societies
were the Bookbinders' Union Society (until 1872) and the Cordwainers.
[3] *Scottish Typographical Circular*, Aug. 1859.
[4] S. and B. Webb, *The History of Trade Unionism* (Revised edn., 1920), Ch. 4.

bureaucratic in their organization, by no means every important union was of the centralized 'new model' type; the Scottish
Typographical Association, for example, was federal in structure, and its local constituents retained considerable autonomy.[1]
In all unions, regardless of differences in formal structure,
significant initiative remained in the hands of the branch, and
often of the immediate work group. All bargaining about
wages and conditions was at a local level, although it is true
that here the activities of branches were, constitutionally speaking, subject to considerable central control. There is, however, a
crucial difference between 'forward' movements—demands for
wage rises etc., which needed the sanction of the national
executive—and the defence of *existing* conditions and practices.[2]
This latter type of activity has been aptly described as 'regulation by union rule'.[3] It depended on constant vigilance and
initiative at workshop and branch level, and was closely related
to the occupational community and the solidaristic values of
craft cultures. Such values are often articulated in the pre-
ambles to union rule-books; the objective of the Bookbinders'
Union Society (1846) was to: 'keep within proper limits all
attempts on the part of the employer to tamper with the rights
and privileges of his workmen'.[4] This form of defensive combination was evidently not confined to the formal membership
of unions. The bookbinders' minutes, for example, on one occasion record the readiness of non-members 'to Help and work in
co-operation with the Society'.[5] It is misleading to focus on the
development of formal union organization to the exclusion of
the wider occupational solidarity which was often crucial to
the upholding of craft conditions and practices.

Industrial disputes arising from 'regulation by union rule'
were often on an extremely small scale. In one instance, the
bookbinders remonstrated with an employer about his new
workshop rules; he refused to withdraw them, in the belief that

---

[1] Scottish Typographical Association, *Rules*. The Edinburgh Typographical
Society was the local branch of this Association.
[2] See various rule-books in Sect. C of the Webb Trade Union Coll. See Edin.
Central Branch, Associated Joiners, Minutes, 14 Mar. 1872, 30 Nov. 1876, for
examples of these rules in operation.
[3] Child, *Industrial Relations in the British Printing Industry*, Pt. III.
[4] Edin. Union Society of Journeymen Bookbinders, *Rules* (1846).
[5] Bookbinders' Union Society, Minutes, 20 Feb. 1864.

he could get blacklegs from abroad. 'The Deputation then left Mr. M'Kenzie to his Dream', and called twenty men out; after four days the employer conceded the point.[1] The bookbinders' minutes, in particular, indicate the importance of vigilance over working practices, especially with the widespread intro-duction of female labour into binding processes. In one such case, typical of many throughout the period, three men struck, 'attempting to resist an infringement of their rights and privileges' through the encroachment of female labour.[2] Among compositors, too, there were many 'small local strikes where there have been disagreements arising as to the variation from the scale of pay'.[3] The compositors' workshop controls were institutionalized in the Chapel.[4] This body, consisting of all the journeymen in a particular office or shift, had, by long-estab-lished tradition, a general responsibility for maintaining order and seeing to the proper conduct of the work. In the nineteenth century this tradition of workshop self-organization became incorporated into the trade-union structure.[5] Chapel meetings 'may be called at any time either to preserve the employer's property, or to settle a dispute regarding prices to be paid for special kinds of work.'[6] Any picture which overlooks these forms of workshop organization will be seriously distorted. In this, as in other periods, vigilance over shop-floor conditions and the day-to-day experience of defensive combination constituted the essential base of trade unionism.

The collective action of the skilled worker was embedded in craft tradition and the defence of trade custom, and this no doubt was reflected in the perception of class interests and relationships. There were, however, important aspects of trade-union activity which implied a wider class identity. As workers became aware of their bargaining strength they tried to enforce avowedly new principles—such as the nine-hour day—to which the norms of established trade custom were irrelevant. The formation of the Trades Council is closely associated with this

[1] Bookbinders' Union Society, Minutes, 20 Feb. 1864.

[2] Edin. Branch, Bookbinders' Consolidated Union, Minutes, 25 Nov. 1874.

[3] *R.C. on Labour, group C*, P.P. 1893–4 XXXIV, q. 23198 (secretary, Edin. Typographical Society).   [4] See Child, op. cit., pp. 35–9.

[5] See Edin. Typographical Society, *Rules* (1892).

[6] *The Ballantyne Press*, p. 150.

process. Although its influence may have been rather limited at this period—only one union, the tailors, were continuously affiliated during the years 1859–73[1]—participation in the Council must none the less have brought a few activists into contact with men in other trades. And there is, as we might expect, a degree of overlap between the personnel of trade unionism and of other artisan institutions. Two of the founders of St. Cuthbert's and an officer of the Mechanics' Libary were at various times delegates on the Trades Council; while its regular meeting-place, Buchanan's Temperance Hotel, is perhaps an indication of the ties with the milieu of working-class 'respectability'.[2]

The Council originated, it would seem, in the agitation for Saturday half-holidays in the early 1850s.[3] The earliest extant minutes (from 1859) indicate its part in encouraging the demand for the nine-hour day. It organized a meeting, attended by 2,000, which, 'calls upon all Tradesmen whether organized or not to come forward and assist the Masons and Joiners so that the Rights of Labour may not be overpowered by the weight of Capital.'[4] Again, in the second great wave of the nine hours' movement, the Council organized a meeting at which Burnet, the Tyneside engineers' leader, declared: 'It was not only for themselves they were fighting, but for the working men throughout the whole country. (Applause.)'; soon afterwards the Edinburgh engineering trades were themselves agitating for the nine-hour day.[5]

These movements often resulted in large-scale industrial disputes, which contrast with the small local strikes that arose from 'regulation by union rule'. The masons were out for three months in 1861 when they won the nine-hour day.[6] The printers' decision, taken at the 'largest trade assemblage at which we have ever been present',[7] to give notice for shorter hours and other demands, led to a bitter struggle; a 'powerful combination of local publishers' forced the men back on the employers' terms, following the organized introduction of blackleg labour.[8] There is also some evidence of tension between local branches and the union executives. When a member

---

[1] MacDougall, op. cit., p. xxi.   [2] Ibid., pp. xxiii, xxv, xli.   [3] Ibid., p. xv.
[4] T.C. Minutes, 13 Mar. 1861.   [5] Ibid., 5, 24 Oct. 1871.
[6] *North Briton*, 2 Mar., 5 June 1861. [7] *Scottish Typographical Circular*, Dec. 1872.
[8] Bookbinders' Consolidated Union, *Trade Circular*, March 1873.

of the Ironmoulders' executive visited Edinburgh in an attempt
to persuade the District to lift their overtime ban, he got a
'warm reception'; and it was only reluctantly that the executive
allowed the District to join the local joint short-time committee.[1]
A critic of the A.S.E. executive alleged that they had forbidden
a local joint committee, and generally allowed the union to fall
into a 'stupor' evidenced by the engineers' sluggishness on the
nine hours' question, despite their self-image as the 'aristocracy
of the working classes'.[2]

The formation of local employers' organizations was both
cause and effect of the spread of industrial militancy. The
builders', printers', and engineers' organizations all date from
the 1860s.[3] The engineers' association was said to have been
formed specifically to resist the demand for shorter hours and
was accused of operating a black list: 'No such sights as an
employer fraternising at any of our social meetings, &c., with
the workmen of his own and other establishments, as we see at
the meetings of other trades.'[4] Given this tendency, and the
growing scale of industry and concentration of ownership, conflicts resulting from 'regulation by union rule' could escalate.
The alteration of work-allocation arrangements at the *Scotsman*
newspaper led to a serious strike and eventually to the closing
of the office to union members.[5] The Trades Council resolved
that, 'all who have taken any interest in the matter cannot but
see that it is intended as a representative struggle, being a blow
aimed it is conceived at Trade Unionism in general, and will if
successful be followed by other employers in other Trades',
and called on all trade unionists in the city to support a
subscription for the strikers.[6] In 1875 the Council expressed
concern at the 'aggressive action of employers, federated or
otherwise, in the matter of wages and hours', and took steps to
encourage mutual aid in resisting cuts.[7] The severe depression of
the later 1870s encouraged the engineering employers to attack

---

[1] Associated Ironmoulders, E.C. Minutes, 30 May 1870, 22 Nov. 1871.
[2] Letter in *Reformer*, 13 Feb. 1869.
[3] *North Briton*, 6 Mar. 1861; *Scottish Typographical Circular*, Dec. 1866; letter in
Reformer, 9 Jan. 1869.   [4] *Reformer*, loc. cit.
[5] MacDougall, op. cit., p. 341, footnote.
[6] T.C. Minutes, 24 Sept. 1872: spelling and syntax in original.
[7] Ibid., 9 Feb., 31 Mar. 1875.

the gains made in the preceding period of boom; a fifty-four-hour week was introduced, despite the formation of a 51 Hours Defence League, 'especially to embrace the large number of unskilled labourers enjoying the great Priviledge and should be allowed the opportunity to defend it'.[1]

The larger-scale industrial disputes of the 1860s and 1870s reflect the increased bargaining power of skilled labour, and the resistance of employers to the wider exercise of this power. The shop-floor defence of trade practices was increasingly complemented, but never superseded, by more centralized collective bargaining. The nine hours' movement is of particular significance in extending the sphere of bargaining between employers and workers' representatives appointed by the unions. The disputes of the 1870s, and the onset of severe depression in building and engineering later in that decade, marked setbacks to the advance of trade-union power. The graph of unionization (Figure III) indicates the growth of organization to the mid-1870s, the subsequent setback, and the very gradual recovery of the eighties. The graph, however, is at best a rough approximation to the real picture. Employers' attacks on the gains

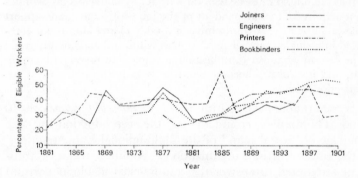

Figure III. Unionization, 1861–1901

Source: Membership returns in union reports. Eligible workers estimated from census tables (inter-censal change in numbers distributed over relevant non-census years).

made in organization and wages and conditions helped to foster a generalized trade-union consciousness, a growing sense

[1] T. C. Minutes, 12 Sept. 1878: spelling and syntax in original.

that trade unionists, as trade unionists, were being attacked.

The growth of an industrially based class-consciousness was also fostered by the dubious legal position of workers' combinations, and the ideological opposition of the powerfully entrenched economic individualism of the middle class. It was here that the artisan was likely to dissent most sharply and explicitly from the dominant ideology. The legal and ideological standing of trade unions was a recurring concern of the Trades Council. It organized a meeting in 1859 to refute the views of Adam Black, the Whig M.P. for the city, and was later closely involved in the nation-wide agitation for the repeal of anti-union statutes; it was on this issue that the alliance of middle-class Liberalism and working-class organizations showed most signs of strain.[1]

An important legitimation of collective action derived from the values of craft solidarity. The articulation of solidaristic values in more generalized and abstract terms could broaden the defence of the craft into a critique of middle-class individualism.

'A man can do what he likes with his own.' Before this plea can be held as tenable, it must be seen how what any man calls his own has been acquired . . . independent of the joint-assistance and support of co-labourers . . . A community or a body of any kind is not comprised in a single member . . . No man within the pale of any trade or profession whatever is, in himself, a whole, but merely a member of it, and is, and has become what he is, only through and by his connection with it . . .[2]

This remarkable passage from the *Typographical Circular* calls to mind Thompson's comment on the reproduction of 'the language of "social man" of the philosophical Enlightenment' in the rules of artisan organizations.[3] Another strand of argument attempted to answer the middle-class ideologues within the terms of their own economic theory. It was argued that 'superabundance of labour', rather than 'improvident habits' was at the root of social problems, and that restriction of labour supply was 'a matter of self-defence'.[4] Sometimes the argument

---

[1] T. C. Minutes, 11 Nov. 1859; MacDougall, op. cit., pp. xxxii–xxxv.
[2] *Scottish Typographical Circular*, May 1858.
[3] Thompson, *Making of the Working Class*, p. 461.
[4] *Scottish Typographical Circular*, Feb. 1859.

could take on a blunter and more militant tone: 'Labour is the commodity the operative has to sell, and if he has the power he has the perfect right to sell as small a quantity as he thinks proper without giving any reason in the shape of an apology of so doing.'[1]

Underlying all these arguments was the conviction of a natural opposition of interest between workers and employers, the assertion of an ethic of solidarity. The *North Briton*'s columnist 'John Wilkes' condemned 'base sneaking fellows' who 'offer themselves . . . at low wages':

Every trade, sir, has its own peculiar name for these good-for-nothing willing-to-work-for-anything characters, but perhaps the most expressive is that of shoemakers . . . In the shoemaking trade, those who go in and take the work of men who are out on strike for an advance of wages are called scabs, and woe be to the outcast whose conduct brings that terrible name upon him.[2]

The blackleg printer was caricatured in a satirical 'situations vacant' column: 'Accustomed to use the Knob Stick. Is a Firm Believer in the Identity of the Interests of Capital and Labour—especially of Capital. Objects to have his Wages Raised by the Agency of Combination . . . A strict Tee-totaler, if required. Prayer Meetings attended Gratis.'[3]

Together with this widely diffused ethic of solidarity went a view of collective action as the essential defence of the rights of working people. In this perspective, the struggle over wages and working conditions was a particular manifestation of a more general movement of resistance to every kind of oppression that workers might suffer at the hands of their employers and social superiors. In the mid-Victorian period this was often enough formulated in the language of popular radicalism. 'If we have a *right* to a vote in the administration, we have in consequence the *right* to a great deal more in other directions. We are no more masters and servants, but equals, having the right, as those above us have, to regulate as we think proper when we shall work, how long we shall work, and to put our own value upon what we sell . . .'[4] The labour laws, as William Paterson

---

[1] *North Briton*, 20 Mar. 1861.   [2] Ibid., 10 Mar. 1866.
[3] *Scottish Typographical Circular*, May 1869. 'Knob Stick' was a term for blackleg, and is here a pun on the 'stick' the compositor used in his work.
[4] Ibid., Aug. 1865.

of the Associated Joiners told the Royal Commission, were resented 'more as . . . a moral wrong', that for the direct hardships they inflicted.[1] As a letter in the *Typographical Circular* put it:

every true unionist may well feel proud of his principles when he knows that taking higher ground than that of desiring to fix the price and hours of labour, trades-unionism aspires to free the British workman from an indignity under which he has so long groaned; and, if not investing him with the social and political equality which he so earnestly desires—and to which, according to high authority, he is so fully entitled—at least cutting from his neck one of the most degrading badges of his serfdom.[2]

We find the same claim to social recognition, the same stress on the independence and moral dignity of the worker, as we traced in the artisan's aspirations outside the work place. This often connected with the argument from economic theory and the freedom of contract. The 'equal freedom of capital and labour' was implied by the political economists themselves.[3] The *Typographical Circular* noted with approval the disappearance of testimonials from employers, as betokening 'the vigorous expansion of ideas of self-reliance and self-respect. A fair field and no favour is now all that is asked by average workmen in the struggle for existence; a right manly sentiment, and one which is bound to yield a better return morally and materially than was to be got when they went about cringing for work on the strength of a bit of paper, or ate their bread per favour of a patron.'[4]

Those closely involved in sophisticated ideological discussion were, however, an articulate minority, even of union members; and the men organized in unions were themselves at this period a minority in every trade. Intellectualized legitimations must be seen against the background of day-to-day experience of industrial relations and trade solidarity. The practical ethic of solidarity, and the rather diffuse view of collective action as the essential defence of the worker's rights were probably the most widely influential elements in the trade-union ideology, and

---

[1] *R.C. on the Labour Laws, Second Report*, P.P. 1875 XXX, q. 212; cf. A. Anderson, 'The Political Symbolism of the Labour Laws', *Society for the Study of Labour History Bulletin*, 23 (Autumn 1971). [2] *Scottish Typographical Circular*, Sept. 1864. [3] Ibid., May 1865. [4] Ibid., July 1872.

certainly played a part in the formation of working-class cultures. We must, however, again emphasize that social attitudes might be incoherent, fragmented, and ambivalent; the experience of collective action in the employment situation must be set beside those other aspects of artisan life explored in earlier chapters.

A sense of class oppression and class interest was also articulated through political activity. Indeed, the pervasive ideology of Victorian liberalism led working men to define their oppression as arising, above all, from their exclusion from the formal political system. This was part of a long tradition of radical social analysis which, despite the important challenges of Owenites and other 'proto-socialists', stretched unbroken from Paine to the socialists of the 1880s.[1] In some industrial communities this tradition could, in its relation to the experience of class struggle, take on new meanings, which implied a challenge to the property relations of industrial capitalism;[2] the process can be seen especially in the Chartist movement. In Edinburgh, however, the development of class-consciousness in the 1830s and 1840s was of a more limited kind. Although there was, for example, a significant Chartist movement in the city there is little evidence of the kind of relationship to deeply felt local grievances of the working people that was so important in the industrial North of England; the Edinburgh leadership inclined to the rational 'moral force' radicalism characteristic of the self-educated artisan élite.[3] There was an established artisan political tradition, going back at least to the reform movement of the late eighteenth century, which tended to become socially and organizationally more distinctive.[4] But Edinburgh did not experience the explosive emergence of class-consciousness to be seen in some communities during the 1830s and 1840s. In the third quarter of the nineteenth century the inherited popular political tradition found expression in a context defined by socio-economic changes in the working class; by important developments in middle-class politics; and by the

[1] See P. Hollis, *The Pauper Press* (1970).
[2] See Thompson, op. cit.; Foster, op. cit., provides a local case-study of the process.
[3] See A. Wilson, *The Chartist Movement in Scotland* (1970), e.g. pp. 67–8, 230–1, 236–8.   [4] Ibid., pp. 23, 28.

formation, after 1867, of a Liberal political bloc incorporating the politically conscious and organized sections of the working class. Even when the rather tenuous *organizational* links between working-class radicalism and bourgeois Liberalism seemed liable to snap, the deeper hegemony of liberal *ideas and values* remained unshaken.[1]

Urban growth, economic expansion, and changes in social structure created new groupings and conflicts within the bourgeois and petty-bourgeois classes. These forces coalesced in a series of challenges, whose cohesion and consistency varied, to the older, gentry-linked urban élites of 'Church, Army, Physic, Law'.[2] The most coherent and successful challenge came with the formation in the 1860s of a Liberal bloc, led by the merchant Duncan McLaren, which, significantly, differentiated itself from Whigs as well as Tories; McLaren's success in the parliamentary election of 1865 was generally attributed to improved registration, and a canvass of the 'new' electorate in the poorer quarters of the city.[3]

The continuing tradition of artisan political consciousness became attached to this movement, especially as McLaren supported parliamentary reform during 1866–7.[4] Ten years earlier the radical *North Briton*, which regarded itself as the inheritor of Edinburgh Chartism, advocated alliance with middle-class radicals, even at the cost of watering down the popular radical programme.[5] The radical tradition became overlaid with the dominant ideology of mid-Victorian Britain. The essentially élitist argument of the 'growing virtue and intelligence of the working classes'[6] received more emphasis than

---

[1] Capitalized words such as 'Liberal', 'Radical', etc. refer to identifiable party groupings; the same words without capitals refer to modes of political thought, to which individuals in a range of different parties might adhere.

[2] J. B. Mackie, *The Life and Work of Duncan McLaren*, vol. ii (1888), p. 27. See Williams, 'Edinburgh Politics' (Ph.D. thesis); and A. J. Cameron, 'Society, Policing, and the Problem of Order: Edinburgh, 1805–1822' (Undergraduate dissertation, Edinburgh University, Department of Economic History, 1974), for these developments.

[3] Mackie, op. cit., p. 48; Williams, op. cit., pp. 374, 384–90, which indicates a considerable increase in the working-class electorate, even before 1867.

[4] *North Briton*, 21 Nov. 1866 (speech by McLaren).

[5] Ibid., 25 Nov. 1857.

[6] Ibid., 16 Mar. 1859 (speech by Alexander Fraser, blacksmith, future secretary of the Trades Council).

the rights of man. There were, however, other elements; different layers of language and analysis were superimposed on each other (sometimes, no doubt, in the minds of the same individuals). The very stress on 'respectability' could, as has been seen in other contexts,[1] be a focal point of class identity and social tension:

... cabs and open carriages, with cynical or simply curious 'swells', were driven slowly past to have, as they said, a view of 'the great unwashed', who were, however, as was at once evident, not only washed but dressed—and that handsomely, too, for the occasion; and it will be unanimously allowed, even by those who habitually sneer at the working classes, that a better dressed procession of *working men* was never seen.[2]

The range of emphases in the radical movement is reflected by the speakers at the reform demonstration, who ranged from Liberal-Radical Town Councillors to the Glasgow Owenite Alexander Campbell. One speaker (a mason) argued that: 'The "great unwashed", as they were called, they must still remain, and must to the end of their lives earn their bread by the sweat of their brows. But if they had the franchise they might be a great deal better in their condition than they now were.'[3] Campbell declared that the workers should be enfranchised, since they 'supported every other class of society', while another speaker (a plumber) put forward the argument from working-class 'respectability', going so far as to argue that a £10 franchise might have been appropriate in 1832, but that the subsequent 'progress of the working classes' now made a wider one appropriate.[4] The political postures of working-class leaders were thus ambivalent, and sometimes mutually contradictory.

The working-class reform movement had a continuous, if erratic, existence from the Chartist period through to the renewed mass agitation of the 1860s. Thereafter, it came to form the left wing of the Liberal party emerging under the hegemony of men like McLaren. The *Reformer*, founded in 1868, represented this conjuncture of political forces. Edited by Bailie Lewis, an ex-journeyman master shoemaker, radical, and temperance advocate, its stated policy was to agitate for extension of the

---

[1] Above, pp. 140–1. [2] *North Briton*, 21 Nov. 1866; emphasis in original.
[3] Ibid. [4] Ibid.

1867 borough franchise to the counties, give coverage to the labour movement and space to its spokesmen, and 'represent the opinions of Advanced Liberals'.[1] It represented the current of opinion that hoped that the Reform Bill could be made the prelude to a more sweeping attack on entrenched privilege; working-class organizations were regarded as potentially a part of the broad radical-progressive movement. The Commons was described as still, despite the Reform Bill, the 'Second House of the Aristocracy' and the people were urged to send representatives of 'their own class'.[2]

Vincent has argued that in particular communities Radical-Liberalism reflected the demand for social recognition of those excluded by entrenched local élites.[3] Many statements by Edinburgh radicals can be seen in this light. The *North Briton*, for example, complained of 'the great tendency in certain quarters of our city to confine all public arrangements to a small section of the community'.[4] The catch-phrase 'class legislation' summed up many of these feelings of social exclusion, as well as more material grievances. We have already noted the symbolic aspect of the labour laws. The land laws, and a whole range of statutes that appeared to endorse some principle of inequality were regarded in a similar light; the Contagious Diseases Acts, for example, were described as 'class legislation'.[5] The *Reformer* regarded further franchise extension as the prelude to 'impartial legislation'.[6] The aspirations of the working-class radicals are further illuminated by the response of the local radical press to the Paris Commune and the British republican movement which emerged at about the same period. The *North Briton*, although it had initially been hostile to the insurgents, was quick to take offence at the aspersions cast on the Communards' social class.[7] The *Reformer*, while opposing 'the wealthy monopolists who grind the faces of the poor with their

---

[1] *Reformer*, 15 Aug. 1868. For Lewis see MacDougall, op. cit., p. 235, footnote. The intention of covering trade-union affairs was largely carried out; letters to the editor indicate a readership of active trade unionists.

[2] Ibid., 22 Aug. 1868.

[3] J. Vincent, *The Formation of the Liberal Party* (1966), pt. II, esp. pp. 76–82.

[4] *North Briton*, 18 Mar. 1871.

[5] *North Briton*, 10 May 1871; *Reformer*, 23 Apr. 1870.

[6] *Reformer*, 15 Aug. 1868.

[7] *North Briton*, 15 Feb., 29 Mar., 8 Apr. 1871.

class legislation', also opposed 'the Socialist sentiment which would confiscate the property of the industrious, well-doing artisan for the benefit of his lazy and profligate fellow-labourer'.[1] Here, too, the attitudes of the wealthy classes provoked a shift of editorial line; and the columnist 'Old Radical' emphasized the differing opinions of the 'democracy' and the 'aristocracy and wealthy classes'.[2] A letter in the same paper referred to the 'strong feeling' of working men in favour of republicanism; six months later a republican club was in existence in the city.[3] This evidence, together with the industrial militancy of the same period and the growing feeling about the labour laws, does suggest a widening gulf between working-class radicalism and the Liberalism of wealthy businessmen like McLaren.

The characteristic objects of class hatred seem, however, to have belonged to the old radical demonology: monarchy, aristocracy, church, militarism. The *North Briton* concluded from a series of articles on 'Republics—Ancient and Modern' that monarchy was synonymous with 'class legislation'—exemplified in Britain by the land and game laws.[4] Bailie Lewis, lecturing on 'Capital, Labour and Wages', advocated the recognition of trade unions and collective bargaining, to avoid 'misunderstanding'; the employer was 'an organiser of labour', whose interests largely coincided with those of his workers: 'The true capitalists viewed in relation to our national industry may with comparatively few exceptions be regarded as those who hold possession of the soil.'[5] Lewis, as an employer trying to cement a political alliance with trade unionists, clearly had an axe to grind. But this view of the 'aristocracy' as the true exploiting class seems none the less to have provided an intelligible analysis of society for politically conscious artisans. In 1884, for example, a Trades Council subcommittee listed the causes of industrial depression as the land laws, the drink traffic, foreign tariffs, and over-production (in that order).[6] The tendency to adopt this image of society must also be seen in

---

[1] *Reformer*, 25 Mar. 1871. [2] Ibid., 6, 13 May 1871.
[3] Ibid., 8 Apr., 11 Nov. 1871. [4] *North Briton*, 10 May 1871.
[5] *Reformer*, 1 Mar. 1873. The lecture was organized by the Trades Council.
[6] T.C. Minutes, 2 Dec. 1884.

its local context. The blanket term 'aristocracy' may have applied loosely, in the minds of working men, to all those groups of the wealthy upper-middle class who appeared to dominate local affairs—a stratum which was in Edinburgh not at all synonymous with the employers of industrial labour. The recruitment to the working class of Highland and Irish immigrants may, moreover, have added a dimension of personal experience to the sense of agrarian injustice.

The influence of agrarian questions on urban politics was a general feature of the 1880s. The traditional urban Liberal hostility to landed property meant that this issue represented the most advanced position possible within the structures of Victorian liberalism; and, by raising the question of property relations, it led some workers on to a socialist view of class exploitation, and to a political break with the Liberal Party.[1] The dynamism of this issue in the 1880s derived partly from the militancy of Irish and Highland peasants.[2] It is hard to gauge the real extent of urban working-class solidarity with these movements; the Highlanders themselves, and probably also most urban radicals, took care to distance themselves from the Irish and anything that smacked of 'Fenianism'.[3] Events in the Highlands increased the saliency of the land question, and brought to the fore a deep-rooted tendency to concentrate social discontent in an attack on landlordism. The Trades Council minutes record a number of debates on the various land reforms then being canvassed.[4] This was at one level a matter of sympathy for people who were seen as the victims of blatant social injustice; thus the Council expressed concern at the repression meted out to the Skye crofters.[5] But it also reflected an economic analysis, and land reform (in whichever variant) was advocated to overcome trade depression, by reducing 'the vast and increasing number of non-producers who live upon the wealth produced by the Industrial Class'.[6] Finally, one must note the political dimension of the land question; the

---

[1] See below, pp. 179–80.
[2] For the Highland movement see J. Hunter, 'The Politics of Highland Land Reform, 1873–1895', *Scottish Historical Review*, 53 (1974).
[3] Ibid., pp. 48–9.
[4] T.C. Minutes, e.g., 28 Aug. 1883, 26 Aug. 1884, 16 Aug. 1887.
[5] Ibid, 14 July 1885, 16 Nov. 1886.   [6] Ibid., 29 Dec. 1885.

concentration of landownership was seen as supporting a reactionary and parasitic caste, and its hangers-on. While trade unionists were well enough aware of social difference and conflict in the work place, the social analysis made available by the radical tradition gave a central place to landed, rather than industrial, property.

Despite these potentially more far-reaching developments, the ideology of working-class activists seems still to have been contained within a tradition of popular radicalism which had become, in practice, a subordinate part of mid-Victorian Liberalism. The Liberal party was a relatively loose electoral coalition, which in Edinburgh had emerged as recently as the election of 1865, so that in the 1870s radical artisans were not attaching themselves to a monolithic, tightly organized party with fixed characteristics, but rather to an emergent movement whose nature they might hope to influence. Mid-Victorian Liberalism was as much a 'movement' as a political party in the conventional sense; and its local manifestations might have only the most tenuous connections with the opinions or activities of the men it sent to Westminster.[1] The main integrative element appears to have been the name of 'Gladstone—vanguard of liberty unshaken', as a political versifier in the *Reformer* called him.[2] Urging the Trades Council to welcome Gladstone to the city in 1879 one delegate (a joiner) described him as 'a Statesman of great Intellectual and moral worth, and in doing Honour to such a Statesman they would at the same time be Honouring themselves'.[3] Here again political attitudes may shed some light on social aspirations; the key to Gladstone's extraordinary popularity with sections of the working class seems to have been his readiness to appeal to the moral sense of ordinary people, to admit them, at a symbolic level, to membership of the 'political nation'.[4]

The Radical-Liberalism of politically active working men involved the same process of bargaining, the same negotiated accommodation between the dominant class and relatively autonomous working-class organizations, as we saw operating in the institutions of artisan 'self-improvement'. On a number

---

[1] See Vincent, op. cit.　　　　　　　[2] *Reformer*, 26 Sept., 1868.
[3] T.C. Minutes, 22 July 1879.　　　[4] Vincent, op. cit., pp. 216–17, 233–4.

of local issues—the agitation to enforce the Factory Acts in Edinburgh, the allocation of educational endowments to found schools for the sons of the wealthy, the opening of Princes Street gardens to the public—the Radical Town Councillors, who seem to have been mainly businessmen, worked with the Trades Council.[1] Sometimes, though not invariably, they came to electoral arrangements; while in parliamentary elections the interviewing of candidates became a regular part of the Council's business, and generally led to the conclusion that working men should vote Liberal.[2] The striving for recognition of their corporate status seems to be reflected in the Trades Council's attitudes to notable political figures; they elected McLaren, and the current and past Lord Advocates honorary presidents, and welcomed Gladstone and Bright on their visits to the city.[3]

This attachment to Liberalism was, however, subject to certain strains. The issue of direct working-class representation on local bodies was one source of tension. When the Advanced Liberals apparently changed their minds about running jointly with a Trades Council nominee (William Paterson of the Associated Joiners) in the municipal election of 1869, the Council condemned 'political jugglery', and resolved: 'That this Council in future connect itself with none of the present pollitical Parties but confine itself to the representation of labour.'[4] The issue of the labour laws was also disruptive. McLaren, 'as an economist and Free Trader', declined to support the trade unionists' demands, and was 'denounced as a "traitor" ' at a large demonstration in 1873.[5] These conflicts may, however, have been rather more complex than a simple split between working-class radicals and the middle-class Liberalism of men like McLaren. The issue of the labour laws was raised at the Advanced Liberals' A.G.M. by Andrew Dewar (blacksmith, a former secretary of the Trades Council);[6] it is not altogether clear what attitude the radical businessmen took

---

[1] T.C. Minutes, 11 Dec. 1868, 7 Mar., 23 Sept. 1873. For the Radical Town Councillors see Marwick, 'Municipal Politics in Victorian Edinburgh'.

[2] See T.C. Minutes, e.g., 18 Mar. 1873, 30 Mar. 1880.

[3] Ibid., 12 Jan. 1869, 16 Oct. 1868, 14 Oct. 1879.

[4] Ibid., 22, 26 Oct. 1869; spelling in original. The Council none the less continued to support Radical or Liberal candidates.

[5] Mackie, op. cit., p. 53.   [6] *Reformer*, 6 Sept. 1873.

—though Lewis, as we have seen, produced a sophisticated argument to reconcile his position as an employer with his trade-union political alliance—but at any rate disenchantment with McLaren does not seem to have driven a wedge between the trade unionists and the Advanced Liberals. Social distinctions within the middle class—reflected in the difference between McLaren and the more radical politics of smaller businessmen—may be important here.[1] It must again be borne in mind that parties at this period were rather loosely articulated political structures. In opposing the exclusion of working men from the party ticket, or the attitudes of Liberal 'economists' to trade unionism, trade unionists could remain within the broad ideological and organizational framework of Radical-Liberalism—if the tensions under discussion had any effect, it was probably to reinforce the 'anti-political' attitudes of many trade unionists, rather than to produce a political revolt against the hegemony of Liberalism.

The third quarter of the nineteenth century saw the emergence of a relatively autonomous working-class industrial and political movement, conditioned by the position and outlook of the labour aristocracy, and effectively contained within the forms of social hegemony characteristic of the period. This should not, however, be allowed to obscure the reality of class conflict and the growth of class-consciousness. The containment of working-class pressures was seen at the time as problematic, and hindsight should not mislead us into supposing that it was preordained. The phenomenon of industrial combination and strikes was deeply disturbing to many members of the middle class, and large questions seemed to hang over the entry into politics of a mass electorate. The Reverend David Aitken (a retired clergyman of some wealth) noted in his diary the 'orderly' character and 'holiday look' of the Edinburgh reform demonstrators; but nevertheless viewed with alarm the nation-wide agitation over the 'unprofitable subject' of the franchise, especially since 'Fenianism seems to increase'.[2] This perhaps

---

[1] It is not true, as Mackie states (loc. cit.), that the Advanced Liberals were first formed to oppose McLaren on this issue; it is clear from the *Reformer* that they represented a grouping that had existed, under that label, at least from 1868.

[2] R. G. Heddle (ed.), 'Extracts from the Diary of the Rev. David Aitken, D.D., 1864–1875', *Book of the Old Edinburgh Club* (1971).

typifies the odd mixture of social complacency and apprehension among conservative-minded members of the upper-middle class.

Workers themselves, on the other hand, showed little tendency to link their experience of industrial struggle to the persistent inequalities of political power. Both kinds of oppression were recognized as such, and vigorously opposed, but they were never connected within any total social critique. Disillusionment with Liberalism led to political passivity, rather than to any attempt to construct an alternative. It is this more than anything else, that distinguished the experience of mid-Victorian Edinburgh from that of the main regions of Chartist militancy earlier in the century, or of Edinburgh itself during the socialist movement of the 1880s and 1890s. The great achievement of the tiny minority of socialist propagandists in the working-class movement was to provide the outlines of a total critique, within which particular class experiences could be interrelated and broadened into a general rejection of established political forms.

9 The Emergence of a Labourist Working-Class Movement, 1884—1900

THE attachment of industrially and politically organized workers to Liberalism had, by the end of the century, been firmly challenged. The 1880s and 1890s saw important changes in the trade-union movement and in working-class political aspirations. It has been argued that these tendencies represented 'a revision of judgement' of an essentially pragmatic character, rather than any significant shift in ideological perspectives.[1] I would argue, however, that there were related changes in working-class life and culture, and that the influence of socialist ideas cannot be ignored; in short, that there was a discernible change in the consciousness of class among working men. As a socialist commentator of the period remarked:

If there is one feature of the Labour Movement more distinctive than another, it is the widespread spontaneity of the revolt against the tyrannous class monopolies, DUE TO A MORAL AND SPIRITUAL UPHEAVAL, a striving among the people for liberty to live a better, freer, and nobler life than is possible for them as wage-slaves in a capitalist society. And it is this struggle for better opportunities of life, NOT FOR THEMSELVES ONLY but for their class and for society, that has caused the series of social, industrial and political struggles known as the Labour Movement.[2]

Given the general theme of this study, it is important to examine the role in this 'upheaval' of different sections of the working class. To what extent did the new developments reflect the emergence of newly organized strata of the working class, as opposed to a shift in the situation and attitudes of the labour aristocracy? Before trying to answer these questions it is necess-

[1] D. W. Crowley, 'The Origins of the Revolt of the British Labour Movement from Liberalism' (Ph.D. thesis, London, 1952), abstract.
[2] *Labour Chronicle*, Nov. 1894. This paper, 'a local organ of democratic socialism', was a joint venture of the various socialist organizations in Edinburgh.

ary to specify more clearly the nature of the changes under discussion. In this chapter the word 'labourist' is used as a shorthand expression for the form of class organization and consciousness which was the typical outcome of the ferment of the 1880s and 1890s. 'Labourist' ideology is perhaps best regarded as the political expression of the 'trade-union consciousness' of British workers: 'the conviction that it is necessary to combine in unions, fight the employers, and strive to compel the government to pass necessary labour legislation, etc.'.[1] In a sense a particular form of 'labourist' outlook had emerged in the 1860s and 1870s—a form closely related to the situation and aspirations of the upper-artisan stratum. The term has been reserved for this chapter, however, because of the distinctive features of the 1880s and 1890s, the period that saw consistent attempts to transmit class ideology to the lower strata of the working class, and to create a broadly based political and industrial class movement. The growing support among organized workers for a political programme of local and national welfare legislation—free school meals, the eight-hour day, old-age pensions, etc.—was an important feature of this. Since the various socialist groups played some part in mobilizing sections of the working class and forming the labourist programme and ideology, it is necessary to clarify the relationship between labourism and socialism. The term 'socialist' refers to persons or organizations advocating collective ownership and control of the means of production, which they generally believed to imply a social order radically different from that of industrial capitalism. The labourist outlook, on the other hand, looks to the defence of working-class interests within the existing society, which may, of course, be thought to demand welfare measures of the kind generally favoured by socialists, or even state ownership of particular industries. The distinction tended, in the historical circumstances of the late nineteenth century, to become blurred. The class-conscious and egalitarian rhetoric of the labourist tradition derived partly from the activities of the socialists, while the vague term 'collectivism' was applied to any predisposition to favour public intervention in the workings of the economy; 'any departure from Manchester practice

---

[1] Lenin, *What is To Be Done?*, p. 122.

in Cobden's day could genuinely appear indistinguishable from socialism.'[1] The distinction is none the less a real one, and many socialists were themselves aware of it. It will be argued that the political changes of the period—and much of the subsequent character of British labour politics—should be analysed in terms of a convergence of socialist agitation with developments that predisposed wider circles of active trade unionists to the adoption of a labourist-reformist perspective. It is thus necessary to establish at the outset the difference between these two sets of forces. For although both, in Edinburgh, affected the labour aristocracy, they affected it in different ways and at different periods.

A number of changes in working-class life, analysed in earlier chapters, might have some relevance to the shift in industrial and political attitudes. This was a period of rising real wages and consumption standards; and, although wage differentials did not narrow and may have widened, the cheapening of basic foodstuffs may none the less have brought unskilled workers and less-favoured sections of the skilled trades above a consumption 'threshold' which gave them access to goods and services that had hitherto been the prerogative of the aristocracy of labour.[2] The improved position of labour, as well as structural change in industry, may also have made for greater homogeneity within the skilled trades; the 'career ladder' of skilled labour, and the characteristically 'petty-bourgeois' fear of falling off it, may have become a less-marked feature of artisan life.[3] Cyclical unemployment, on the other hand, possibly became heavier; while technical innovation certainly appeared to pose a threat to the security of some skilled workers.

Changes in industrial structure also affected the work situation of skilled labour.[4] In engineering, for example, the 1890s saw a new wave of machine-tool innovation, speeding up the trend to greater specialization and precision and encouraging the rationalization of labour-use and work flow.[5] In printing the linotype and monotype type-setting machines appeared at the

---

[1] Hobsbawm, *Labouring Men*, p. 267.
[2] As Hobsbawm suggests: ibid., p. 325.   [3] See above, pp. 129–30.
[4] Crowley, op. cit., Ch. 4(c), draws attention to this otherwise neglected topic.
[5] Jeffreys, *The Story of the Engineers*, pp. 122–5; Landes, *The Unbound Prometheus*, pp. 309–14.

same period—at first mainly in news work, where speed was at a premium. The capital cost of the new machines led to a growing 'cost consciousness', reflected in the concern of the Linotype Users' Association and the British Federation of Master Printers with 'scientific costing'.[1] A well-informed article by the business manager of the *Manchester Guardian* stressed union opposition to work-measurement and bonus schemes as an obstacle to the efficient use of the new machines; significantly, he diagnosed the weakness of managerial control in the composing department as the root problem of the industry.[2] In both printing and engineering there were important disputes arising from mechanization. And, in addition to any threat to the economic position of skilled labour, the increased size of capital investment encouraged employers to reorganize their plant and to introduce incentive systems, in ways which encroached on valued traditions of workshop autonomy.[3] 'This Juggernaut Car is in the hands of the high priests of trade, and the earth's feeble toilers must become its votaries, and submit their souls to be warped and their bodies crushed in the sacred cause of this fetish, which is dignified with the name of Progress.'[4] In this context, the socialist analysis of mechanization and of the nature of work under capitalism must have provided a recognizable account of the industrial experience of the skilled worker.

Even in the absence of important technical innovations, skilled workers might be affected by the growing scale of industry, closer managerial control, and tighter work discipline. The Edinburgh masons in the 1880s complained that one man now had to do the work of three, the ironmoulders that 'speed had so much improved and quality so much deteriorated'.[5] In printing, even before the introduction of linotypes, 'the previously fleet and graceful but now unfashionable compositor has to "take a back seat", and make room for this latest novelty, the Rusher'.[6] Changes in work organization were also related to the growing size of business units, and concentration of

---

[1] Child, *Industrial Relations in the British Printing Industry*, pp. 164, 197–201.
[2] G. B. Dibblee, 'The Printing Trades and the Crisis in British Industry', *Economic Journal* (1902).   [3] Cf. Hobsbawm, op. cit., pp. 358–63.
[4] Scottish Typographical Association, *Annual Report*, 1900.
[5] T.C. Minutes, 18 Nov. 1884.   [6] *Scottish Typographical Circular*, March 1885.

ownership. 'Large syndicates are being formed by individuals who know nothing about the trade; they distribute their capital to drive men in the same way as steam is distributed to drive machinery.'[1]

We may summarize the foregoing discussion by saying that pressures of structural change were, by the end of the century, impinging on the distinctive class situation of the Victorian artisan. There is also evidence of the emergence at the same period of a more homogeneous working-class community.[2] Outside the employment situation the distinction between the 'superior' artisan and the remainder of the working class was becoming less marked—though it was still of great importance. Hobsbawm suggests, moreover, that the growth of a 'status conscious' clerical lower-middle class encouraged the artisan to identify more strongly with the manual working class[3] (although it is unfortunately impossible to offer any concrete evidence either for or against this hypothesis). It is in relation to these changes in class structure and class culture that we must view trade-union and political developments.

In the first place there was a wave of unionization among unskilled workers during 1888–90. In Edinburgh and Leith, gas workers, dockers, carters, tramwaymen, scavengers, building, foundry and brewery labourers became organized and made some notable gains.[4] It is true, as the revisionary work of recent historians has suggested, that this 'new unionism' had precedents in earlier periods of boom and trade-union expansion (especially the early 1870s) and that its gains were often ephemeral.[5] A defeat by three major firms badly weakened the Leith carters; and there, as in other ports, the union-breaking activities of the Shipping Federation made themselves felt.[6] An attempt in 1893 to form or re-form a Labourers' Union failed.[7] The major office-bearers of the Trades Council up to 1900

---

[1] Associated Joiners, *Annual Report*, 1895.   [2] See above, pp. 115–20.
[3] Hobsbawm, op. cit., p. 325.
[4] T.C., *Annual Report*, 1888–9; Minutes, 19 Feb. 1889.
[5] See e.g. A. E. P. Duffy, 'The New Unionism in Britain, 1889–90: a reappraisal', *Economic History Review*, 2nd ser., 14 (1961); H. A. Clegg, A. Fox, and A. F. Thompson, *A History of British Trade Unions since 1889*, vol. i (1964), Ch. 2.
[6] T.C. Minutes, 25 Nov. 1890, 3 Feb. 1891.
[7] T.C. *Annual Report*, 1893–4.

included only one delegate (a paviour) from unions formed during 1888–90.[1]

Efforts to organize hitherto unorganized groups were none the less more widespread and persistent than at any previous period. And it is significant that the skilled unionists of the Trades Council played a prominent part in those efforts. An Organization Committee was established in 1888, and held a number of organizing meetings; the Council seems, indeed, to have taken it upon itself to appoint its own members as officials for the Labourers' Union.[2] What is significant is not the immediate success or failure of this organizing drive, but the consistency with which it was pursued. It suggests a fairly conscious attempt to widen the scope of class organization: '. . . when we speak of a trade we mean not only those workers who have served an apprenticeship to any given occupation to the exclusion of those whose occupations require comparatively little skill, but rather the word in its broader sense, by which . . . we mean all the workers who earn their bread by the exercise of one particular calling.'[3]

Another notable feature of the period, which the concern of contemporaries and historians with the 'new unions' has tended to obscure, is the growing strength of the craft unions. The graph of unionization (see Figure III) indicates a strengthened position in the 1890s. (The slump suffered by the engineers follows the lock-out of 1897–8.) This increased density of organization may be reflected in the 'forward' movements of the 1890s, which were more widespread than any since the great wave of union advance in the early 1870s. The Typographical Society gained improvements on the piece scale, following a demand for shorter hours in 1892; while the Press and Machinemen's Society gained shorter hours.[4] In 1897 the bookbinders acted jointly with the lithographers to gain fifty-two and a half hours (the lithographers gained fifty) and the Press and Machinemen's Society got 1s. rise (to 33s.) but failed to shorten hours, after seven months' strike.[5] In 1898 the Typographical Society demanded the abolition of piece-work; although this agitation

[1] T.C. *Annual Reports.*
[2] T.C. Minutes, 24 July 1888, 19 Mar., 11, 25 June 1889.
[3] *Labour Chronicle,* May 1895.   [4] *Scottish Typographical Circular,* Feb. 1892.
[5] Ibid., Feb. 1897, Feb. 1898.

'ended in smoke', the attempt to take the bull by the horns is perhaps in itself a significant indication of a sense of increasing union power and the demand for a unified trade policy.[1] In the spring of 1895 the masons and joiners gave notice for the eight-hour day, and the joiners struck unsuccessfully in the summer.[2] The most important dispute in the city arising from a 'forward' movement was perhaps the Scottish rail strike of 1890–1, mainly for the ten hours' day, which collapsed after six weeks.[3] In the local context this is of significance as the first direct involvement of Edinburgh workers in a national dispute. The Trades Council organized support for the railwaymen, as well as expressing concern at the effect on employment generally of the stoppage of rail traffic, and calling for intervention from the Board of Trade.[4]

Craft unionists were also involved in a number of hard-fought defensive struggles, often against combinations of employers, which had a notable impact on trade-union opinion in the city and contributed to a general atmosphere of industrial conflict. The most important of these disputes affected the compositors, shoemakers, and engineers. In May 1890 the Typographical Society were locked out of the *Scottish Leader* news office after resisting an agreement binding compositors there to work the new linotypes 'without having had an opportunity of ascertaining whether the rate fixed would be sufficient to remunerate them for their labour', and to remain with the firm for two years on completion of training on the linotype.[5] Matters came to a head when the employer—who had allegedly threatened 'it would be fought out to the bitter end—aye, even in blood'—accused the men of going slow, and threatened to bring in matter set elsewhere: 'Immediately thereafter the father of Chapel read Association rule 30, which stipulates that no matter is to be borrowed from or lent to an unfair office . . . and . . . it was decided to lay down their sticks.' When the men refused to leave the premises they were forcibly evicted by police.[6]

[1] *Scottish Typographical Circula*, Feb. 1898, Apr. 1899.   [2] *Labour Chronicle*, July, Sept. 1895.   [3] P. S. Bagwell, *The Railwaymen* (1963), pp. 143–7.
[4] T.C. Minutes, 13 Jan. 1891.
[5] Edin. Typographical Society, *Eviction of Trades Unionists from the Scottish Leader Office* (leaflet).
[6] Ibid.; Scottish Typographical Association, *Annual Report*, 1890.

Mechanization also had an impact on industrial relations in
✓ shoemaking. The series of innovations that made possible the
rise of a mass-production factory industry also created problems of demarcation between this and the 'quality' craft sector.
In 1893 the Cordwainers' Society—the local union of craft
shoemakers—protested that Messrs. Allan had introduced an
output norm, and thus 'transformed what was intended to be a
time payment system into a piece system of a very unsatisfac-
tory character'.[1] Three years later the Cordwainers struck at
the same firm against the use of members of the machine-
workers' union—the Boot and Shoe Operatives—to do machine
'jobbing' (i.e. repair) work, presumably at a lower rate.[2] The
local employers' association, founded in 1890 then dissolved
two years later, was revived at the initiative of Allan himself, to
'assist them to withstand the tyrannical demands of the Men's
Society'; a general lock-out was then imposed, and the employers discussed such measures as the blacklisting of militants
and 'importing labour'.[3] After nearly four months, following
Board of Trade intervention, the employers agreed to fix rates
for machine jobbing with the two unions jointly, and concilia-
tion machinery was set up—a result, according to the Trades
Council minutes, 'entirely in the men's favour'.[4]

The engineering lock-out of 1897–8 is notable, not only as
another defensive craft-union struggle involving technical
change and a strong employers' organization, but also as the
second case where Edinburgh workers were engaged in a
national dispute. Although the dispute began ostensibly with the
London engineers' demand for shorter hours, it quickly developed into a nation-wide lock-out in which the main issue
was 'workshop control and the limits of trade union inter-
ference', especially with regard to manning arrangements on
new types of machine;[5] the settlement guaranteed the employers' right to 'introduce . . . any condition of labour'
previously worked by any member anywhere of the unions

[1] Edin. Cordwainers' Society, *To Messrs. James Allan* (1893).
[2] Edin. Master Boot and Shoemakers' Association, Minutes, 9 Nov. 1896.
[3] Ibid., 12, 21 Nov., 14, 21 Dec. 1896.
[4] Ibid., 22 Feb., 4 Mar. 1897; T.C. Minutes, 9 Mar. 1897. Cf. the figures of
Allan's workers' earnings in 1899, in Tables 4.7–4.9.
[5] *Report on the Strikes and Lock-outs in 1897*, P.P. 1898 LXXXVIII.

party to the negotiations, and 'to appoint the men they consider suitable'.[1] The A.S.E. Edinburgh District reported that
men returned to find labourers at their machines; while a
Trades Council investigation substantiated allegations of vic-
timization of shop stewards, in breach of national agreement.[2]
The lock-out was a serious defeat—although it did not lead to
any catastrophic decline in the engineers' position—and one
made all the more impressive by the reputation of the A.S.E. as
a powerful, if somewhat over-cautious, craft union, and by the
reputation of its members as a working class élite.

Important sections of the skilled labour force were therefore
engaged in large-scale industrial confrontations related to the
impact of technical innovation and the threat to craft conditions and practices. These disputes were also important for
their effect on trade-union opinion outside the bodies directly
involved. The Trades Council held a public meeting about the
Leader affair, while the local socialists produced a leaflet on its
significance—in which they no doubt made much of the paper's
Liberal-Radical and Home Rule political outlook.[3] A committee was established to aid the shoemakers, on the ground that:
'These Employers meant to deal a crushing blow at the Union.'[4]
Demonstrations and street collections were held for the railwaymen and engineers, and also for the shale workers and coal-
miners of the region surrounding the city.[5]

These industrial experiences were an important factor in
changing the outlook of skilled trade unionists. The socialists
provided an interpretation of experience, a language for con-
ceptualizing class relations, that helped to sharpen and broaden
the sense of class-consciousness. The Typographical Society
were 'driven to socialism' by the struggle over linotypes.[6] In
1898, after 'another lively tussle between the . . . old and new
unionism', they mandated their delegate to the Scottish T.U.C.
(himself an S.D.F. member) to move a resolution calling for the

---

[1] Clegg *et al.*, op. cit., p. 167. See Crowley, op. cit., Ch. 15(a), for the dispute's
significance.
[2] A.S.E. *Monthly Journal*, Feb. 1898; T.C. Minutes, 8 Mar. 1898.
[3] Edin. Typographical Society, *Eviction of Trades Unionists; Commonweal*, 31 May
1890. Cf. T.C. Minutes, e.g. 12 Mar., 24 Dec. 1889 for other protests about the use
of police in industrial disputes.   [4] T.C. Minutes, 15 Dec. 1896.
[5] Ibid., 13 Jan. 1891, 4 Sept. 1894, 5 Oct., 1897; *Commonweal*, 10 Sept. 1887.
[6] *Labour Chronicle*, May 1895.

collective ownership of 'the land and the means of production, distribution and exchange'.[1] At the meeting in support of the shale workers in 1887, the socialists criticized the mealy-mouthed line which the Trades Council, 'with the hankering after respectability which usually discredits it', had taken, and went on to hold their own meeting, which declared that it 'refuses to be content with the mere limitation of the robbery of labour, and declares that the abolition of wages-slavery is the real aim of the working-class movement'.[2] At a more practical level, the Trades Council 'had to acknowledge the services of several members of the Independent Labour Party' in collections for the miners five years later.[3] Those union activists who became consciously committed to the struggle for 'the abolition of wages-slavery', rather than to more immediate labourist goals, were, no doubt, a small minority. The importance of the socialist propaganda was rather that it provided an analysis of the changing industrial experience of the artisan—of mechanization, employers' combinations, and more generally, perhaps, of the loss of autonomy at work—and helped to determine his response: a broadening class organization and class-consciousness.[4]

The convergence of socialist analysis with the aspirations and experiences of trade unionists became focused on two issues: the legislative eight-hour day, and the drive for trade-union unity to counter the increasing cohesion and organization of the employers. In 1889 the Typographical Society and the joiners' branch both voted for the legislative eight-hour day; the Press and Machinemen's Society were also on record as supporters of the measure by 1895.[5] Table 9.1, based on mandating of Trades Council T.U.C. delegates, shows that supporters of the measure include delegates of the building trades, some engineering trades, glass-cutters, and miners, while opponents include the craft-workshop trades of shoemaking and cabinet-making, the 'élitist' engineers and the ironmoulders. The ironmoulders,

---

[1] *Scottish Typographical Circular*, June 1898.   [2] *Commonweal*, 10 Sept. 1887.
[3] T.C. Minutes, 11 Sept. 1894.
[4] Cf. E. J. Hobsbawm, 'Trade Union History', *Economic History Review*, 2nd ser., 20 (1967).
[5] *Scottish Typographical Circular*, June 1889; T.C. Minutes, 7 May 1889; *Labour Chronicle*, April 1895.

who long held that an eight-hour day was impractical in foundry work, finally swung round in 1899, when they decided to support only parliamentary candidates pledged to the eight-hour day.[1] The Trades Council decided in favour of the measure in 1887, against in 1890, and thereafter more consistently in favour; in 1893 they took the possibly more radical step of co-operating with the socialists in a May Day demonstration.[2] Although we cannot generally tell to what extent delegates were mandated by their branches the alignments are none the less of some interest.

The role of employers' organizations at this period has already been mentioned. The defeat of the engineers, in particular, drove home the lesson. A letter to the *Typographical Circular* shortly after the end of the lock-out argued: 'Employers are everywhere federating that they may annihilate trade unionism.'[3] And the editorial of the following edition drew the conclusion that: 'It is unnecessary to repeat arguments in favour of federation at the present time. Every workman in the country had convincing proof of its necessity in the great industrial struggle of 1897 . . . If such struggles are to be prevented in the future, it will only be by an organisation which shall be able to preserve the balance of power and restore the status quo ante.'[4] The *Clarion* scheme for trade federation had a wide

TABLE 9.1
*Movers and Opposers of Legislative Eight-Hour Day
at Edinburgh Trades Council, 1887–1893*

Movers	Opponents
Masons, joiners, slaters, pattern-makers, tinplate workers*, glass-cutters*, blind workers†, miners†	Painters, engineers, ironmoulders*, shoemakers, tailors, cabinet-makers, railwaymen

Source: Trades Council Minutes, meetings to mandate T.U.C. delegates (generally in August).

Notes: Each delegate is counted only once, regardless of the number of separate occasions on which he moved or opposed the measure.

* Delegates with a record of activity in socialist organizations (the ironmoulders' delegate was presumably mandated by his branch against his personal views).

† An association of inmates of the local Blind Asylum was represented on the Council, as were the miners of the nearby Lothians coalfield.

[1] T.C. Minutes, 5 Sept. 1899.
[2] Ibid., 16 Aug. 1887, 12 Aug. 1890, 28 Mar. 1893.
[3] *Scottish Typographical Circular*, May 1898.   [4] Ibid., June 1898.

appeal as a defensive measure, just as the threats of depression and technological unemployment, and the failure of strong craft unions (in Edinburgh the masons and joiners) to obtain shorter hours, made trade unionists receptive to the socialist agitation for a legislative eight-hour day. The Trades Council participitated in a meeting with the local I.L.P. to discuss the *Clarion* scheme;[1] the scheme was moved at the 1898 T.U.C. by the Edinburgh Typographical Society, and a year later a branch meeting of the bookbinders voted unanimously in its favour.[2] This part of the socialist line seems to have appealed to moderate, as much as to militant opinion. 'What is wanted is not strikes, but what will tend to prevent them,' the *Typographical Circular* argued in support of the *Clarion* scheme.[3] This tendency was no doubt accentuated by the scepticism of many socialists (especially adherents of Hyndman's version of Marxism) as to the possible effectiveness of trade unions. *Justice* looked forward to a turn by the railwaymen to political organization for the eight-hour day should their strike fail, and later applauded the 'common sense' of the men in accepting the employers' terms.[4] And the *Labour Chronicle* commented that: 'Trades Unionists are beginning to see what Socialists have been preaching for years—that the strike is an obsolete weapon, and that the workers must use their political power to work out their social salvation.'[5]

The political activity of socialists was thus an important factor affecting workers' responses to their industrial experience. One distinctive feature of the early socialist movement was the great stress on propaganda, on trying to diffuse the socialist analysis and the critique of existing institutions (including those of the labour movement) by such direct means as open-air meetings.[6] Another aspect was the attempt to gain representation in local government on an independent basis (whether under a 'socialist' or 'labour' label), to attack the political monopoly of the existing parties and develop pressure for a local 'working-

---

[1] T.C. Minutes, 23 Mar. 1897.
[2] *Scottish Typographical Circular*, Aug. 1898; Bookbinders' Consolidated Union, Minutes, 6 Oct. 1899.   [3] *Scottish Typographical Circular*, June 1898.
[4] *Justice*, 3 Jan., 7 Feb. 1891.   [5] *Labour Chronicle*, Apr. 1895.
[6] For propaganda activities by the S.D.F., Socialist League, and I.L.P. see the columns of *Justice* and *Commonweal*, and Edin. Branch, I.L.P. Minutes.

class programme' of reforms within the scope of local authority bodies (including School Boards, as well as municipalities). This often involved the formation of electoral coalitions, around a local programme (generally a watered-down one), with such bodies as the Trades Council. These types of activity were not, of course, necessarily mutually exclusive. Thus the Socialist League decided that its members could join the I.L.P. as individuals, 'but . . . the work of the League was education in Socialist principles';[1] and there was in fact a considerable overlap in the membership of the socialist organizations, at least in the early 1890s.[2]

Just as it was the changing experience of skilled labour, rather than the organization of the unskilled, that explained trade-union interest in the reforms advocated by socialists, so the socialists themselves consisted predominantly, though not exclusively, of artisans. According to a report in *Commonweal*, half of the fifty-two members of the Socialist League were 'artisans', nine were students, and the remainder were 'clerks, warehousemen, artists and one woman'.[3] 'In Edinburgh, which is the most bourgeois town perhaps in Britain, we are able to get our halls filled Sunday after Sunday by the very best class of work-

---

[1] *Commonweal*, 11 May 1889.

[2] *Commonweal*, 11 May 1889. The socialist organizations have a complicated history of secession and unification. The following outline is based mainly on the columns of *Justice*, *Commonweal*, and the *Labour Chronicle*, and on Greaves, *James Connolly*. The Scottish Land and Labour League, formed sometime in the early 1880s was clearly socialist-inclined, and became in effect the local branch of the S.D.F., then of the Socialist League formed (Dec. 1884) by William Morris and other dissident seceders from the S.D.F.; an S.D.F. branch seems to have been reformed in 1886 or 1887. In practice locally the split meant little, and the two organizations worked together. There was also a rather shadowy body called the Scottish Socialist Federation (c. 1889–94) which seems to have been a united front, or possibly an amalgamation, of the S.D.F. and Socialist League branches. Keir Hardie's Scottish Labour Party was regarded as the counterpart of the English I.L.P., but had been formed some years earlier. The Party branch established in Edinburgh in 1892 was strictly speaking a branch of the Scottish L.P., and was variously referred to as the Scottish L.P., (Scottish) I.L.P., I.L.P., etc. For clarity I refer throughout to the S.D.F., Socialist League, and I.L.P. to mean the local bodies which functioned as branches or affiliates of those organizations. The I.L.P. branches, of course, survived to the end of the century and beyond. Of publications cited in this chapter, *Justice* was the paper of the S.D.F., *Commonweal* of the Socialist League, *Clarion* was independent but linked to the I.L.P., and *Labour Chronicle* was a local joint venture of all the bodies mentioned.

[3] *Commonweal*, Feb. 1885.

men.'[1] The printing of leaflets for the Edinburgh S.D.F. was
'done by a comrade with the aid of a small printing press (his
own property) and during his leisure hours as a labour of love';
in the municipal elections of 1896, the committee rooms were
renovated by 'craftsmen of all kinds', and building work needed
to convert the S.D.F.'s new premises was all done by branch
members.[2] The tiny handful of working-class socialist activists
who can be identified include two printers, two bookbinders,
two masons, two engineers, and twelve other skilled workers;
the three unskilled men include James Connolly and his
brother (both carters) and the secretary of Leith dockers.[3]
Although this suggests a preponderantly artisan membership,
we should not ignore the significance of unskilled participation;
no case was found of an unskilled worker playing a role, as
important as that of Connolly in socialist politics, in the Reform
movement of the 1860s or the Radical-Liberal politics it
inaugurated.[4]

The evidence cited above does, however, suggest that the
socialist groups may be regarded, from one point of view, as
belonging to the milieu of the artisan stratum. And like other
institutions of that milieu they were marked by a certain degree
of participation by middle-class individuals. A university
Socialist Society was founded in 1884 and invited Morris to the
city, where his lecture on 'Useful Work versus Useless Toil' was
supported by 'the proletariat in the gallery'.[5] The Society also
produced a pamphlet, *Beauty for Ashes*, which appears to reflect
the influence of Morris.[6] The size and precise composition of
the middle-class elements, is, however, obscure, as is the extent
to which they gravitated to such separate bodies as the Fabians.

Both for artisans, and for the middle-class people to whom
socialism made some appeal, the movement has to be seen in

---

[1] *Commonweal*, 26 Feb. 1887.

[2] *Justice*, 1 Sept. 1888, 14 Nov. 1896, 31 July 1897.

[3] References to committee members, speakers, candidates, etc. in *Justice,
Commonweal, Clarion*, and I.L.P. Minutes; Leith was included in so far as Leith
branches were not separate. Delegates' trades in T.C. *Annual Reports* were the main
source of occupational information; although this may mean a bias to skilled trades,
one would expect delegates of the unskilled 'new unions' to be socialist activists
were there significant participation by unskilled workers.

[4] See Greaves, op. cit., pp. 35–7 for Connolly's considerable role in Edin.
socialism.   [5] *Commonweal*, Feb. 1885; *Justice*, 29 Mar. 1884.

[6] Excerpt in *Scottish Typographical Circular*, Nov. 1884.

relation to a wider cultural rebellion. This included a self-conscious rejection of such catchwords as 'respectability' which were seen by the socialists, in theory at least, as part of a system of oppressive and mystifying norms and values: 'Edinburgh is indeed afflicted with a bowing of the knee to unworthy gods. The clergy obtain a ridiculous amount of respect, as do also savants with the academic hall-mark; but Mrs. Grundy claims the most devoted and the largest number of worshippers.'[1] The earlier analysis of the values of the mid-Victorian artisan stratum[2] suggests that this kind of cultural rebellion had implications, not only for the more 'bohemian' fringes of the middle class, but also for artisans. And it is certainly true that the socialist movement of the 1880s and 1890s formed a minority sub-culture within the working class, and thus played a pervasive part in its members' lives.[3] At a meeting of the Socialist League: 'Part of the evening was spent in discussing subjects of deep interest to Socialists, methods of propaganda, etc. Singing of revolutionary songs, as well as Scotch ones, helped also to pass the time pleasantly.'[4] The continuing popularity of Burns—in the context, no doubt, of a somewhat different interpretation—was one point of continuity with the mid-Victorian culture of artisan 'respectability'; the League had meetings on 'Socialism in Scottish Song' and the 'Politics of Burns'.[5] At an early meeting of the I.L.P. branch, 'The meeting then became free and easy, and after a song by the Chairman, several . . . songs were sung by members of the Branch.'[6]

The appeal of socialism to artisans must also be seen in the context of the movement's early development from the radical anti-aristocratic and republican ideology of an earlier period of working-class politics. One prominent I.L.P. member, Thomas Blaikie (an ironmoulder by trade) was Treasurer of the Trades Council in 1871, Vice-President in 1882, 'veteran of a hundred agitations, a veteran trade unionist, a land nationaliser, and now, still in the van, a Socialist and member of the I.L.P.'[7] We

---

[1] *Labour Chronicle*, Oct. 1894.   [2] See above, Chs. 5–7.
[3] Cf. D. Cox, 'The Labour Party in Leicester', *International Review of Social History* 14 (1969); S. Yeo, 'A Phase in the Social History of Socialism', *Society for the Study of Labour History Bulletin*, 22 (Spring 1971).   [4] *Commonweal*, 7 Apr. 1888.
[5] Ibid., 21 Jan. 1888, 25 Jan. 1890.   [6] I.L.P. Minutes, 26 Nov. 1892.
[7] *Clarion*, 8 Sept. 1894.

shall never know precisely how many men made this transition from the land question to socialism. It may have been a largely generational matter; for people formed in the reform and Radical-Liberal movements of the 1860s and 1870s anti-landlordism might be the end of their politics, while for younger people it might be only the beginning. Robert Banner, an Edinburgh bookbinder, was aged twelve at the time of the Reform Bill, became active in the land and republican agitations of the seventies, then in the S.D.F., before moving to London where he was a member of the dissident group that left the S.D.F. to found the Socialist League.[1] The land question may also have been the main bridge between the politically conscious artisan and the poorer sections of the working class—especially the Irish. During the crofters' trial in 1888 the police were overawed by large demonstrations outside the court.[2] James Connolly worked consistently to unify the national consciousness of the Irish poor with the class-consciousness of British workers:

Perhaps they will realise that the Irish worker who starves in an Irish cabin, and the Scotch worker who is poisoned in an Edinburgh garret, are also brothers with one hope and one destiny. Perhaps they will also observe how the Liberal Government which supplies police to Irish landlords to aid them in their work of exterminating their Irish peasantry, also imports police into Scotland to aid Scotch mineowners in their work of starving the Scottish miners. Perhaps they will begin to understand that the Liberals and Tories are not two parties, but rather two sections of one party—the party of property.[3]

There is, however, little evidence that the socialists succeeded in integrating the Irish and their community organizations within a common movement, despite the importance of the land question in the 1880s and the efforts of Connolly in the nineties.

The convergence that did occur was with sections of the industrially and politically organized skilled working class, rather than with the Irish poor. One aspect of this, which has already been examined, is the appeal of a socialist vocabulary

---

[1] Biographical sketch in *Bookbinding Trades Journal* (1904).
[2] *Justice*, 28 Jan. 1888.   [3] *Labour Chronicle*, Nov. 1894.

as a way of understanding the industrial developments of the period, and, at a more practical level, of the measures advocated by the socialist current within the unions. It also had a political expression. The attempt to break the hold of the existing parties on local and parliamentary representation is associated especially with the formation and early activity of the I.L.P.; the most distinctive feature of the party was its broad and eclectic ideological basis—though most of its members were undoubtedly socialists in some sense of the term—and its concentration on the immediate aim of creating a separate workers' party. A number of candidates stood for local bodies during the nineties, under a variety of auspices—there was considerable electoral co-operation between the I.L.P. and the S.D.F. at this time—and some of them received an appreciable share of the vote, though no seats on the Town Council were won.[1] The most notable success was not on the Town Council, but on the School Board, to which Alex Dickinson was elected on an Independent Labour platform—a success made all the more gratifying by the fact that the Trades Council decided at the last moment to contest the election on a 'Lib-Lab' basis, specifically to prevent Dickinson's election, and lost.[2] The Trades Council had long pursued a policy of 'Lib-Lab' local representation, with some measure of success.[3] The mid-1890s seem to be a critical period in this respect, with a definite shift towards co-operation with the socialists, on an 'independent labour' basis. This shift may well reflect the industrial experiences of these years, and the role of the socialists in providing a programme with which to respond to them; turnover in the personnel of the Council itself may also be important. At any rate, the later 1890s saw distinctly more cordial relations with the socialists; the Council co-operated with the I.L.P. over the *Clarion* trade-federation scheme and with the S.D.F. over the eight-hour day for municipal employees.[4] Finally, it was agreed to set up a Workers' Municipal Committee, in readiness for a 'municipal general election' due in 1900 as a result of local

---

[1] See Marwick, 'Municipal Politics in Victorian Edinburgh'.

[2] *Clarion*, 10 Mar., 7 Apr. 1894. The fact that School Board elections were city-wide and that several candidates were elected no doubt made it easier for a new party to break in by concentrated use of its voting power.

[3] Marwick, op. cit.   [4] T.C. Minutes, 23 Mar., 7 Sept. 1897.

government reorganization.[1] The constitution of this body antici-
pated in the local context the structure of the national Labour
Representation Committee, providing for affiliation of political
bodies, trade-union branches, co-operative societies, etc., for
the purpose of creating a bloc of labour representatives; a substantial number of union branches, as well as the I.L.P. and
S.D.F., had affiliated within a year.[2] Three candidates were
elected to the School Board (including Thomas Blaikie, another
I.L.P.-er, and the cabinet-makers' delegate) and in the municipal election of 1900 the first Labour Councillor was elected
for Dalry ward.[3]

The significance of this electoral activity—both before and
after the establishment of the Workers' Municipal Committee—
lies as much in the emergence of a distinct 'workers' programme',
a separate labour presence in local politics, as in the success or
failure of socialist or Labour candidates. Alex Dickinson on the
School Board, for example, opposed repressive measures to deal
with truancy, urging that the educational system should instead
be adapted to make the experience of the working-class child a
relevant and attractive one, and exposed the 'educational injustice that is done to the working classes' through inadequate
accommodation and staffing;[4] a crowd of 2,000 attended his
funeral when he died only a year and a half after his election.[5]
In 1893 the I.L.P. adopted a municipal programme of temperance reform, the fair-wages clause, municipal coal depots,
the eight-hour day for municipal employees, public housing at
low rents, and curbs on expenditure on visits by royalty;[6] the
Workers' Municipal Committee in 1900 called for fuller use of
local powers under housing legislation, rehousing of tenants of
demolished property, enforcement of the fair-wages clause, etc.[7]

There are a number of senses in which the Labour Party—
the characteristic political expression of the labourist working-
class movement—can be seen as showing a basic continuity
with the radical and 'Lib-Lab' traditions of the Victorian

---

[1] Ibid., 24 Jan. 1899.
[2] Constitution, balance sheet for 1899, in Edin. and Leith Workers' Municipal
Committee, Minutes.   [3] Ibid., 21 Jan. 1900; Marwick, op. cit.
[4] *Labour Chronicle*, Jan., Feb. 1895.   [5] *Justice*, 14 Dec. 1895.
[6] I.L.P. Minutes, 11 Sept. 1893.
[7] Manifesto (1900), in Workers' Municipal Committee Minutes.

artisan stratum. Certainly the coincidence of shifts in attitudes among politically active workers and among sections of the central political and intellectual élites, together with the 'acculturation' of Labour representatives by parliamentary institutions, made possible the construction of a new liberal-reformist political bloc—a bloc characterized by a commitment to welfare legislation, in which the working class would, however, continue to play a subordinate role.[1] But at grass-roots level the dynamic of the labourist coalition came from the socialists, especially from the I.L.P., rather than from the trade-union leaderships which provided the money—and often the candidates as well. It was only because a socialist language—in however diffuse a form—provided a meaningful interpretation of their class experience, and changed the consciousness of class that working people felt the need to create their own political party. For one characteristic of 'Lib-Labism' was the tendency to make the return of working men to representative bodies an end in itself—the relationship of this to the status aspirations of the mid-Victorian labour aristocracy is clear enough. The distinctive feature of the type of labourism that emerged by the end of the century was, however, the attempt to mobilize and unify all manual workers around a programme of reforms in their perceived class interest. The typical demand of the 1870s was for the removal of 'class legislation' held to infringe the worker's rights as a citizen, that of the nineties was for the implementation in his interest of new legislative measures. There was, then, a definite change in the form of class-consciousness and in political ideology, associated with the changing life and culture of the manual working class. This change has far-reaching implications for the role of the upper stratum of the working class, who became more clearly committed to mobilizing support from a broad class movement.

---

[1] Cf. J. Hinton, 'The Beginnings of Modern British Politics', *Society for the Study of Labour History Bulletin* 24 (Spring 1972).

IO   The Labour
       Aristocracy and Reformism

In the third quarter of the nineteenth century the formation of
a labour aristocracy had a twofold significance. The upper
stratum created relatively autonomous class institutions and
had a distinctive cultural life, articulating a sense of class
identity. The typical aspirations of the 'superior artisan' were
for improvement in the position of his social group, and recognition of its corporate claim to moral and political equality,
rather than for purely personal advancement—were this not
the case, indeed, we would be able to speak only of a common
class situation, rather than of the cultural and political formation of a separate stratum. On the other hand, the aspirations
of the stratum were often enough expressed in a language
'adopted' from the dominant class, so that the institutions and
modes of behaviour of the artisan world were contained within
a larger local society dominated by the 'hegemonic' bourgeoisie.
Such values as 'respectability', 'independence', 'thrift', were
mediated by the institutions of the artisan world, their meanings
to some extent translated and adapted to the conditions of the
would-be 'respectable' working man. And the democratic aspirations of the popular-radical tradition were, after 1867,
effectively contained—despite certain important tensions—
within a Liberal movement dominated nationally by middle-
class and aristocratic élites.

    This containment of working-class aspirations and institutions
was, however, a complex process—certainly not readily explicable by any 'conspiracy theory' of the indoctrination of the
working class. It is rather to be understood in terms of the
essentially incoherent and fragmented character of ideology. A
complex set of political and cultural processes—some, but not
all, of which were the result of purposive activity by a middle-
class group—inhibited the generalization of the more 'sub-
versive' elements in the class experience and outlook of working
people. These processes—which Gramsci referred to as the

'contrast between thought and action'[1]—might operate in two directions. On the one hand, people might legitimate, suppress, or reinterpret their awareness of activities and situations problematic to the formal ideology to which they were, in other social contexts, committed. The practices of solidarity and mutual aid which were a necessary part of the artisan's protective response to his environment might coexist with individualism, 'home-centredness', and cultural exclusiveness. In this way dominant values are adapted to the situation of the subordinate class, to create what Parkin calls a 'negotiated version' of the ruling ideology.[2] Equally important to 'accommodative' attitudes in the subordinate class, however, is the 'negotiated version' of more radical and dissident values. A conscious desire to create a radically different society might, in practical terms, lead only to courses of action readily contained by minor adaptations of the established order. Thus the stress on financial viability in such bodies as co-operative associations made them—regardless of the ideology of their founders—into organizations catering for the more prosperous strata of the working class and institutionalizing the values of thrifty and provident conduct. The sectional character and conciliationist postures of many unions imply a similarly accommodative and protective response to the exigencies of survival within capitalist society.

The emergence of new patterns of class formation has to be seen in relation to this complexity and ambivalence of the world view of the Victorian skilled worker. It is important here to see ideology, as Gramsci did, as having two levels: the meanings attached to particular aspects of social experience; and the systems of 'formal ideology' within which those meanings are partly, but never totally, 'rationalized' and integrated.[3] At the level of formal ideology, there is a Utopian strand of thought, a hope for total emancipation from competitive capitalism. The *North Briton* in 1861 expressed the hope that there would 'eventually rise that grand system of cooperation which will render men individually independent of capital . . .' and in 1864 even published Owenite articles on 'Social Economy'.[4]

---

[1] Gramsci, *Prison Notebooks*, p. 327.
[2] Parkin, *Class Inequality and Political Order*, p. 92.
[3] Gramsci, op. cit., pp. 325 ff.
[4] *North Briton*, 25 Mar. 1861, 5, 12 Oct. 1864.

At the level of day-to-day behaviour and meaning-systems, the experience of class solidarity implied modes of conduct at variance with the dominant ideology. A writer in the *Labour Chronicle* saw socialism as a new, and more valid, interpretation of experiences and aspirations that had hitherto been expressed within the framework of a false consciousness: 'Lured on by such catch phrases as "equality before the law" and "political equality", men seek to extend the bounds of their freedom. In course of time, however, it is seen . . . that there can be no all-embracing freedom apart from substantial equality in social condition . . . Men then organise themselves for the conscious winning of this goal.'[1]

The emergence of the new labourist class organization and consciousness of the 1890s must be explained in terms of the complex relation between class structure, class action, and ideology. It was because labourist and socialist ideas seemed to offer a more meaningful interpretation of their situation that working people sought to build broader industrial and political institutions. This implies a shift in the outlook and role of the aristocracy of labour. The upper stratum came to form a political, social, and cultural élite within a wider working-class movement and community. In a sense this role of leadership can be seen as deriving from the feeling of superiority of the mid-Victorian 'superior artisan'. For example, the pretensions of the middle-class Central Benevolent Association were criticized on the ground that: 'The working men, who are the nearest to the "lapsed classes" in physical and social proximity, and therefore know all their bad habits, and how to cure and prevent them, and have also the deepest interest in the work for their wives' and children's sake, should not have been slighted so'[2] In this context, the rise of labourism can perhaps be seen as paralleling, at the social level of the upper working class, shifts in middle-class reform ideology. There was, as Stedman Jones notes, a change from purely individualistic moralism, to emphasis on the need for reforms which would create the structural preconditions of 'moral' conduct among a wider section of the population.[3] It would, however, be quite wrong to see

[1] *Labour Chronicle*, Oct. 1894.   [2] *North Briton*, 11 Apr. 1868.
[3] Stedman Jones, *Outcast London*, pp. 285–6.

the emergence of socialism and labourism *solely* in these terms; there was a more basic change in perceptions of the social order and subjective definitions of class identity and interest.

This role of the labour aristocracy within the working class is analytically quite distinct from the phenomenon of professionalized leadership in the labour movement, with which it is sometimes confused.[1] Whereas the aristocrat of labour makes his living by manual labour—even if he is marked off by material advantages and a different style of life—the 'professional' leader belongs to 'a group of persons permanently and directly engaged in the service of the collectivity', consisting of party and union officials, parliamentarians, journalists, etc.[2] Men employed in this way move in a bureaucratic or political world different from that of manual labour, enjoy a higher and more secure income, and develop a different life-style; as a consequence, they may come to see the problems of the labour movement in a perspective different from that of the manual workers who compose its membership. Like the theory of labour aristocracy, that of the 'corruption' of labour leaders is often offered as an explanation of the limited character of working-class opposition to capitalist society. An acceleration of the growth in numbers of M.P.s, officials, journalists, etc., recruited from the working class was certainly among the consequences of the trend to labourism in the late nineteenth and early twentieth centuries. How, then, is this phenomenon related to that of the labour aristocracy, and to what extent can it provide an alternative, or complementary, explanation of the reformist moderation of British labour? The classic statement of the thesis of the conservative influence of labour leaders is that of Michels.[3] He argues that pressures of *embourgeoisement* erode any commitment to transforming society; the leader becomes an 'intermediary', a professional expert.[4] Such processes are undeniably visible in the history of the labour movement. But any real explanation must take account also of the wider historical conditions in which these processes operate; and these conditions relate to the structures of the working class and of society as a whole, not simply to the position of labour leaders. The relevant factors

---

[1] Hobsbawm, e.g., brackets 'the professional labour movement of politicians, union officials', etc. with the upper artisan stratum: *Labouring Men*, p. 324.
[2] Michels, *Political Parties*, p. 276.   [3] Ibid., *passim*.   [4] Ibid., p. 299.

include: the room for manoeuvre in bargaining over concessions (whether in terms of wages or of welfare legislation); the readiness of the membership to *accept* compromises arrived at in this way, their reluctance to formulate more ambitious demands, etc.; and the influence on both leaders *and members* of hegemonic ideas and values, in the absence of a strong articulated 'counter-ideology'.[1] The tendency for leaders to become a conservative force is related to particular conditions of existence of the working class itself (including the ideological, as well as material, environment), rather than to 'iron laws' of large-scale organization. The conditions mentioned were especially marked in the second half of the nineteenth century; the formation of the labour aristocracy was partly a product of these same conditions. The moderate and accommodative outlook of labour leaders was deeply rooted in the aristocratic stratum of the working class.

The labour aristocracy thus implanted accommodative responses to capitalism, and subsequently transmitted them to a broader class movement. Their role in this context is distinguished from that of the 'professional' leaders by its 'voluntary' character, as union and party activists, municipal representatives, etc. These were the *objective consequences*, within a wider political structure, of the local activities of the aristocracy of labour—consequences not necessarily the direct outcome of conscious intention. The importance of the labour aristocracy, in this objective sense, is to be seen in the development of two sets of links with groups outside the manual working class. Locally, the upper working-class stratum channelled the activities and aspirations of the working class *vis a vis* the middle-class élites of the local community; the earlier account of social and political alignments in Victorian Edinburgh indicates the importance of this activity (see especially Chapters 7 and 8 above). In addition, the aristocracy of labour formed a link between professionalized labour leaderships—and even political élites generally—and particular working-class institutions, communities, and subcultures. Party structures, of course, articulate such links, and local activists are of key importance.

---

[1] Cf. R. Hyman, *Marxism and the Sociology of Trade Unionism* (1971), pp. 26–33; Parkin, op. cit., p. 133.

It is *precisely because their conditions of life remained those of manual labour* that the aristocracy of labour could form a link of this type. And their own voluntary participation in local affairs may, at the same time, have made them receptive to an 'accommodative' viewpoint. These comments must remain rather speculative, since they look beyond the scope of the present study, to the growth of the Labour Party in the twentieth century, and its relation to local working-class communities. It is none the less necessary to make some attempt to sketch in—however roughly—the broader historical context of the analysis.

The labour aristocracy, then, mediated accommodative responses to capitalist society. In the first place, this may have arisen simply from the fact that only the upper strata of the working class were able to create viable protective institutions, to arrive at a *modus vivendi* with the capitalist order, at a time when that order appeared to have become firmly consolidated. As the power and scope of these organizations increased, the ideologies and traditions of collective action of the labour aristocracy affected the class formation of broader working-class strata. However, as the earlier comments on the nature of ideology and class-consciousness would suggest, the 'accommodative' response coexisted problematically with other tendencies. It is, for example, hard to assess from the existing evidence the likelihood of a convergence of the political radicalism of the artisan with that of the Irish poor, around the land and republican agitation and the early socialist movement.[1] But the possibility was there. None the less the dominant tendency remained the accommodative and reformist one. The convergence that occurred was with the changing class-consciousness of artisans, engaged in defensive industrial struggles. Its characteristic expression, both nationally and locally, was not a mass socialist party similar to German Social Democracy, but an *ad hoc* committee with no defined programme beyond one of immediate reforms and the creation of a bloc of Labour representatives. Socialism was transmuted into labourism—a programme of gradualist reforms, combined with a

---

[1] A closer study of the institutions and attitudes of the Irish community would help to answer this question.

diffuse moralistic critique of competitive capitalism, and an equally diffuse egalitarian and class-conscious rhetoric. These tendencies—associated especially with the I.L.P.—show a certain continuity with the ideology of many spokesmen for the mid-Victorian labour movement; the transition to a form of socialism did not mean too radical a break with earlier traditions of labour ideology.[1]

The accommodation of the British working class to capitalist society was, however, a *negotiated* one—and subject, moreover, to constant renegotiation. This is of key importance in understanding the class outlook of manual workers, and especially of the upper stratum. The process of negotiation presupposes strong and autonomous protective class institutions. The defence of those institutions—however it may have been overlaid at some periods with a rhetoric of 'self help' borrowed from the dominant class—was a distinctive feature of the class-consciousness of the artisan. Associated with this was a strong sense of class pride and an ethic of class solidarity. This class identity was transmitted in the later nineteenth century to a wider class movement and culture—it is not the least of the legacies of the Victorian labour aristocracy.[2]

This study has been concerned to trace these processes in one city. It may therefore be appropriate to conclude with the customary plea for further research, which in this case has a substantive relevance to what has gone before. For if the book has shown anything at all it must surely be the crucial importance—especially in the far more localized society of the nineteenth century—of the specific economic, social, and political structures of the city. The conclusions drawn can therefore refer only to the local case; the problems raised must be investigated in a range of other local settings. Only when we have some comparative account of class structure and class formation in a range of localities can we begin to write working-class history as the history of any class must be written—by beginning from the life situation, the hopes and fears of the members of the class.

---

[1] As Crowley argues: 'The Revolt of the British Labour Movement from Liberalism' (Ph.D. thesis), abstract. And see also the characterization of I.L.P. socialism by F. Reid in *Society for the Study of Labour History Bulletin* 16 (Spring 1968).

[2] See Hobsbawm, op. cit., p. 323.

APPENDIX I

The Interpretation of
Census Occupation Tables

THE difficulties attaching to Victorian censuses make it impossible
to arrive at precise measures of the occupational or class structure
at any particular census, still less of changes between censuses. The
objective of the procedures adopted is the more modest one of at least
reducing distortions, and making the censuses *more* comparable *with
each other* than they otherwise would be. The resultant figures are
clues to the shape of the occupational structure, rather than precise
quantitative statements. It is not, for example, possible to assimilate
census categories to the occupational classification discussed in
Appendix II.

Only the censuses of 1841, 1861, and 1881–1901 are suitable: the
1851 occupational tables combine Edinburgh and Leith, and the
1871 census gives detailed tables only by county. My own tables
based on the censuses (Tables 2.3, 2.4, and 2.5) include figures for
various broadly defined middle-class sectors of employment, for
domestic service, and for industrial occupations. I have used Booth's
scheme, as presented by Armstrong, to reconstruct five important
industrial groups in part A of Table 2.4;[1] part B of Table 2.4 includes all occupations not included in part A with 100 or more in
1881, many of these being combined for purposes of analysis.
(Where this has been done the classification is my own.)

A number of points demand more detailed discussion: changes in
the boundaries to which the tables refer; the definition of occupied
population, on which the whole analysis of occupational structure
rests; the occupational designations used in my tables, where these
are not obvious abbreviations of categories in the census as published; estimation procedures used to disentangle certain occupations
which are combined in some censuses but not others, and to distinguish 'makers' from 'dealers', etc. For the sake of clarity, occupational designations taken from the census as published (or obvious
abbreviations of them) are placed in quotation marks, whereas my

---

[1] Armstrong, in Wrigley (ed.), *Nineteenth Century Society.*

own designations, as used in my tables, are italicized. Where reference is made to the 'orders' and 'sub-orders' of the census these are
cited by roman numerals (orders) with arabic suffixes (sub-orders).

Boundaries[1]

The tables for 1841 are for 'Edinburgh City and suburbs', and
cover an area (probably based on Registration Districts) with a total
population 283 greater than that of the Parliamentary Burgh; the
1861 tables are stated to be for Edinburgh Registration District,
covering a total population 2,323 greater than that of the Parliamentary Burgh. The 1881 and 1891 tables are for the Parliamentary
Burgh, and those of 1901 for the Municipality with a population
18,724 greater than that of the Parliamentary Burgh. The last of
these changes is by far the most serious. There were, however, extensions of the parliamentary boundaries during the eighties, so that
no two censuses refer to precisely the same boundaries. The 1881
parliamentary boundaries included most of the then built-up area;
in 1891 they had been extended slightly, following the expansion of
the built-up area, to include more of the middle-class suburb of
Newington, and part of the industrial and working-class area newly
growing up in Gorgie–Dalry. The municipal extensions of 1896,
1900, and 1901 took in parts of Liberton and Duddingston, the
former Burgh of Portobello, all of Granton, the Gorgie area as far as
Saughton, and other large areas to the West. The inclusion of these
areas probably had an appreciable effect on the occupational distribution, but one is reduced to informed guessing as to the likely
direction of that effect; on balance, it probably added disporpor-
tionately to the middle-class suburban population. Little can be
done about the problem of boundary changes, beyond drawing
attention to its existence.

Occupied Population

In 1841, the unoccupied population are grouped together at the
end of the tables and a figure for occupied population can be easily
calculated; there appear to be no 'unoccupied' groups lurking elsewhere in the tables, as there are at most subsequent censuses. In
1861 dependent relatives, property owners, pensioners, etc., are
scattered throughout the tables, as are the wives of shoemakers,
farmers, and sundry other occupations; these were all picked out
and subtracted from total population. Subsequent censuses are more

---

[1] The following sources were consulted: street maps in *Post Office Directories;
Encyclopaedia Britannica* (11th edn.), entry on 'Edinburgh' (lists areas incorporated
in extensions of 1896, 1900, and 1901).

conveniently arranged, but nevertheless present some difficulties. Orders XXIV and XXV in 1881 and 1891 and XXIII in 1901, comprising 'persons returned by property, rank etc.,' unoccupied children, schoolchildren, etc., were subtracted from total population to arrive at a figure for total occupied population; in 1881 'legislator' and 'army and navy pensioner' are listed separately and these were added to the orders mentioned. In 1901 'students' are placed in the unoccupied group; as I had not previously treated students as unoccupied (though they do not appear among the occupations analysed in any of my tables) it was necessary to adjust for this, by reducing order XXIII in 1901, according to the ratio of students to unoccupied population in 1891.

Occupational Categories: Non-industrial Occupations (Table 2.3)

Administration: order I, except 'legislator' (1881). *Church, law, medicine*: professional practitioners only (ancillary employees are included under *other services*, etc.). *Teaching*: order III.4. *Other services, etc.*: order III. 5–8, and also professional ancillaries (missionaries, law clerks, nurses, etc.). *Commerce*: order V. *Domestic service*: order IV.

Occupational Categories: Industrial Occupations (Table 2.4)

The analysis of industrial occupations presents many problems of comparability, to which there is no hard-and-fast solution. No two censuses are precisely the same, but those of 1841 and 1901 are least like the others. The 1841 tables include many more separate occupations, presented in an alphabetically ordered, but analytically random, list; many of the designations differ from those of later censuses. It is, however, generally quite clear which are the comparable designations at later censuses, and it is not worth entering a detailed discussion of this point. (In many cases the 1841 occupations must evidently be aggregated to achieve comparability.) In 1901 dealers in some occupations are distinguished for the first time. There may thus be distortions due to the fact that these dealers are excluded, whereas they had previously been indistinguishable (it is not always clear under what designation such dealers were included in previous censuses, so that estimation is not feasible). If included these categories would increase the engineering group by 0·08 per cent and the clothing group by 0·24 per cent.

The industrial groups in part A of Table 2.4 are based on the following sections of Armstrong's classification:[1] *printing*: manufac-

---

[1] Armstrong, op. cit., pp. 284–93.

ture, 30; *building*: building, 2; *engineering and metals*: manufacture, 1, 4, 5; *clothing*: manufacture, 22; *transport*: transport, 4, 5. But designations definitely referring mainly to employers or managers are excluded from all these groups (e.g. 'builder', as opposed to the specific manual occupations in building). The only other divergences from Armstrong are that 'paper ruler' is placed in *printing*, not papermaking, since ruling was closely allied to the commercial branch of binding; and *messenger, porter* is placed in *transport*, together with rail and road transport, whereas Armstrong places it with dock transport, which is not included in Table 2.4.

Other printing, other building, other engineering, other clothing: indicate all occupations not separately listed placed by Armstrong in these industrial groups. Some of the other occupational designations demand explanation, and are disscused below in the order in which they are given in Table 2.4, together with any special problems.

Bookbinder: in 1841 it was necessary to estimate the numbers in this category (see below); in 1861 females under the designation 'bookfolder, newsagent' are placed under *bookbinder*, bookfolding being a semi-skilled binding process, and numbers in that category being comparable to numbers of females under 'bookbinder' in later censuses (numbers under 'newsagent' in later censuses are negligible). *Building labourer*: 'masons', 'bricklayers' lab.' and 'plasterers' lab.' combined. These designations do not appear in 1861, when 'mason' and 'plasterer' presumably include labourers. *Engineer*: 'engine and machine maker' combined with 'fitter and turner'. *Iron, brass manufacture*: the census designations referred to are 'iron-' and 'brass-founder' in 1861 and 1901; 'brass finisher' (1901) is also included here. *Rail*: all railway workers have been combined. *Furniture trades*: 'cabinet maker, upholsterer', 'French polisher', and 'carver and gilder'. *Other wood*: 'sawyer', 'wood turner', 'box maker'. *Leather*: 'tanner', 'currier, leather goods', 'saddle, harness, whip maker'. *Baker*: 'bread, biscuit, cake, etc.- maker' (1901). *Other food and drink*: 'miller', 'confectioner, pastry cook', 'maltster', 'distiller', 'tobacco manufacture'. *Papermaking*: 'paper manufacture,' 'envelope maker', 'paper bag, box, etc.' *Undefined manufacture*: designations such as 'mechanic, undefined', etc.

Finally, attention must be drawn to cases where it proved necessary to disentangle occupations combined in some censuses but not others. The procedures used generally involve allocating the total between two categories, according to their ratios at the nearest census to distinguish them. The problem obviously arises only where the occupations so combined belong to different categories (e.g. where retail and manufacture are combined). The occupations where this has been necessary are as follows: *domestic service, coach-man, cabman,* in 1891 'domestic' coachmen and gardeners are not distinguished from others; *other building, furniture trades,* in 1901 'wood carver' (under *other building*) and 'carver and gilder' (under *furniture trades*) are combined; *other clothing,* includes 'hatter' allo-cated between manufacture and retail; *other food and drink,* includes 'tobacco manufacture', combined with 'tobacconist' in 1881 and 1891. These procedures are as described by Armstrong, to whose work the reader is referred, and do not demand further discussion. A similar procedure has been used in one case not mentioned by Armstrong, perhaps because it occurs only in the Scottish tables: in 1841 'bookbinder' is combined with 'bookseller and publisher', and the total is therefore allocated by the ratio of these occupations in 1861. The one recommendation of Armstrong and Booth I have not followed is their allocation of half 'goldsmith, silversmith, jeweller' to retail; Edinburgh was a centre of jewellery manufacture, and the 1901 figures indicate a large preponderance of manufacture over retail. This occupation has therefore been placed entirely in manufacturing.

APPENDIX II

Occupational Classification

THE data presented in this book include analyses of the social composition of voluntary organizations (Table 5.3), patterns of inter-marriage (Tables 5.4–5.6), and membership of savings institutions (Table 6.1). It was therefore necessary to develop a scheme of occupational classification, which is most conveniently discussed in this appendix. The present appendix refers *only* to the problems encountered in assigning individuals to occupational categories, *not* to the separate problem of interpreting *published* census occupation tables (see Appendix I).

Information as to occupation is sometimes given in the source itself (Tables 5.4–5.6, Table 6.1), sometimes traced in census enumerators' books and/or *Post Office Directories* from a list of members' names and addresses (Table 5.3). Where occupations were traced in this way a varying proportion (indicated in the table concerned) had to be recorded as not traceable. The most obvious reason for this is change of address (especially as the sources do not relate to census years), but other possible reasons include incorrectly recorded addresses, misreading of handwritten membership lists, difficulty in finding some addresses (e.g. because of indexing errors by the census clerks), etc. Addresses in the Closes and Courts of the Old Town were especially hard to trace; while the factor of change of address will bias the data against the more mobile. On the other hand, misrecording and misreading of addresses is presumably a more random source of error. At any rate, little can be done about these problems except to draw attention to their existence; and the intrinsic interest of figures for the social composition of recreational organizations at this period seems to me to outweigh these deficiencies.

It remains to explain the categories used, which were developed in a pilot study of a sub-sample of the Savings Bank clients.

1. *Professions, higher administrative, gentlemen, etc.*

This category is intended to refer to the upper and more firmly established strata of the middle class. There are problems in defining the boundaries of the 'professions' (especially as these changed over the period studied), for which I have consulted the sources listed at the end of this appendix. In general, the concern has been with the *social status* of the occupation, in the eyes of bourgeois society, rather than with the questions of training and code of ethics which have preoccupied many students of the professions; occupations are therefore assigned on the evidence of information about their social position, rather than about education etc. *per se*. A number of 'marginal' semi-professional groups (e.g. school teachers) are placed in a white-collar category (Category 4 below). In addition to the established professions, Category 1 includes higher civil servants, 'gentlemen', etc.

2. *Business*

All in retail occupations not described as employees, and those in industrial occupations likely to be employers or self-employed by criteria mentioned below. Occupational designations of unknown employment status are therefore treated as employers or self-employed in retailing, but as employees in industry; this seemed appropriate, in view of the differing ratios of employers to employees in the two sectors. In assigning industrial occupations to the business category (rather than to the appropriate manual category) any or all of the following criteria have been used: described as 'master' or 'on own account' in census schedule; one or more domestic servants included in household; listed in trades section of Directory. Cross-checking with the *Directory* did not seem worth while for the larger scale analyses (marriage and Savings Bank clients), especially as a sub-sample of the Savings Bank clients showed no appreciable proportion listed. Some placed in manual categories will, in fact, be non-wage-earners, and many of the smaller businesses may not have appeared in the *Directory* at all. For the recreational organizations (Table 5.3) all such cases were cross-checked and classified accordingly.

Category 2 is highly heterogeneous, ranging from large and successful businessmen (who may belong most properly to Category 1) to self-employed artisans and shopkeepers of clearly working-class origins and affiliations. A breakdown between large and small business, while not impossible, would demand a considerable amount of work with such indicators as residence, numbers of domestic servants, etc. This did not seem worth while in a study concerned primarily with the manual working class. Provided that it is remembered that this category is inevitably more heterogeneous than any other, the absence of such a breakdown will not be too damaging.

3. *White-collar I: clerical and commercial*

Clerks of all sorts, book-keepers, cashiers, commercial travellers, salesmen, etc.

4. *White-collar II: supervisory, technical, minor officials*

Whereas Category 3 covers those in mainly routine and subordinate clerical posts, for which the basic skill was proficiency in the 'three Rs', Category 4 covers a more varied range, generally distinguished by some element of technical skill or supervisory responsibility. Verbatim examples of such occupations include: assistant inspector of poor; furniture draughtsman; gas surveyor; cemetery superintendent; market inspector; librarian; rail inspector. All teachers are also included in Category 4, as are merchant marine officers, and supervisory employees in agriculture (farm overseers etc.). But all industrial foremen are classified as skilled manual (Category 6).

5. *Retail, warehouse, etc.: employees*

All in retail occupations of definitely employee status (i.e. described as 'assistants', etc.). But message boys and porters (except those described specifically as 'shop porters') are classified as unskilled manual (Category 7); and various personal services of ambiguous employment status (e.g. hairdressers) are placed in a special category (Category 10).

6. *Manual—skilled*

Manual categories (6, 7, 8) include all industrial occupations not classified as non-wage-earners by the criteria stated (see above, Category 2). The criterion used to define skilled labour is that of apprenticeship. But this raises the problem of the existence in every trade of a more or less numerous section who had not served regular apprenticeships but had picked up the trade and entered it by the 'back door'; a further complication is the impact of technical change in down-grading established skills, and creating newer ones to which the traditional apprenticeship might be irrelevant. The general rule adopted is therefore to treat as skilled all occupational designations which refer to *at least some* apprenticed workers. And there is little difficulty in classifying most locally important occupations by this rule (printers, masons, engineers, etc., were clearly regarded by general consent as skilled trades). An exception must be made for certain sectors of industry (notably the railways, for which I have followed Kingsford's classification of skill grades) which had a series of grades, rather than the familiar distinction between the craftsman and the labourer. The railways also exemplify the problem of how to weight the factor of responsibility and initiative, as against manual skills needed to perform the actual physical tasks of the job (e.g. guards, signalmen). In cases of this sort a separate decision must be made for each occupation.

Finally there is the problem of those occupations where we simply lack the information to make a reliable skill classification. Sometimes this is the result of ambiguities in the wording of the source (e.g. 'rubber worker'); sometimes it reflects a general lack of information about the occupation. A proportion of these cases will not be soluble, and for this reason a category for manual workers of unclassifiable skill is included (Category 8). The size of that category has, however, been minimized by treating as skilled various occupations (mostly makers of musical instruments, sports equipment, etc.) known from the published census occupation tables to have employed extremely small numbers, on the assumption that such occupations were carried on on a handicraft basis.

7. *Manual—semi- and unskilled*

See above, Category 6, for procedures of skill classification.

8. *Manual—skill unclassifiable*

See above, Category 6, for procedures of skill classification. Apart from occupations of little importance in Edinburgh which enter into some of the populations studied (e.g. brides' fathers from other parts of the country), the most important local unclassifiable manual occupations were in the rubber and paper mills.

9. *Domestic service, catering employees, etc.*

All types of domestic servant; all employed in catering. It is in practice not possible to draw a distinction between the domestic and catering sector; similarly grooms and stablemen may be either domestic servants or employed in transport undertakings. Where no distinction can be drawn such occupations are always classified as domestic. Certain personal services provided on a business basis are however placed in a separate category (Category 10), and catering employers and self-employed (e.g. publicans) are placed in the business category (Category 2).

10. *Miscellaneous personal and public services*

All service occupations of ambiguous employment status not classified as domestic servants (e.g. hairdressers), public-service employees not easily classifiable as either manual or white collar (e.g. post-office telegraphists, and one man described as 'mace bearer, Court of Session'); and all entertainers, artists, etc. All transport workers (other than coachmen, who are placed in Category 9) and public-utility manual workers are placed in appropriate manual categories, and many public-service employees are placed in white-collar categories; similarly, personal services placed in Category 10 are those not easily classifiable as business or domestic-service occupations. Category 10 is therefore a residual category of service occupations not elsewhere classified.

11. *Police*

Includes all ranks. Also includes prison officers.

12. *Armed forces*

Not officers; officers are placed in Category 1.

13. *Agriculture, fishing, seamen*

These groups are of little importance in the city's occupational structure, but appear in certain of the populations studied (notably the brides' fathers). Merchant marine officers, supervisory and managerial grades in agriculture, and farmers and crofters are placed elsewhere (Categories 4 and 14).

14. *Farmers and crofters*

The frequency of this occupation among the brides' fathers justified creating a separate category, which occurs only in the marriage data (Tables 5.4–6). The category is a heterogeneous one, possibly ranging from the fringes of the gentry to Highland or Irish subsistence agriculture. Farm overseers etc. are placed in Category 4.

15. *Other and miscellaneous*

Includes mainly 'marginal' forms of petty trading that cannot be placed in Category 2 without distortion: hawkers, 'dealers', 'brokers', etc. (the two latter phrases are used for Irish dealers in second-hand goods in the Cowgate area); also various designations of completely unknown meaning, illegible occupations, etc.

Sources of Information about Occupations

The sources used in classifying occupations are too scattered to be exhaustively listed, but the more important specific sources are listed below:

D. Bremner, *The Industries of Scotland* (1869).
A. M. Carr-Saunders and P. A. Wilson, *The Professions* (1933).

O. Gordon, *Handbook of Employments* (1908).
P. W. Kingsford, *Victorian Railwaymen* (1970).
Oxford English Dictionary.
W. J. Reader, *Professional Men* (1966).
R.C. on Labour, Glossary of Technical Terms, P.P. 1893–4 XXXVIII.
Webb, Manuscript Notes on apprenticeship etc. (Webb collection, section A).

Bibliography

Note: The following abbreviations are used to indicate location of manuscript and other rare sources:

BM   British Museum Newspaper Library.
EPL   Edinburgh Public Library.
LSE   British Library of Economic and Political Science, London School of Economics.
NLS   National Library of Scotland.
Webb   Webb Trade Union Collection, at LSE.
*   Items preserved in the archives of the organization concerned.

I MANUSCRIPT SOURCES

James Allan Ltd., Wage books *.
A.S.E. head-office questionnaire to Districts, return from Edinburgh District (1876): at A.U.E.W. headquarters, London.
Associated Ironmoulders of Scotland, EC Minutes: NLS.
John Bartholomew Ltd., Wage books *.
Bruntsfield Links Allied Golf Club, Minutes: EPL.
Census of Scotland, 1871, 1891, Enumerator's books: at Register House, Edinburgh.
T. & A. Constable Ltd., Wage books, 'List of Parties Employed, 1833–1856' (Manuscript notebook) *.
Edinburgh and Leith Workers' Municipal Committee, Minutes: at offices of Edinburgh Trades Council.
Edinburgh Bowling Club, Minutes: EPL.
Edinburgh Branch, Bookbinders' Consolidated Union, Minutes NLS.
Edinburgh Branch, I.L.P., Minutes: NLS.
Edinburgh Central Branch, Associated Carpenters and Joiners of Scotland, Minutes: at East of Scotland District offices, Amalgamated Society of Woodworkers.
Edinburgh Master Book and Shoemakers' Association, Minutes: at offices of James Allan Ltd.
Edinburgh Savings Bank, Declaration forms, 1865–9, 1895–9 *.
Edinburgh Trades Council, Minutes *.
Edinburgh Union Society of Journeymen Bookbinders, Minutes: NLS.

Hamilton & Inches Ltd., Wage books *.
MacKenzie & Moncur Ltd., Wage books *.
Marriage certificates for Edinburgh Registration Districts, 1865–9,
    1895–7: at Register House, Edinburgh.
Scotsman Publications Ltd., Wage books *.
S. and B. Webb, Manuscript Notes: Webb coll. sect. A.

2 PRINTED REPORTS ETC. OF ORGANIZATIONS

Amalgamated Carpenters and Joiners, *Annual Reports*: Webb D.22.
A.S.E., *Reports, Monthly Journal*: Webb D.69, 71, 72.
Associated Carpenters and Joiners of Scotland, *Annual Reports*:
    Webb D.26.
Associated Ironmoulders of Scotland, *Reports*: NLS.
Bookbinders' Consolidated Union, *Reports, Trade Circulars*: NLS.
Bookbinding Trades Journal: Bishopgate Institute, London.
Central Ironmoulders' Association, *Reports*: NLS.
Edinburgh Cordwainers' Society, *To the Master Boot and Shoemakers
    of Edinburgh* (1872): Webb B.119.xxv.
Edinburgh Cordwainers' Society, *To Messrs. James Allan* (1893):
    Webb B.119.xxiii.
Edinburgh Master Painters' Association, Printed broadside (1858):
    EPL.
Edinburgh Mechanics' Subscription Library, *Laws and Catalogue*
    (6th edn., 1859): NLS.
Edinburgh Press and Machinemen's Society, *Memorial to the Master
    Printers of Edinburgh and District* (1892): Webb B.119.xxxviii.
Edinburgh Press and Machinemen's Society, *Annual Report*, 1892–3:
    St. Bride Institute, London.
Edinburgh School Board, *Minutes*: EPL.
Edinburgh Trades Council, *Annual Reports*: EPL.
Edinburgh Typographical Society, *Eviction of Trades Unionists from
    the Scottish Leader Office* (leaflet, 1890): Webb B.119.xxxvii.
Edinburgh Typographical Society, *To the Master Printers of the City
    of Edinburgh* (1891): Webb B.119.xxxvi.
Edinburgh Typographical Society, *Rules* (1892): Webb C.81.xv–xvi.
Edinburgh Union Society of Journeymen Bookbinders, *Rules* (1846):
    NLS.
Masons' Association, *To Lodge Members and Non-members* (n.d., *c.*
    1885): Webb B.34.xvii.
Scottish Amalgamated Union of Boot and Shoemakers, *Report*, Feb.–
    Aug. 1868: Webb D.5.
Scottish Typographical Association, *Rules* (1852): Webb C.81.i.
Scottish Typographical Association, *Reports*: Webb D.205.

Scottish Typographical Circular: Webb D.206.
United Patternmakers, *Monthly Reports*: Webb D.162.

3 OFFICIAL PUBLICATIONS

Census of Population, 1841, P.P. 1844 XXVII (occupation tables);
  Census of Scotland: 1861, vol. i (population), P.P. 1862 L, vol. ii
  (occupations, birth-places), P.P. 1864 LI; 1871, vol. i (population),
  P.P. 1872 LXVIII, vol. ii (occupations, birth-places), P.P. 1873
  LXXIII; 1881, vol. i (population), P.P. 1882 LXXVI, vol. ii
  (occupations, birth-places), P.P. 1883 LXXXI; 1891, vol. i
  (population), P.P. 1892 XCIV, vol. ii, pt. 1 (birth-places), P.P.
  1893–4 CVII, vol. ii, pt. 2 (occupations), P.P. 1893–4 CVIII;
  1901, vol. i (population), P.P. 1902 CXXIX, vol. ii (birth-places),
  1903 LXXXVI, vol. iii (occupations), P.P. 1904 CVIII.
General Report on Wages, P.P. 1893–4 LXXXIII, pt. ii.
R.C. on Friendly Societies, Second Report, pt. ii, P.P. 1872 XXVI.
R.C. on the Housing of the Working Classes (Scotland), P.P. 1884–5
  XXXI.
R.C. on Labour, P.P. 1892 XXXVI, pts. ii, iii, 1893–4 XXXII,
  XXXIV, XXXVIII.
R.C. on the Labour Laws, Second Report, P.P. 1875 XXX.
R.C. on the Poor Laws, appendix vol. viii, P.P. 1910 XLVIII.
Report of the Committee . . . to Enquire into . . . the Census, P.P. 1890
  LVIII.
Reports on Strikes and Lock-outs, 1890, 1897, P.P. 1890–1 LXXXVIII,
  1898 LXXXVIII.
Return of Factories, P.P. 1871 LXII.
Returns of Wages, 1830–86, P.P. 1887 LXXXIX.
Select Committee on the Sweating System, P.P. 1889 XIV, pt. i.

4 NEWSPAPERS AND PERIODICALS

Clarion: LSE.
Commonweal: LSE.
Edinburgh Athletic Times: EPL.
Edinburgh News (series of articles on 'The Condition of the Working
  Classes in Edinburgh and Leith', 1852–4): BM.
Justice: LSE.
Labour Chronicle: EPL.
North Briton: BM.
Reformer: BM.
Scotsman.

5 OTHER PRINTED SOURCES (INCLUDING REPRINTS OF SOURCE MATERIAL)

AITCHISON, T. S., and LORIMER, G., *Reminiscences of the Old Bruntsfield Links Golf Club* (Privately printed, 1904): EPL.

The Ballantyne Press and Its Founders, 1796–1908 (1909): EPL.

BEGG, J., D. D., *Happy Homes for Working Men and How to Get Them* (1866).

BLACKIE, J. S., *Notes of a Life*, ed. A. S. Walker (1908).

BOWLEY, A. L., and WOOD, G. H., 'Statistics of Wages in the United Kingdom', series of articles in *Journal of the Royal Statistical Society*, 62–8 (1899–1905).

BREMNER, D., *The Industries of Scotland* (1869).

CITY OF EDINBURGH CHARITY ORGANISATION SOCIETY, *Report on the Physical Condition of Fourteen Hundred Schoolchildren in the City* (1906).

COSSAR, J. J., and FROUDE, A., *The Census Returns of Edinburgh* (*c.* 1911): EPL.

DIBBLEE, G. B., 'The Printing Trades and the Crisis in British Industry', *Economic Journal* (1902).

Edinburgh and Leith Post Office Directories.

FLEMING, L., *An Octogenarian Printer's Reminiscences* (1893): EPL.

GORDON, MRS. O., *A Handbook of Employments* (1908).

GROOME, F.H., ed., *Ordnance Gazetteer of Scotland* (1885).

HEDDLE, R. G., ed., 'Extracts from the Diary of the Rev. David Aitken, D.D., 1864–75', *Book of the Old Edinburgh Club* (1971).

HEITON, J., *The Castes of Edinburgh* (2nd edn., 1860).

History of the Firm of Neill and Co. (1900): EPL.

HOWE, E., ed., *The Trade: passages from the literature of the printing craft* (1943).

JACOBI, S. T., *Printing* (5th edn., 1913).

'J.B.S.', *Random Recollections and Impressions* (privately printed, 1903).

'JOURNEYMAN ENGINEER', *The Great Unwashed* (1868).

KEITH, A., *Edinburgh of Today* (1908).

KERR, A. W., *History of Banking in Scotland* (2nd edn., 1908).

KINNEAR, S., Miscellaneous Writings: scrapbook in EPL.

——*Reminiscences of an Aristocratic Edinburgh Printing Office* (1890): EPL.

MACDONALD, J. H. A., *Fifty Years of It: the experiences and struggles of a Volunteer of 1859* (1909).

MACDONALD, J. R., ed., *Women in the Printing Trades* (1904).

MACDOUGALL, I., ed., *The Minutes of Edinburgh Trades Council, 1859–73* (1968).

McDowall's New Guide to Edinburgh (n.d., *c.* 1851).

MACKIE, J. B., *The Life and Work of Duncan McLaren*, vol. ii (1888).

MALLINSON, J., *Statistics Bearing on the State of Employment . . . in the City of Edinburgh, December,* 1893 (1893): EPL.

MAXWELL, W., ed., *First Fifty Years of St. Cuthbert's Co-operative Association Ltd.,* 1859–1909 (1909).

MILLER, H., *My Schools and Schoolmasters* (1854).

OLDFIELD, A., *A Practical Manual of Typography* (n.d., c. 1891).

'OLD MACHINE MANAGER', *The Printing Machine Manager's Complete Handbook and Machine Minder's Companion* (1889).

PATON, D. N., et al., *A Study of the Diet of the Labouring Classes in the City of Edinburgh* (n.d., c. 1900): EPL.

PRESTELL, J., ed., *Edinburgh Bowling Annuals*: EPL.

Reminiscences of the Grange Cricket Club, Edinburgh (1891): EPL.

SCOTTISH NATIONAL ASSOCIATION OF OPERATIVE TAILORS, EDINBURGH BRANCH, *The Sweating System in Edinburgh* (n.d.): EPL.

SMILES, S., *Self Help* (Sphere Books edn., 1968).

SMILES, S., *Industrial Biography* (1863).

SOMERVILLE, A., *The Autobiography of a Working Man* (1951 edn.; original edn. 1848).

STEPHEN, W., *History of the Queen's City of Edinburgh Rifle Volunteer Brigade* (1881).

THOMPSON, E. P., and YEO, E., eds., *The Unknown Mayhew* (1971).

THORBURN, T., *Statistical Analysis of the Census of the City of Edinburgh* (1851): NLS.

WILSON, D., *William Nelson: a memoir* (privately printed, 1889).

6 UNPUBLISHED DISSERTATIONS AND THESES

BURGESS, K., 'The Influence of Technological Change on the Social Attitudes and Trade Union Policies of Workers in the British Engineering Industry, 1780–1860' (Ph.D. thesis, Leeds University, 1970).

CAMERON, A. J., 'Society, Policing, and the Problem of Order: Edinburgh, 1805–1822' (undergraduate dissertation, Edinburgh University, Department of Economic History, 1974).

CANNON, I. C., 'The Social Situation of the Skilled Worker: a study of the compositor in London' (Ph.D. thesis, London University, 1961).

CROWLEY, D. W., 'The Origins of the Revolt of the British Labour Movement from Liberalism' (Ph.D. thesis, London University, 1952).

DOCHERTY, A. G., 'Urban Working Class Recreation before 1914' (undergraduate dissertation, Edinburgh University, Department of Economic History).

GORDON, G., 'The Status Areas of Edinburgh' (Ph.D. thesis, Edinburgh University, 1971).

STRACHAN, A. J., 'The Rural-Urban Fringe of Edinburgh' (Ph.D. thesis, Edinburgh University, 1969).

WILLIAMS, J. C., 'Edinburgh Politics, 1832–52' (Ph.D. thesis, Edinburgh University, 1972).

7 OTHER WORKS CONSULTED

ALLAN, C. M., 'The Genesis of British Urban Re-development with Special Reference to Glasgow', *Economic History Review*, 2nd ser., 18 (1965).

ALTHUSSER, L., *For Marx*, trans. B. Brewster (Allen Lane, Harmondsworth, 1969).

ANDERSON, A., 'The Political Symbolism of the Labour Laws', *Society for the Study of Labour History Bulletin*, 23 (Autumn 1971).

ARMSTRONG, W.A., 'The Use of Information about Occupation', in WRIGLEY, E. A., (ed.), *Nineteenth Century Society* (Cambridge University Press, Cambridge, 1972).

BAGWELL, P. S., *The Railwaymen* (Allen & Unwin, London, 1963).

BAIRD, G., 'The Operative House Painters of Scotland' (typescript, 1959): EPL.

BARTHOLOMEW, P., 'House of Bartholomew' (typescript, loaned by the author).

BECHHOFER, F., and ELLIOT, B., 'An Approach to a Study of Small Shopkeepers and the Class Structure', *European Journal of Sociology*, 9 (1968).

BENDIX, R., *Work and Authority in Industry* (Harper Torchbook edn., New York, 1963).

BEST, G., *Mid-Victorian Britain, 1851–75* (Weidenfeld and Nicolson, London, 1971).

√ BLAUNER, R., *Alienation and Freedom* (Chicago University Press, Chicago, 1964).

BOWLEY, A. L., *Wages and Income in the United Kingdom since 1860* (Cambridge University Press, Cambridge, 1937).

√BRIGGS, A., and SAVILLE, J., eds., *Essays in Labour History, 1886–1923* (Macmillan, London, 1971).

CARR-SAUNDERS, A. M., and WILSON, P. A., *The Professions* (Clarendon Press, Oxford, 1933).

CHILD, J., *Industrial Relations in the British Printing Industry* (Allen and Unwin, London, 1967).

City of Edinburgh Lodge, No. 1 Branch of the Scottish Order of Oddfellows (duplicated, n.d., c. 1940, loaned by Mr. T. Donoghue).

CLEGG, H. A., Fox, A., and THOMPSON, A. F., *A History of British Trade Unions since* 1889, vol. i (Clarendon Press, Oxford, 1964).

COHEN, S., ed., *Images of Deviance* (Pelican, Harmondsworth, 1971).

COURT, W. H. B., *British Economic History, 1870–1914: commentary and documents* (Cambridge University Press, Cambridge, 1965).

Cox, D., 'The Labour Party in Leicester', *International Review of Social History,* 14 (1969).

DEANE, P., and COLE, W. A., *British Economic Growth, 1688–1959* (2nd edn., Cambridge University Press, Cambridge, 1967).

DUFFY, A. E. P., 'The New Unionism in Britain, 1889–90: a re-appraisal', *Economic History Review*, 2nd ser., 14 (1961).

FOSTER, J., *Class Struggle and the Industrial Revolution* (Weidenfeld & Nicolson, London, 1974).

Fox, A., *A History of the National Union of Boot and Shoe Operatives* (Blackwell, Oxford, 1958).

GILLESPIE, S. C., *A Hundred Years of Progress: the record of the Scottish Typographical Association,* 1853–1952 (Scottish Typographical Association, Glasgow, 1953).

GOLDTHORPE, J. H., and LOCKWOOD, D., 'Affluence and the British Class Structure', *Sociological Review*, 11 (1963).

GORMAN, J., *Banner Bright*, intro. G. A. Williams (Allen Lane, London, 1973).

GRAMSCI, A., *Selections from the Prison Notebooks*, ed. and trans. Q. Hoare and G. Nowell Smith (Lawrence & Wishart, London, 1971).

GREAVES, C. DESMOND, *The Life and Times of James Connolly* (Lawrence & Wishart, London, 1961).

HANDLEY, J. E., *The Irish in Scotland,* 1798–1845 (Cork University Press, Cork, 1943).

HARRISON, R., 'Afterword' in SMILES, S., *Self Help* (Sphere Books, London, 1968).

HEDDLE, R. G., ed., 'Extracts from the Diary of the Rev. David Aitken, D.D., 1864–75', *Book of the Old Edinburgh Club* (1971).

HINTON, J., 'The Beginning of Modern British Politics', *Society for the Study of Labour History Bulletin* 24 (Spring, 1972).

HOBSBAWM, E. J., *Labouring Men* (Weidenfeld and Nicolson, London, 1964).

——'Trade Union History', *Economic History Review*, 2nd ser., 20 (1967).

——'Lenin and the "Aristocracy of Labour"', *Marxism Today* (July 1970).

HOLLIS, P., *The Pauper Press* (Clarendon Press, Oxford, 1970).

HORNE, H. O., *A History of Savings Banks* (Clarendon Press, Oxford, 1947).

Howe, E., ed., *The Trade: passages from the literature of the printing craft* (Walter Hutchinson, London, 1943).

A Hundred Years of Publishers' Bookbinding, 1857–1957 (privately printed for Hunter & Foulis Ltd., Edinburgh, 1957).

Hunter, J., 'The Politics of Highland Land Reform, 1873–95', *Scottish Historical Review*, 53 (1974).

Hyman, R., *Marxism and the Sociology of Trade Unionism* (Pluto Press, London, 1971).

Ingham, G. K., *Size of Industrial Organisation and Worker Behaviour* (Cambridge University Press, Cambridge, 1970).

Institute of Public Administration, *Studies in the Development of Edinburgh* (Institute of Public Administration, London and Edinburgh, 1939).

Jamieson, D. A., *Powderhall and Pedestrianism* (W. and A. K. Johnston, Edin., 1943).

Jeffreys, J. B., *The Story of the Engineers* (Lawrence and Wishart, London, 1945).

Johnson, R., 'Educational Policy and Social Control in Early Victorian England', *Past and Present*, no. 49 (1970).

Jones, G. Stedman, *Outcast London* (Clarendon Press, Oxford, 1971).

Kingsford, P. W., *Victorian Railwaymen* (Cass, London, 1970).

Landes, D. S., *The Unbound Prometheus* (Cambridge University Press, Cambridge, 1969).

Lenin, V. I., *Selected Works* (3 vols., Progress Publishers, Moscow, 1967).

Lockwood, D., *The Blackcoated Worker* (Allen & Unwin, London, 1958).

MacDougall, I., ed., *The Minutes of Edinburgh Trades Council, 1859–73* (Scottish History Society, Edin., 1968).

MacLaren, A. A., *Religion and Social Class: the Disruption years in Aberdeen* (Routledge and Kegan Paul, London, 1974).

Marwick, W. H., 'Municipal Politics in Victorian Edinburgh', *Book of the Old Edinburgh Club* (1969).

Marx, K., and Engels, F., *On Britain* (2nd edn., Foreign Languages Publishing House, Moscow, 1962).

Michels, R., *Political Parties* (Dover edn., New York, 1959).

Mitchell, B. R., and Deane, P., *Abstract of British Historical Statistics* (Cambridge University Press, Cambridge, 1962).

Neale, R. S., 'The Standard of Living, 1780–1844: a regional and class study', *Economic History Review*, 2nd ser., 19 (1966).

Parkin, F., *Class Inequality and Political Order* (MacGibbon and Kee, London, 1971).

Payne, P. L., ed., *Studies in Scottish Business History* (Cass, London, 1967).

PELLING, H., *Popular Politics and Society in Late Victorian Britain* (Macmillan, London, 1968).

POLLARD, S., *The Genesis of Modern Management* (Pelican edn., Harmondsworth, 1968).

POULANTZAS, N., 'Marxist Political Theory in Great Britain', *New Left Review*, 43 (1967).

PRICE, R. N., 'The Working Men's Club Movement and Victorian Social Reform Ideology', *Victorian Studies*, 15 (1971).

READER, W. J., *Professional Men* (Weidenfeld & Nicolson, London, 1966).

REID, F., Review article in *Society for the Study of Labour History Bulletin* 16 (Spring 1968).

REID, F., 'Keir Hardie's Conversion to Socialism', in BRIGGS, A., and SAVILLE, J., (eds), *Essays in Labour History, 1886–1923* (Macmillan, London, 1971).

REID, W., *The Story of the Hearts* (Edinburgh, n.d., c. 1924).

ROBERTS, R., *The Classic Slum* (Manchester University Press, Manchester, 1971).

SAMUEL, R., 'Class and Classlessness', *Universities and Left Review*, 6 (1959).

SCOTLAND, J., *The History of Scottish Education*, vol. i (London University Press, London, 1969).

Scotsman, 25 April 1960, 'The Edinburgh Story' (special supplement).

SIGSWORTH, E. M., and BLACKMAN, J., 'The Home Boom of the 1890s', *Yorkshire Bulletin of Economic and Social Research*, 17 (1965).

SLAVEN, A., 'Earnings and Productivity in the Scottish Coal-mining Industry during the Nineteenth Century', in PAYNE, P. L., (ed.), *Studies in Scottish Business History* (Cass, London, 1967).

SMOUT, T. C., *A History of the Scottish People 1560–1830* (Fontana edn., 1972).

STINCHCOMBE, A. L., 'Bureaucratic and Craft Administration of Production', *Administrative Science Quarterly*, 4 (1959).

SUTHERLAND, G., *Elementary Education in the Nineteenth Century* (Historical Association pamphlet, 1971).

TAYLOR, I. R., 'Soccer Consciousness and Soccer Hooliganism', in COHEN, S., (ed.), *Images of Deviance* (Pelican, Harmondsworth, 1971).

THOMPSON, E. P., *The Making of the English Working Class* (Pelican edn., Harmondsworth, 1968).

——'Time, Work-discipline and Industrial Capitalism', *Past and Present*, no. 38 (1967).

——and YEO, E., (eds.), *The Unknown Mayhew* (Merlin Press, London, 1971).

Tuckett, A., *The Scottish Carter* (Allen and Unwin, London, 1967).

Vincent, J., *The Formation of the Liberal Party* (Constable, London, 1966).

Webb, S., and Webb, B., *The History of Trade Unionism* (revised edn., Longman's, London, 1920).

——*Industrial Democracy* (Longman's, London, 1926).

Weir, J. B. de V., 'The Assessment of the Growth of Schoolchildren', *British Journal of Nutrition*, 6 (1952).

White, C., 'A Century of Bookbinding in Edinburgh', *Edinburgh Journal of Science, Technology, and Photographic Art*, 16 (1941).

Williams, R., 'Base and Superstructure', *New Left Review*, 82 (1973).

Wilson, A., *The Chartist Movement in Scotland* (Manchester University Press, Manchester, 1970).

Wrigley, E. A., ed., *Nineteenth-century Society* (Cambridge University Press, Cambridge, 1972).

Yeo, S., 'A Phase in the Social History of Socialism', *Society for the Study of Labour History Bulletin*, 22 (Spring 1971).

Index

n indicates reference to footnotes   t indicates reference to tables